EASTERN
CHRISTIANITY
IN INDIA

The oldest Persian Cross of Kottayam with a Pahlavi inscription which is generally interpreted as 'My Lord Christ, have mercy on Afras, son of Chaharbukt the Syrian, who cut this' — Knanaya Jacobite Church, Kottayam.

EASTERN CHRISTIANITY

IN INDIA

*A History of the Syro-Malabar Church
from the earliest time to the present day*

His Eminence

CARDINAL EUGENE TISSERANT

Authorized adaptation from the French by
E. R. HAMBYE S.J.

LONGMANS, GREEN AND CO

LONDON • NEW YORK • TORONTO

LONGMANS, GREEN AND CO LTD
6 & 7 CLIFFORD STREET LONDON W I
BOSTON HOUSE STRAND STREET CAPE TOWN
605-611 LONSDALE STREET MELBOURNE C I

LONGMANS, GREEN AND CO INC
55 FIFTH AVENUE NEW YORK 3

LONGMANS, GREEN AND CO
20 CRANFIELD ROAD TORONTO 16

ORIENT LONGMANS PRIVATE LTD
CALCUTTA BOMBAY MADRAS
DELHI HYDERABAD DACCA

First edition 1957

Imprimi potest
F. Timmermans, S. J.
Praepositus Vice-Provinciae
Calcuttensis, die 2a Aprilis, 1957

Imprimatur † Ferdinandus S. J. *Archiepiscopus*
Calcuttensis, die 2a Aprilis, 1957

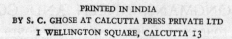

PRINTED IN INDIA
BY S. C. GHOSE AT CALCUTTA PRESS PRIVATE LTD
I WELLINGTON SQUARE, CALCUTTA 13

PREFACE

THE Syro-Malabar Church has the distinction of being the most ancient Christian community of India and the Far East. For more than fifteen centuries its members have occupied the south-western shores of India. They have played—and still do—a vital role in the expansion of Christianity in Asia. They have been so rooted in the native soil that their customs have developed in conformity with the social atmosphere of Ancient India, and, except for their faith and morals, they have been—and are still—hardly distinguishable from their compatriots of other creeds. Their spontaneous adaptation stands as a perpetual and concrete manifestation of the natural universality of Christianity.

When mention is made of the Syro-Malabar Church, we refer to those Christians of India who, before the advent of the Portuguese, were hierarchically connected with the Chaldean Church of Mesopotamia and Persia. It was from the Chaldean Church that they received their ways of worship, which are diversely known as the Chaldean, East Syrian, or even Nestorian rites, although the last of these is a misnomer. Thence is derived the first part of their epithet, *Syro*-Malabar. It signifies that they form part of an oriental branch of the Church, which makes use of one of the Syrian rites.

The latter part of the name, *Malabar*, was given to them, following the rediscovery of South India by European travellers, although Malabar is rather the name of the country than of the people.

We also make occasional use of the appellation, St. Thomas Christians, since even nowadays St. Thomas the Apostle is commonly regarded by the Christians of Malabar, both Catholic and dissident, as their father in the faith. But, owing to some differences as to the interpretation of this title, we have preferred to preserve that of the Syro-Malabar Church in the title of this book.

The present work is a translation of a scholarly French monograph written by His Eminence Eugene Cardinal Tisserant, Bishop of Ostia, Porto and Santa Rufina, Dean of the Sacred College, Secretary of the S. Congregation for the Oriental Church, for the *Dictionnaire de Théologie Catholique* (Vacant et Mangenot). It was published in 1941 as a section of volume XIV, part 2, under the title 'Syro-Malabare (Eglise)'.

The original text forms the bulk of the translation, but, with the approval of the learned author, we have deemed it necessary to make corrections and additions. These chiefly include the problem of St. Thomas the Apostle in India, the relations between the Syrians and the Jesuits, summed up in the Synod of Diamper and its aftermath, the contributions of Bishop Lavigne and Bishop Medlycott to the re-establishment of the Syro-Malabar hierarchy, the history of the Indian Jacobites during the nineteenth century, and the recent reunion movement among them. It is also obvious that statistics have been revised and brought up-to-date. Besides this, we have compiled appendices III and IV, as well as the bibliography. We have attempted to make the latter as complete as possible, with regard to printed works.

When reviewing the relations between the Christians of Malabar and the Chaldean Church of the early Middle Ages, we have embodied most of section IV of the article 'Nestorienne (L'Eglise)', entitled 'Les établissements nestoriens dans l'Inde' which was also written by His Eminence Cardinal Tisserant and published in the same dictionary, volume XI, part 1, for the year 1931.

The corrections and additions were considered suitable for the adaptation of an article of a dictionary to the requirements of a separate book.

It is not out of place to characterize in a few words the work of His Eminence the Cardinal. It does not aim at presenting a detailed and analytical account of the long history of the Syro-Malabar Christians. Rather is it a general, yet accurate review of all the problems connected with their chequered life, which, while not giving the impression of a stained glass window of the thirteenth century with all its minute patches of colour, produced the effect provided by the large scenes with which the genius of great artists adorned the windows of the late Gothic and first Renaissance churches. Such a plan presents the history of the Syrian Christians in a vivid and appealing light, for it traces the main lines of their struggles, their successes, and their failures, as well as their share in the general development of Christianity and the cultural history of India. Further researches may contribute to greater precision and better shading, but the colours will remain the same.

We are deeply grateful to His Eminence Cardinal Eugene Tisserant for the permission he gave us, as early as 1950, to proceed with the translation of his work. From then on his unfailing interest has been for us an unforgettable source of encouragement. A great debt of gratitude is due also to our many friends of Malabar, particularly the late Archbishop-Bishop of Tiruvalla, His Grace Joseph Mar Severios, and the Reverend Father Placid of St. Joseph T.O.C.D., who were of such service in contacting the Syrians of Malabar and visiting many of their ancient churches. Yet those visits and studies on the spot could not have been undertaken without the financial support of a Belgian scientific institution, *Le Fonds National de la Recherche Scientifique*, which, despite distance and the foreign aspect of our work, did its utmost to further our personal researches. Our translation could not have been made and completed without the co-operation, sometimes entailing heavy services, of some of our students of the Society of Jesus, among whom mention should be made of FF. R. Correia-Afonso, D. Dias, and C. De Brouwer of De Nobili

College, Poona, and Fr. S. Matthews of St. Mary's College, Kurseong.

E. R. Hambye s. j.

CONTENTS

page

PREFACE   *vii*

INTRODUCTION   *xv*

LIST OF ABBREVIATIONS   *xix*

I   THE ORIGINS   I

The Land and the Christians—1. The Apostolate of St. Thomas in India—2. Beginnings of Christianity—6. Relations with the Persian Church—8. Historical appreciation of the origins—10.

II   THE SYRO-MALABAR CHURCH FROM 450 A.D. TILL   II
THE ADVENT OF THE PORTUGUESE

The Persian Church and Indian Christianity—11. Nestorianism and Indian Christians—17. Medieval contact with the West—19. Last glimpse of Mesopotamia—24.

III   THE SYRIAN CHRISTIANS UNDER PORTUGUESE   27
RULE AND THE SYNOD OF DIAMPER

Portuguese discoveries and Padroado—27. Early frictions and tensions —30. Conflicts and oppositions. The tribulations of Mar Joseph—35. Mar Abraham, the Padroado and the Jesuits—42. Mar Abraham's succession and the visitation of Archbishop Alexis de Menezes—47. The Synod of Diamper—56. An appreciation of the Synod of Diamper—65.

IV   THE ST. THOMAS CHRISTIANS UNDER THE JURISDIC-   69
TION OF THE JESUITS AND THE CARMELITES

The Jesuits in India and in Malabar—69. The election of Fr. Roz, the first Latin prelate of the Indian Syrians—70. Bishop Francis Roz and his successors—73. Preliminary embarassments—75. The breach of 1653 —78. The Syrians and their apostolic vicars—84. The Carmelites settled in Malabar—89. The nineteenth century and the strengthening of the Syrian Catholics of Malabar—97.

V   RELATIONS WITH MESOPOTAMIA AND SCHISMS   IOI

page

Memories of the past—101. Fidelity to the Catholicos of the East—102. Renewed contacts—103. Direct action—105. Chaldean attentions—106. Mar Rokos and his Indian adventure—108. The forerunners of a schism —111. Mar Mellus and his dealings—114. Failure and schism—118.

VI THE INDIAN CATHOLIC HIERARCHY 121

Glimpses from the past—121. The dawn of better days—122. False steps—124. The eve of more auspicious days—125. The work of Bishop Lavigne and of Bishop Medlycott—127. The fulfilment—134. Wonderful progress—136.

VII THE JACOBITES IN INDIA AND THE CREATION OF THE 140 CATHOLIC COMMUNITY OF THE ANTIOCHIAN RITE

Syria, Mesopotamia and India—140. Early Jacobite influences—141. Protestantism versus Jacobitism—145. The origins of the Mar Thomites —147. The Patriarch's dealings—151. New discussions and internal rifts—153. Reunion movements—155. The origins of the Syro-Malankara Catholics—157.

APPENDICES

I CANON LAW AND CUSTOMS OF THE SYRIAN 163 CATHOLICS OF MALABAR

Canon Law of the Syro-Malankara Church—172.

II THE LITURGY OF THE SYRIAN CATHOLICS 175 OF MALABAR

Practice before the Portuguese—175. Early Latinization—175. Diamper's work—177. Vicissitudes of the Syro-Malabar missal—179. Present situation—181. Pontifical, Ritual and Office—183. The Syro-Malankara Liturgy — 184.

III LIST OF BISHOPS IN MALABAR AND OF EASTERN 187 PATRIARCHS

IV CHRONOLOGICAL EVENTS 199

BIBLIOGRAPHY 205

INDEX 251

ILLUSTRATIONS

The oldest Persian Cross of Kottayam — *frontispiece*

plate   *facing page*

I 1. Section of a pre-Portuguese lintel, Archbishop's museum,   12
S. Thomé-Mylapore

2. Traditional dance — Syro-Malabar Suddist church,
Kadutturutti

II 1. Open-air cross, Syro-Malabar Suddist church of Chungam,   13
Todupuzha

2. Pre-Portuguese Church (13th century?), Jacobite church,
Chengannur

III 1. Hindu or Buddhist temple at Thiruvancode, now a   60
Jacobite church

2. Pre-Portuguese Baptismal Font, Syro-Malabar Church,
Edapally

IV 1. Carved lintel, eastern gate, Knanaya Jacobite Church, Kottayam   61

2. Ruins of the Portuguese fort, Cranganore

V 1. View of the forane church, now the cathedral, of Palai   108

2. Interior of the cathedral of Palai

VI 1. Parish house of the old seminary church, Syro-Malabar   109
church, Vaipicotta

2. The 18th century church of Our Lady of Dolours at Trichur

VII 1. His Eminence Cardinal Eugene Tisserant at Trivandrum in   156
November 1953

VIII 1. The late Mar Severios, Syro-Malankara Bishop of Tiruvalla,   157
singing the Gospel of the Nativity, cathedral ground,
Tiruvalla

2. His Lordship Mar Thomas Tharayil, Syro-Malabar Suddist
Bishop of Kottayam, at an interdenominational meeting
held at Kottayam in December 1952

MAPS

facing page

The Central Region of Kerala   162

Christian Kerala   204

INTRODUCTION

IT IS not possible to write a complete history of the Christians in South-West India, because the ancient documents of their churches were destroyed by fire at the Synod of Diamper in 1599; but the main lines of that history are fairly well-known.

At the beginning of our era, communication between India and the Roman Empire was not difficult. Trade relations existed, new proofs of which were discovered a few years ago on both the west and east coasts. The tradition that the Apostle St. Thomas evangelized India is strong in many places, and affirmed by Mesopotamian records, and it is plain that relations continued for centuries between the Christians of Malabar and the religious centres first of Edessa, and then of Seleucia-Ctesiphon.

As in Ethiopia, so also in India there was no development of a local hierarchy. As far as we know, the Christians there had never had bishops taken from among themselves until the arrival of the Portuguese about 1500. Fortunately we still have the account of a visit which occurred twenty years before that time, of a delegation entrusted with the task of choosing candidates from monasteries of Mesopotamia for the episcopal sees of India.

However, there were many differences between the Ethiopian situation and the Indian one. The Patriarch of Alexandria used to send exclusively for the see of Axum a single Coptic monk, ordained a bishop but without the faculty of consecrating indigenous prelates. This foreign-born metropolitan, knowing only Coptic and Arabic, and ignorant of both the liturgical language of Ethiopia—Gheez—and the local

This introduction was written by the author expressly for this translation.

dialects, remained out of contact with his clergy and people. For this reason, very few of the Coptic metropolitans in Ethiopia had any real influence on the community they had to govern. The bulk of the literature translated into Gheez came directly from the Greek, while the remainder was from Arabic, and, to a much less extent, from Coptic texts.

Things were quite different in South India. Even the simplest parish priest had to learn Syriac, since the St. Thomas Christians in their liturgy and culture adhered steadfastly to it as the language of the Apostolic preaching east of Antioch. The bishops, who came from Mesopotamia to India, had no difficulty adapting themselves to their clergy. Moreover, they enjoyed the prestige of a culture which remained flourishing until 1401, when the hordes of Timur Leng destroyed Mesopotamian churches, monasteries, and libraries.

The Christians in India lived in the midst of Hindus, who had an elaborate religion and loved philosophical speculation. They were obliged to struggle for the defence of their faith. Now the Syriac literature was to provide them with excellent weapons. Since the fourth century, Greek writings, Christian and profane, had been abundantly translated into Syriac, and knowledge of Greek wisdom was profound in Mesopotamia until the reign of the first Abbasid Caliphs, when Syriac texts were changed into Arabic. We know of several Christian scholars at that time, one of them the Catholicos Timothy I, who was extremely careful and conscientious when selecting metropolitans and bishops for the distant bishoprics of his jurisdiction, which extended not only to India, but also to Tibet and China.

Consequently, there was a strong tradition of learning among the St. Thomas Christians, who were highly esteemed by their Hindu fellow-countrymen, and who therefore obtained social privileges which they still enjoy. The present zeal of the Syro-Malabar clergy and laymen for the acquisition of knowledge is in perfect keeping with the tradition of their ancestors.

The Christians of Malabar were able to keep in touch only with the Mesopotamian Christians, who themselves were soon cut off from Rome and the Eastern patriarchates owing to the wars between the Roman and Sassanide empires. Moreover, after standing up to the most severe persecutions, the Christians under Persian rule drifted away into a separate body which soon fell under Nestorian influence through the famous 'School of the Persians' at Nisibis. Moreover, the Christians of those regions did not share in the later western or Byzantine theological progress. Thus, by default, the chief authors of the Indian Christians were Theodore of Mopsuestia and his eastern followers, however rich and abundant was this literature. This happened through no fault of their own, nevertheless it proved disastrous to them, because they did not receive the help that communion with the Holy See afforded others.

The Christians of Malabar suffered also an impoverishment of their Christian treasure, especially after the heavy losses inflicted by the Mongols on Mesopotamian Christianity. Consequently, when the Portuguese arrived a century later, the Christians of Malabar were spiritually underfed. The missionaries, realizing this, rapidly provided them with schools and seminaries, which opened a new era of better educated clergy.

Unfortunately, the Portuguese prelates and missionaries, because they had neither experience of different rites, nor understanding of the need for respecting the traditional liturgical practices of the local Christians, made no effort to consecrate indigenous bishops. This was all the more lamentable, since the Holy See would have done it, and tried to do it, following a policy applied a long time ago to for the Maronites of Mount Lebanon. A century and a half after the arrival of the missionaries, part of the Catholic community, in most dramatic circumstances, swore that they would never again obey foreign prelates. Thus was born the Jacobite movement in Malabar.

Not until European missionaries had been on Indian soil for

about three centuries did India receive a regular hierarchy from Leo XIII. A few months later the Syro-Malabars were given a hierarchical organization of their own. The recent statistics which are found in this work show how the Pope of the Encyclical *Orientalium Dignitas* was well inspired, when he created the first two Syro-Malabar dioceses. Logically, the Jacobites ought to return to the Catholic faith, because the pretext which separated their ancestors from Rome, namely unwillingness to obey foreign prelates, had been removed by the organization of a complete Syrian hierarchy.

The Syro-Malabar community developed very quickly, and at present it has numerous clergy, secular and regular, a great number of nuns in their own congregations, and many flourishing institutions of every kind. Their development had been remarkable. Moreover, their true and vigorous missionary zeal had prompted hundreds of them to serve as secular priests of the Latin rite throughout India. Besides this, Latin orders and congregations of both men and women recruit amongst them many, and for some, most of their Indian members.

When I prepared for the *Dictionnaire de Théologie Catholique* the article which Father Hambye is now presenting in English, I came to admire greatly the Syro-Malabar Christians, who remained constantly faithful to their religion despite centuries of adversity. My visit to them in November-December 1953 immeasurably increased this admiration. I hope the present volume helps them keep alive the gratitude they owe their ancestors, and makes them ever more zealous for the defence and propagation of our common Catholic heritage.

Rome, the 6th of August 1955
Transfiguration of Our Lord

EUGENE CARDINAL TISSERANT
Bishop of Ostia, Porto and
Santa Rufina

LIST OF ABBREVIATIONS

A.A.S.	Acta Apostolicae Sedis, Rome & Vatican City
AA.SS.	Acta Sanctorum, Ed. Bollandistae, Antwerp, Paris & Brussels
A.B.	Analecta Bollandiana, Brussels
A.F.H.	Archivum Franciscanum Historicum, Karachi-Rome
A.F.P.	Archivum Fratrum Praedicatorum, Rome
A.H.S.I.	Archivum Historicum Societatis Iesu, Rome
A.O.C.D.	Archivum Ordinis Carmelitarum Discalceatorum, Rome
An. P. Cat.	Annuaire Pontifical Catholique, Paris
A.P.F.	Archivum S. Congregationis de Propaganda Fide, Rome
A.R.S.J.	Archivum Romanum Societatis Jesu, Rome
A.V.	Archivum Vaticanum, Vatican City
B.I.C.H.S.	Bulletin of the International Commission of Historical Sciences, London
B.J.R.L.	Bulletin of the John Ryland's Library, Manchester
B.S.O.S.	Bulletin of the School of Oriental Studies, London
B.V.	Bibliotheca Apostolica Vaticana, Vatican City
C.C.O.	Codificazione Canonica Orientale, Rome & Vatican City
C.M.	The Clergy Monthly, Kurseong-Ranchi
C.O.V.	Her Christelijk Oosten en Vereeniging, Amsterdam
C.Q.R.	The Church Quarterly Review, Madras
C.R.	The Clergy Review, London
C.S.C.O.	Corpus Scriptorum Christianorum Orientalium, Louvain & Washington
D.A.C.L.	Dictionnaire d'Archéologie Chrétienne et de Liturgie, Paris
D.B.	Dictionnaire de la Bible, Paris
D.B.S.	Dictionnaire de la Bible, Supplément, Paris
D.D.C.	Dictionnaire de Droit Canonique, Paris
D.H.G.E.	Dictionnaire d'Histoire et de Géographie Ecclésiastique, Paris
D.T.C.	Dictionnaire de Théologie Catholique, Paris
E.C.Q.	Eastern Churches Quarterly, London-Ramsgate
E.O.	Les Echos d'Orient, Paris
E.R.E.	Encylopaedia of Religion and Ethics, London
G.C.S.	Griechische Christliche Schriftstellers, Berlin
I.A.	Indian Antiquary, Bombay
I.H.Q.	Indian Historical Quarterly, Calcutta
J.A.	Journal Asiatique, Paris
J.A.S.B.	Journal of the Asiatic Society of Bengal, Calcutta
J.B.B.R.A.S.	Journal of the Bombay Branch of the Royal Asiatic Society, Bombay
J.B.H.S.	Journal of the Bombay Historical Society, Bombay
J.B.O.R.S.	Journal of the Bihar & Orissa Research Society, Patna
J.I.H.	Journal of Indian History
J.R.A.S.	Journal of the Royal Asiatic Society, London
J.T.S.	Journal of Theological Studies, London
K.S.P.	Kerala Society Papers, Trivandrum

L.F.T.K.	Lexicon für Theologie und Kirche, Freiburg. i. B.
M.G.H.	Monumenta Germaniae Historica, Berlin
M.H.S.I.	Monumenta Historica Societatis Iesu, Rome
M.M.S.I.	Monumenta Missionum Societatis Iesu, Rome
N.Z.M.W.	Neue Zeitschrift für Missionswissenschaft, Beckenried
O.C.	Orientalia Christiana, Rome
O.C.A.	Orientalia Christiana Analecta, Rome
O.C.P.	Orientalia Christiana Periodica, Rome
P.G.	Migne, *Patrologiae series Graeca*, quoted by volume and column
P.L.	Migne, *Patrologiae series Latina*, quoted by volume and column
P.O.C.	Proche-Orient Chrétien, Jerusalem
Q.J.M.S.	Quarterly Journal of the Mythic Society, Bangalore
R.H.E.	Revue d'Histoire Ecclésiastique, Louvain
R.H.M.	Revue d'Histoire des Missions, Paris
R.O.C.	Revue de l'Orient Chrétien, Paris
Y.M.I	Young Man of India, Madras
Z.D.M.G.	Zeitschrift der deutsche morgenländer Gesellschaft, Leipzig
Z.K.T.	Zeitschrift für katholische Theologie, Innsbruck & Vienna

Note for the Reader

When the manuscript of this book went to the press the recent changes in State boundaries had not been finalized. The text has been amended where necessary, but the following note may be useful to the reader.

Following the recommendations of the States Re-organization Committee, the political divisions of India have been considerably modified. These modifications have affected Malabar. Together with the other new States the State of Kerala was inaugurated on 1 November 1956. It comprises all the Malayalam-speaking regions of the west coast, i.e. the former State of Travancore-Cochin— except for the southernmost part which was handed over to Madras State on account of its Tamil character —, the Malabar District, and a small section of the South Kanara District, both of which formerly belonged to Madras State. The name of Kerala — usually interpreted as meaning the 'land of coco-nuts'—has been chosen on account of its antiquity and popular appeal.

The boundaries of Travancore-Cochin and the Malabar District as shown on the general map coincide now with those of Kerala State, except for the southernmost section which has been merged in Madras State. The central region of the former State of Travancore-Cochin as illustrated on the particular map is now entirely situated in Kerala State.

E. R. H.

I

THE ORIGINS

THE LAND AND THE CHRISTIANS

IN POLITICAL geography the name of Malabar indicates the Malayalam-speaking area in South India, which covered the Travancore-Cochin State and included a part of the bordering State of Madras. In physical geography the appellation 'Malabar Coast' was applied, during the Portuguese occupation, to the whole sea-shore overlooked by the Western Ghats from Bombay down to Cape Comorin. But recently the word 'Malabar' was more commonly used in connection with the territory covered by the former United State of Travancore-Cochin.[1]

From the sixteenth century until the eighteenth, Europeans used the name of 'Malabar' for Indians dwelling between the western and eastern coasts of Southern India; but those Indians living in the area comprising part of the Madras State, together with the whole Travancore-Cochin territory, called themselves and still do so, Malayalees. They speak Malayalam, which is one of the Dravidian languages.

The Christians who form the Syro-Malabar Church are frequently known as 'Christians of St. Thomas'. They were recognized by the first missionaries as belonging to the group of Eastern Syrians or Chaldeans, from their hierarchical relations and their rite. Till the beginning of the twentieth century ecclesiastical documents generally name them as 'Syrians', 'Soriani'. Hence the tautological phrase, 'Syrians-Sorians', used in the first twenty years of the *Annuaire Pontifical Catholique*.[2]

---

[1] See note following the Preface.

[2] A. Battandier (continued by E. Chardavoine A. A.), *Annuaire Pontifical Catholique*, Paris, 1898-1918.

THE APOSTOLATE OF SAINT THOMAS IN INDIA

The problem of the origins of Syrian Christianity in India is closely connected with the evangelization of India by the Apostle Saint Thomas. This apostolate is asserted by ancient traditions, both literary and local.

The *Acts of Judas-Thomas*[1] probably originated in a milieu of Upper-Mesopotamia, perhaps Edessa, and go back either to the last quarter of the second century A.D. or to the first years of the third. The author is a Syrian who is able to recognize the name '*Thomas*' as a nickname derived from *t'omo*, which means twin; therefore he has preserved the real name, *Judas*, which, according to the old Syriac version of the Gospels, was the name of Thomas-Didymus. From this detail the author assumes that, in those days, the old version of the Gospels had not yet been replaced by the *Peshitto*. There are those who have attributed the composition of the *Acts* to Bardesanes.

According to the *Acts*, the Apostle St. Thomas preached the Gospel in the land of Gondaferes or Gundaphares. This prince is the Parthian King Guduphara, who was ruler of Afghanistan and the Punjab during the second quarter of the first century A.D. Most of the critics of the nineteenth century have refused to concede any historical value to the *Acts of Judas-Thomas* and nobody can deny that they are full of fabulous details.[2]

---

[1] For the text of the *Acts* (Greek version corrected on the Syriac) one can consult M.R.James, *The Apocryphal New Testament*, Oxford, 1924, pp. 364-438. On the value of the Acts cf. E. Amann, 'Apocryphes du Nouveau Testament', in *D.B.S.* vol. I (1928), col. 501-4; P. Peeters s.J. reviewing J. Dahlmann s.J. in *A.B.* 32 (1913), pp. 75-7; J. Quasten, *Patrology*, Westminster (U.S.A.), 1950, vol. I, pp. 139-40.

[2] Among those who refuse any value to the Acts, let us mention P. Peeters s.J. 'Bulletin des publications hagiographiques', in *A.B.* 18 (1899), pp. 275-9, 25 (1906), pp. 196-200, 32 (1913), pp. 75-7, 44 (1926), pp. 402-3; R. Garbe, *Indien und das Christentum*, Tübingen, 1914; A. Harnack, *Die Mission und Ausbreitung des Christentums*, Leipzig, 1924, 4th ed., vol. II, p. 698; L. de la Vallée Poussin, *L'Inde aux temps des Mauryas*, Paris, 1930; U. Monneret de Villard, 'La Fiera di Batnae e la tralazione di S. Tommaso a Edessa', in *Rendiconti della Academia Naz. dei Lincei, Classe di scienze morali . . .*, 6 (1951), pp. 77-104.

Nevertheless it has recently been observed that it was unlikely for a writer of the third century to have invented the story contained in the document. For it is remarkable that the sovereign's name, which is an historical one, should have been preserved intact in a rather remote country, and all the more so as it has left no traces in any historical or legendary work of India, and has reappeared only in the nineteenth century on coins and on an inscription of Gandhara.

The highly documented study of Mgr. A. E. Medlycott in 1905,[1] the thesis of Fr. Dalhmann s. J. in 1912,[2] and the articles of J. N. Farquhar in 1926,[3] have effectively contributed towards lessening the suspicions of the critics. The bundle of ancient testimonies is all the more striking as the tradition of an apostolate at the court of a Parthian prince of the Indus Valley prevents opposition between authors who speak of India and others who mention Parthia in connection with the labours of St. Thomas. The first group of testimonies, which apparently depend more or less directly on the tradition of the *Acts* (Edessenian tradition), is more numerous.[4] Other ancient testimonies appear to have hailed from Alexandria.[5] The

[1] A. E. Medlycott, *India and the Apostle Thomas. An Inquiry with a critical Analysis of the 'Acta Thomae'*, London, 1905.

[2] J. Dahlmann s. J. *Die Thomas-Legende und die ältesten historischen Beziehungen des Christentums zum fernen Osten*, Freiburg i.B. 1912.

[3] J. N. Farquhar, 'The Apostle Thomas in North India', in *B.J.R.L.* 10 (1926), pp. 80-111; 'The Apostle Thomas in South India', ibid. 11 (1927), pp. 20-50.

[4] Some testimonies of this tradition, S. Ephraem, *Carmina Nisibena*, Ed., Bickell, Leipzig, 1866, no. 42, text p. 79, transl. p. 163; T. J. Lamy, *S. Ephraemi Hymni et Sermones*, Mechlin, 1902, vol. IV, col. 694, 704, 706; 'Doctrine of Addai', Ed. Cureton in *Ancient Syriac Documents*, London, 1864, p. 32; S. Gregorii Nazianzi, 'Sermo 33', *P.G.* 36, 227; S. Ambrosii, 'Enarrationes in Psalmum XLV', 21, *P.L.* 14, 1198; S. Hieronymi, 'Epistola LIX ad Marcellam', *P.L.* 22, 588, ff.; and in general the Latin writers, viz. Gaudentius of Brescia, *P.L.* 20, 962, ff.; St. Paulinus of Nola, *P.L.* 61, 514; St. Gregory of Tours, 'In Gloria Martyrum' cap. 21, 22', in *M.G.H. Scr. Rer. Merov.* I. b, pp. 507, ff.

[5] Origen, extract of 'In Genesim' Bk. III, *P.G.* 12, 92; 'Recognitiones Clementinae' Bk IX, 29, *P.G.* 1, 1415.

author of the *Book of the Bee*, the Nestorian Solomon of Basrah, writing in the thirteenth century and well aware of both the Indian and Mesopotamian traditions, summarized the story of St. Thomas in conciliatory terms: 'Thomas was from Jerusalem, belonging to the tribe of Juda. He preached to the Parthians, the Medes and the Indians; then because he had baptized the daughter of the King of the Indians, he died by the sword. The merchant Habban brought his body and laid it down at Edessa, the city blessed by Christ our Lord. Others say that he was buried at *Mahluph*, a city of the Land of the Indians.'[1]

Besides this literary tradition favouring a Thomistic apostolate on the north-west borders of Hindustan, there is another, of a local and popular character, in favour of a preaching among the Dravidian populations of the south. To support the northern tradition of the *Acts* no ancient Christian monument has so far been discovered. On the other hand, in the south the living presence of a strong body of Christians, the findings of Palayur, Arthad, Nilamperur,[2] and so on, the sanctuary of Mylapore, venerated as the *Martyrium* of the Apostle, all these bear strong testimony to the reliability of the local tradition of Malabar.

As a matter of fact, the Romans had as close or closer trade relations with Southern India, as they had with the north, particularly in connection with the pepper-growing country. The numerous golden coins of the Empire which have been found all over the south, as well as many recent discoveries,

[1] Solomon of Basrah, 'The Book of the Bee', Ed. E.A. Wallis Budge, in *Anecdota Oxoniensa, Semitic Series*, Oxford, 1886, I. b, text p. 119, transl. p. 105.

[2] Palayur, at present situated in Kerala State, is well known for the popular traditions of an early apostolate of St. Thomas, and for the recent excavations, cf. Placid of St. Josepeh т.o.cd. *The Church of Palayur*, Chundal, 1951 (in Malayalam). At Arthad a strang. cross painted on a roughly hewn stone block was found under the open-air cross of the Catholic church. At Nilamperur, near the site of a Hindu temple, the effigy of a king, wearing a pectoral cross, was unearthed *c.* 1889, cf. T.K. Joseph, 'The St. Thomas Traditions of South India', in *B.I.C.H.S.* London, 5 (1933), p. 560.

offer abundant proof that Roman trade-centres existed along the southern coasts of India, even on the eastern shores.[1]

Having reached this point in his thesis, one would think that Fr. Dahlmann would be ready to accept as an historical fact that St. Thomas preached in Malabar; but he prefers to hold that the apostolate was limited to the Punjab. He supposes therefore that the Christians of Mesopotamia, who settled in South India after Sapor II's persecution, probably brought thither what they knew from the Edessenian tradition of the *Acts*. It would be a kind of wandering tradition, a *Wander-legende*.[2]

But Mgr. Medlycott and, generally speaking, all authors who have had personal contact with India, are reluctant to lessen the weight of the southern tradition. For instance, J. N. Farquhar finds the first favourable clue to the southern tradition in the *Acts* themselves. The *Acts* tell of the departure of St. Thomas from the court and kingdom of Gundaphares in order to continue preaching the Gospel in some other part of India. This journey of the Apostle according to Farquhar, must have been connected with the Kushans' invasion of the Indus Valley, which occurred about A.D. 50.[3] It is therefore quite possible that when driven away by the invaders, Habban, the King's merchant, and his friend St. Thomas chose as a place of safety one of those harbours of South India, Muziris for example, where there were many Jews, Syrians and Greeks. At this point in his explanations Farquhar asserts the

[1] J. Dahlmann, op. cit. pp. 51-76; on the recent excavation of a Roman trading-centre south of Pondicherry—R.E.M. Wheeler, A. Ghosh and Krishna Deva, 'Arikamedu: an Indo-Roman Trading-station on the East Coast of India', in *Ancient India*, no. 2 (1946), pp. 17-124. The article contains three maps of India, the first one showing the principal places mentioned in the Arikamedu report, the second one giving the distribution of Roman coins found so far in India, the third one the distribution of semi-precious stones obtained in India for the Roman market.

[2] J. Dahlmann, ibid., G. Rae, *The Syrian Church in India*, London, 1892, pp. 24-6.

[3] J. N. Farquhar, '*The Apostle Thomas in South India*', pp. 21, ff.

local tradition of Malabar, for he readily confesses that the *Acts of Judas-Thomas* in the narration of the Apostle's second mission do not name any place or person suitable to India proper.

In accordance with this tradition, the Apostle probably left the mouth of the Indus for Socotra, and from Socotra he must have reached Muziris-Cranganore.[1]   Mgr. Medlycott believes that details given by the *Acts* on the life at Gundaphares's court are better fitted to a maharajah's court than to the residence of a Parthian prince.[2]   It is impossible to go into details here. The southern tradition must be more ancient; but we do not possess any dated testimonies before the sixth century A.D. What the monk Theodore told Gregory of Tours must apply to Mylapore.[3]   Mgr. Medlycott specifies that the meteorological data pertain to South India, and not to the Punjab.[4]

BEGINNINGS OF CHRISTIANITY

In the Christian community of the south there was no doubt a good proportion of indigenous Christians, because the author of the *Acts of Judas-Thomas* could not have written in Mesopotamia something which, to contemporaries sufficiently aware of the situation in India, would have seemed unlikely. Moreover, we know from Eusebius that at the end of the second century A.D. the Alexandrine Pantaenus found Christians in India who read St. Matthew's Gospel in Hebrew. The word 'Hebrew' is probably the result of a scholarly adaptation

[1] Ibid. pp. 22-4.
[2] A. E. Medlycott, op. cit. pp. 277-89.
[3] Cf. *infra* p. 19.
[4] A. E. Medlycott, ibid. pp. 71-9. Besides we have the testimony of the *Song of St. Thomas*, the text of which must be very old, but which cannot be dated with accuracy., cf. P. J. Thomas, 'The South Indian Tradition of the Apostle Thomas', in *J.R.A.S.* Centenary supplement, 1923, p. 214; T. K. Joseph, op. cit. pp. 560-9; F. X. Rocca, 'La Leggenda di S. Tommaso Apostolo', in *O.C.* 22 (1933), pp. 168-79; Placid of St. Joseph T.O.C.D., 'The South Indian Apostolate of St. Thomas', *O.C.P.* 18 (1952), pp. 234-6.

of Eusebius. Actually that Gospel must have been written in Aramaic, in Syriac.[1]

No positive testimony of the third century A.D. is available regarding organized communities in India. Such a silence is all the more surprising because Mingana has collected a large number of quotations referring to the bishoprics of the Persian Gulf and of the neighbouring countries.[2] Not until A.D. 295 does the *Chronicle of Seert* refer to Bishop David leaving his see of Basrah to devote himself to a missionary life in India.[3]

Following many others, Mingana quotes among the subscribers of the Council of Nicaea 'John, the Persian, Bishop of the whole of Persia and Greater India.'[4] But, according to H. Gelzer,[5] the lists contain only a 'John, the Persian' or 'of Persia.' The testimony of Gelasius should be given less importance because he wrote in the latter half of the fifth century (A.D. 475), at a time when it could be held as certain that the Indian Christian communities received their prelates from Persia; Gelasius would transfer a state of affairs existing in his days to the time of the Council of Nicaea.

It cannot be proved that there was a hierarchical connection with Mesopotamia in the middle of the fourth century, and in fact the mission of the monk Theophilus in 354 A.D. contradicts it. For this native of the Maldives Islands was sent by the Roman Emperor Constantius as a propagandist of the Arian doctrine to Himyar, in the country of Axum, to his native island and to India. Philostorgos tells us that Theophilus

[1] Eusebii, 'Historia Ecclesiastica', Bk. V, 10, *P.G.* 20, 456; S. Hieronymi, 'De Viribus Illustribus', 36, *P.L.* 23, 683.

[2] A. Mingana, 'The Early Spread of Christianity in India', in *B.J.R.L.* 10 (1926), pp. 489-95. On the subject of the historical value of the *Chronicle of Arbela*, cf. I. Ortiz de Urbina, 'Intorno al Valore Storico della Cronica di Arbela', in *O.C.P.* 2 (1936), pp. 5-33, and also *infra*, p. 12. n. I.

[3] 'Chronique de Seert, Histoire Nestorienne inédite', Ed. Mar Addai Scher, in *P.O.* 4, p. 236

[4] A. Mingana, op. cit. p. 395; according to Gelazii Cyzicensis, 'Concilium Nicaenum', *P.G.* 85, 1314

[5] H. Gelzer, *Patrum Nicaenorum Nomina*, Leipzig, 1898.

reformed several abuses, particularly the use of sitting during the public reading of the Gospel, a custom then prevalent among the Indian communities.[1] It may be rightly asked how such an intervention was possible, if India had Mesopotamian bishops from that time onwards?

RELATIONS WITH THE PERSIAN CHURCH

It should be remembered that about the same period Persian Christians, who were running away from the persecution of the Sassanide Emperor Sapor II, arrived in Malabar. Their attitude can be compared to that of the Zoroastrians, who, after the Muslim victory over the Sassanides, founded the Parsi colony of Gujarat in the eighth century; yet no attestation of a similar exodus of Christians can be gathered from contemporary documents. Only a local tradition reports that, at the same time, a group of Christians arrived to whom might be attributed the division of the Syrians into two sections, still extant today, the Nordists and the Suddists, *Vadakkumbhagar* and *Thekkumbhagar*. At a certain period they must have dwelt separately, the Vadakkumbhagars to the north, and the Thekkumbhagars to the south of Cranganore. Moreover, according to the same tradition, the Nordists are the descendants of the converts of St. Thomas, whereas the Suddists go back to the Syrian immigrants.

This tradition had already been expounded by Antonio de Gouvea. It is generally based, in recent contributions, on a record written in Malayalam and Syriac about 1770, and secured through the care of Gavril (Gabriel), a Jacobite bishop. The document is now preserved in the University library of Leyden.[2]

[1] Philostorgos, 'Historia Ecclesiastica', Bk. III, 4-6, *P.G.* 65, 482-90, and in *G.C.S.* 21 (1913), pp. 33-5; A.E. Medlycott, op. cit. pp. 188-202.

[2] J. P. N. Land, *Anecdota Syriaca*, Leyden, 1862, pp. 7, 24-30, 123-7. Text and translation reproduced in S.Giamil, *Genuinae Relationes...*, Rome, 1902, pp. 552-64. A similar story was published from a manuscript of the

According to this record of the Jacobites, the descendants of St. Thomas's converts, numbering 160 families, had been deprived of priests for a long time and had therefore partly reverted to idolatry. Their situation however was revealed to the Bishop of Edessa in a vision. This divine intervention led the Catholicos of Seleucia-Ctesiphon to send Thomas, a merchant of Jerusalem, to India. After his first contact with India, he introduced there the core of a permanent colony, that consisted of Christians from Jerusalem, Baghdad and Nineveh. They were led by deacons and priests as well as by the metropolitan who had had the vision. The merits of that Palestinian merchant went further. He was farsighted, and obtained from the local prince the land where at a later date the city of Kuramaklur was built, and also a grant of privileges. The text of the document, conferring both the land and those privileges, was engraved on brass plates but unhappily the plates were lost when the Portuguese decided to bring them to Portugal.

Such is the tradition as recorded in the aforesaid document, though it has different shades of meaning, especially among Nordists. Gouvea records it with slight differences. He says that the merchant must have had two houses at the same time, one north and the other south of the river which divided the town of Cranganore. His true wife lived in the south, and the concubine in the north. Hence some division according to the caste system can be easily understood.[1]

Bodleian Library by F. Nau, 'Deux notices relatives au Malabar', in *R.O.C.* 17 (1912), pp. 74-82.

[1] But, according to the Nordist tradition and certain written accounts, the Suddists are the descendants of Thomas Cana by his concubine. The Nordists claim that Thomas Cana had under his protection a woman of the washerman caste. Thomas Cana arranged for her to be married with a boy of the Marar caste. The seven daughters of this woman were married to seven boys of the colonists living in the southern street. These seven boys are the progenitors of the Suddists. This is how the Nordist accounts depict the origin of the Suddists. In the beginning there were Nordists and Suddists only in Cranganore. In course of time all the non-Suddists came to be called Nordists [translator's note].

J. S. Assemani, who came across the story, makes reference
to the arrival in India of Bishop Thomas Cana, about A.D. 825.
He believes that his 'wives' were the two cities of Cranganore
and Angamale where he had jurisdiction.[1]

Furthermore, S. Giamil when studying the Leyden text
and Assemani's explanation logically concluded that there
were two missions: first came the merchant, Thomas of Jerusalem, accompanied by Joseph, the anonymous Metropolitan
of Edessa; then there arrived, in A.D. 800, Bishop Thomas Cana.[2]

According to A. Mingana, even if there is some historical
background for the mission attributed to A.D. 345, it must be
distinguished from the coming of Bishop Thomas Cana.[3]

Among the Chaldean documents which give such a full
account of the Persian Church during the first quarter of the
fifth century, no mention of any Indian Christianity is made.

HISTORICAL APPRECIATION ON THE ORIGINS

Summing up the present results of historical scholarship on
the origin of Christianity in India, particularly in Malabar,
we may say this: there was a very ancient evangelization,
started by St. Thomas the Apostle, and mainly in South India.

From very early times, certainly before the end of the second
century, Indian Christians came into close connection with
Edessa, as can be surmised from the composition in this town,
or in its environs, of the *Acts of Judas-Thomas*, and from that
Aramaic or Syriac Gospel found by Pantaenus in India. Indian
Christianity was definitely connected with the see of Seleucia-
Ctesiphon only about A.D. 450, at a time when the Mesopotamian, also called the Persian, Church was itself being strongly
established and was a well-knit unit.

[1] J. S. Assemani, *Bibliotheca Orientalis*, vol. III b, pp. CCCCXLI, ff.
[2] S. Giamil, op. cit. pp. 578-82.
[3] A. Mingana, op. cit. p. 476, n. 1.

II

THE SYRO-MALABAR CHURCH FROM A.D. 450 UNTIL THE ADVENT OF THE PORTUGUESE

THE PERSIAN CHURCH AND INDIAN CHRISTIANITY

THE FIRST detailed and objective text we have is the report of Cosmas Indicopleustes. It is the starting-point of this period.

In his *Topographia Christiana*, Cosmas summarizes his own travelling experiences in India which took place between A.D. 520 and 525.[1] Cosmas mentions a Christianity in Socotra (Dioscurides Island). Its inhabitants, he says, are the descendants of the colonists introduced by Ptolomaeus, and they speak Greek. Having passed within sight of the island but without landing there, he had secured his information from some natives with whom he was travelling. But they told him that there were many Christians in the island and that their clergy were ordained in Persia.

Had the island not become a Persian dominion when, according to the Arabian geographers, Al-Hamdani and Yaqut,[2] Khosroas deported inhabitants of countries wrested from Byzantium, it would be strange if those descendants of Ptolomaeus' colonists had no connection with Alexandria. The early Greek colonists must have merged among the new immigrants. In any case, the influence of the Persian Church was predominant in the island. This can be explained. As in Beith

[1] *P.G.* 88, 169 and 445; E.O. Windstedt, *The Christian Topography of Cosmas Indicopleustes*, Cambridge, 1909, pp. 119, 321, ff, and notes pp. 332, 344 and 346; J.W. McCrindle, *The Christian Topography of Cosmas*, London, 1897, pp. 118-9; on Cosmas consult H. Leclercq, 'Kosmas Indicopleustes', in *D.A.C.L.* vol. VIII (1), 820-49; V. Barthold, *La Découverte de l'Asie*, Paris, 1947, p. 68.

[2] J. Tkatsch, 'Sokotra', in *Encyclopaedia of Islam*, Leyden, 1934, vol. IV, p. 478.

Qataraye,[1] so also there had been an actual evangelization of the mixed population of Socotra, consisting of Greeks, Arabs, Indians, etc. Socotra remained Christian for a long time; it still received a bishop from Catholicos Sabrisho III (1064-72).[2] Arabian geographers of the fourteenth century also regarded the island as Christian, as did Marco Polo: 'And you must know that the inhabitants of this island are baptized Christians, and have an archbishop. Their archbishop has nothing to do with the Pope of Rome, for he depends upon an archbishop who lives at Baudac [Baghdad] called, as we have said before, Jatolic [catholicos]. It is this Jatolic of Baudac, who sends the archbishop to the island. He also sends prelates to many other parts of the world, just as the Pope of Rome does. And all these clergy and prelates obey not the Roman Church, but this great prelate of Baudac, whom they consider their Pope.'[3]

[1] According to the *Chronicle of Arbela* there was a bishopric, or at least a residing bishop, by A.D. 225, in Beith Qataraye, on the northern section of the Arabian shore of the Persian Gulf. But the *Chronicle* must be used with great care, since it appears full of anachronisms. Cf. A. Mingana, 'La Chronique d'Arbèles', in *Sources Syriaques*, Mosul, 1907, vol. I, text. pp. 1-75, transl. pp. 76-108; M.E. Sachau, 'Die Chronik von Arbela. Ein Beitrag zur Kenntnis der ältesten Christentums im Orient', in *Abhandlungen der kgl. preuss. Akademie der Wissenschaften, phil.-hist. Klasse*, Berlin, 1906, n. 6; A. von Harnack, *Mission und Ausbreitung des Christentums*, vol. II, pp. 683-91; P. Peeters s. J., 'Le passionnaire d'Adiabène', in *A.B.* 43 (1925), pp. 261-304; F. Zorell s. J., 'Chronica Ecclesiae Arbelensis', in *O.C.* 8 (1927), n. 31, pp. 141-204.

[2] H. Gismondi s.J., *Maris Amri et Slibae de Patriarchis Nestorianorum Commentaria*, Rome, 1896-9, p. 125, transl. p. 11.

[3] Translation taken from A. Ricci, *The Travels of Marco Polo*, London, 1931, pp. 338 and 340. Cf. also H. Yule and H. Cordier, *The Book of Ser Marco Polo*, London, 1921, vol. II, pp. 406-7. Here is the original text: 'Et sachiés que celz de cest ysle sunt cristienz bateçés et ont arcevesque . . . Ceste arcevesque ne a que fer con le apostoille de Rome: mes vos di qu'el est sotpost a un arcevesque que demeure a Baudac [Bagdad]. Et cestui arcevesque de Baudac mande ceste arcevesque de ceste ysle; et encore mande en plosors parties dou monde aussi com fait l'apostoille de Rome. E tui cesti clereges et prelais ne sunt obeisant a le yglise de Rome, mes sunt tuit obeisant a celz grant prelais de Baudac, qu'il ont por leur pape', in *Il milione*, Ed. L. Foscole Benedetto, Florence, 1928, pp. 203-5. Cf. also the last edition of Marco Polo's travels, A. C. Moule and P. Pelliot, *Marco Polo: The Description of the World*, London, 1938, vol. I, pp. 425-7.

1. Section of a pre-Portuguese lintel, showing the head of a king—
Archbishop's museum, S. Thomé-Mylapore.

2. Traditional dance and song in honour of St. Thomas the Apostle,
November 1953 — Syro-Malabar Suddist Church, Kadutturutty.

II. 1. Open-air cross on a large elaborately carved base, standing on the south-west side of the Syro-Malabar Suddist Church of Chungam, Todupuzha.

2. Pre-Portuguese church (13th century ?). View taken towards the east — Jacobite Church, Chengannur.

In the seventeenth century there were still some Christians in Socotra.[1]

The Christians in Ceylon seem to have had a different origin. Cosmas speaks of Taprobana in the two references mentioned above. In the first he tells us only that there is a church with its faithful and clergy, but in the second text he is more accurate: there is a church of Persian settlers with a priest ordained in Persia, a deacon and some minor clergy. The natives and the king belong to another religion. Therefore there was no real missionary centre in Ceylon but only an establishment of Persian traders, who were dwelling in a place abounding in merchandise imported from China and Indonesia. They had their parish, just as the Melkite, Maronite and Syrian communities have in a port like Marseilles today.

Cosmas does not know whether there are Christian communities beyond Ceylon but affirms that there do exist Christians in Male, and at Quilon (Kalliana) where a bishop, ordained in Persia, lives.[2] The exact site of Male is not yet identified, but it is the centre of the pepper trade; hence, like Quilon, it is situated on the Malabar Coast.[3]

There are other texts of Chaldean origin concerning Christians in India. Unfortunately they are less accurate regarding the number of Christians, the places where they formed communities, and their organization.

Mana, who wrote during the last quarter of the sixth century, sent his translations of Diodorus to seaboard countries, like

[1] J. Tkatsch, op. cit. ibid.

[2] According to a slightly corrected translation of the Greek text, Cosmas seems to speak also of a bishop living in the country of Male. Cf. E. R. Hambye s.j., 'The Syrian Church in India', in C.M. 16 (1952), p. 368, n. 9. The Malayalam name of Quilon is to-day Kollam. According to some authors, the Kalliana of Cosmas is to be identified with the town of Kalyan, in North Konkan, which was the main trading centre of that region in Ancient India. Nowadays it is a suburb of Bombay. Cf. A. C. Perumalil s.j., 'The Apostles of Kalyana (Bombay)', in J.I.H. 22 (1943), p. 76.

[3] E. O. Windstedt, op. cit. p. 354.

Bahrayn, and also to India.[1] During the pontificate of Catholicos Sabrisho I (596-604), Maruta, the future Maphrian of
Takrit, received from his superior perfumes and gifts brought
from India and China. Doubtless they had been presented to
the catholicos by Christian merchants of those places.[2]

In the correspondence of Catholicos Ishoyabh III (c. 647-
50-7-8), mention is made of the schismatic tendencies
of the Metropolitan of Rewardashir (in the present south-
western part of Iran) who by his stubbornness led the bishops
of India astray from the catholicos. Ishoyabh says that Christianity had expanded not only as far as India, but farther east to
Qalah or Qillah. Qillah is probably the Kalah mentioned by
the Arabian geographers, situated in the Malacca Straits.[3]

According to the great Catholicos Timothy I (780-9-823),
those who were married but were separated from their partners
were not allowed to embark on a new marriage without being
sure of the death of the other party. Even if the absent party
were in India or China, a certificate of death could be obtained
through the hierarchy, namely, the catholicos, metropolitan
or bishop residing there. Hence we can see how well kept
was the *liber status animarum* of the Persian colonies even in
those days.[4]

Timothy also mentions that many Persian monks voyaged
across the seas towards India and China. Timothy struggled
as much as did Ishoyabh III against the separatism of Fars
(South Persia). This separatism fostered a schismatic situation in India. But, says Barhebraeus, the reluctant bishops
answered: 'We are the disciples of St. Thomas; we have

[1] 'Chronique de Seert . . . ', *P.O.C.* 7, p. 117.

[2] Ibid. 13, p. 497.

[3] In spite of the reluctance of A. Mingana. Cf. M. Streck, 'Kalah', in
Encylopaedia of Islam, Leyden, 1927, vol. II, pp. 669-70; 'Ishoyabh III Liber
Epistolarum', Ed. R. Duval, in *C.S.C.O. Script. Syri, ser. 2*, 64, p. 252.

[4] J. Labourt, *De Timotheo I . . . et Christianorum Orientalium Condicione
sub Chalifis Abbasidis*, Paris, 1904, quest. XXXI, p. 63, ff. On Catholicos
Timothy I, cf. E. Tisserant, 'Timothée I', in *D.T.C.* vol. XV, 1121-39.

nothing to do with the See of Mari.'[1] This is the first allusion to the phrase 'Christians of St. Thomas', which was so frequently used during the following centuries.

Although at the time of Catholicos Ishoyabh II (628-46) bishops and priests had already been sent to India, Timothy made the Indian Church fully independent from Fars (South Persia) by giving it a metropolitan of its own. According to Abdisho (714-28), a contemporaneous writer, the Metropolitan of India held the tenth place and came before that of China on the list of episcopal sees.[2]

In the meantime, according to local tradition, two more groups of Persian immigrants had landed in Kerala: one arrived with Bishop Thomas about A.D. 774 or 795; another, some forty years later, with two bishops, Mar Sabrisho and Mar Peroz. This immigration can possibly be compared with the arrival in India, some fifty years earlier, of Parsis escaping from Muslim persecution.[3] There is also the possibility of identifying Bishop Thomas with a certain monk, Thomas, who was ordained as a missionary prelate by Timothy I.[4] We are told that they settled mainly at Quilon, strengthening the group of local Christians already living in that important trading centre.

Most western scholars, like Burnell, attribute to that period the two documents or copper plates, the *Sathanam*, granting privileges to the Christians.[5] The Jews had already received

[1] *Gregorii Barhebraei Chronicon Ecclesiasticum*, Ed. J.B. Abbelloos and T.J. Lamy, Paris-Louvain, 1877, vol. III, p. 171.

[2] J. S. Assemani, op. cit. vol. III a, pp. 346, ff; A. Mai, *Scriptorum Veterum Nova Collectio*, Rome, 1838, vol. Xa, text p. 304, trans. p. 142. According to J. Dauvillier, it held only the thirteenth place, if one follows Amr, and the fifteenth from what Selibha says. It was reckoned after the Metropolitan of China, J. Dauvillier, 'Les provinces chaldéennes de l'extérieur', in *Mélanges F. Cavallera*, Toulouse, 1948, p. 313.

[3] D. J. Karka, *History of the Parsis*, London, 1884, vol. I, p. 26-35.

[4] J. S. Assemani, op. cit. vol. III b, pp. CCCCXLIV-V.

[5] G. M. Rae, *The Syrian Church in India*, London and Edinburgh, 1892, pp. 155-65. According to Fr. Schurhammer's hypothesis, the lost copper plates

a similar favour. If this date is maintained, does it not mean that ancient privileges were only renewed and, perhaps, enlarged at a time when local rulers attempted to strengthen some sort of caste system among the Dravidian population expelled from the north? To the same immigration we may also ascribe the four Persian crosses of Malabar: at Kottayam where the oldest of the two crosses is preserved in the Jacobite Suddist Church called *Velliapally*, belonging today to the patriarchal party, at Kadamattam, Muttuchira and Alangad; also the Persian cross of Mylapore.[1] At any rate the local tradition gives some credit to this hypothesis; for it states that Mar Sabrisho and Mar Peroz made a good number of conversions, built new churches and erected open-air crosses.[2]

of Mar Jacob are actually the two sets found later at Tevalacara, G. Schurhammer, *The Malabar Church and Rome*, Trichinopoly, 1934, p. 23, n. 69. K. N. Daniel expressed the possibility of dating the grant to Iravi Korttan, which is one of the plates, as 6 March A.D. 230. But he has not yet convinced the scholars. On the other hand, the so-called Quilon plates are certainly of the time of the second immigration, since they bear some Cufi script. Cf. K. N. Daniel, 'Kottayam plate of Vira-Taghava Chakravartti', in *I.A.* 53 (1924), pp. 185-96, 219-29, 244-51; T. K. Joseph, *The Malabar Christians and their Ancient Documents*, Trivandrum, 1929, p. 32.

[1] On the Kottayam cross, cf. A.E. Burnell, 'Some Pahlavi Inscriptions in South India', in *I.A.* 3 (1874), pp. 308-16. On the cross of Muttuchira, cf. A. Mingana, 'The Early Spread of Christianity in India', *B.J.R.L.* 10 (1926), p. 506. On the Kadamattam cross, cf. A.S.R. Ayyar, 'A New Persian Cross from Travancore', in *The Ceylon Antiquary and Literary Register*, 9 (1924), pp. 188-96; T. K. Joseph, 'Malabar Miscellany. I. Another Persian Cross in Travancore...', *I.A.* 52 (1923), pp. 355-59; Id. 'A Pahlavi Inscription round a Persian Cross at Katamaram, Travancore', ibid. 53 (1924), p. 123; A. Modi, 'A Christian Cross with a Pahlavi Inscription recently discovered in the Travancore State', in *J.B.B.R.A.S.* (new series) 2 (1926), pp. 1-18. Thanks to the type of script used, most of those crosses can be attributed to the sixth or the eighth century. Only the second cross of Kottayam, that has a Syriac inscription in Estrangelo, is generally dated from the tenth century, cf. G.M. Rae, op. cit. pp. 120, 124, ff; E.W.West, 'Inscriptions around Crosses in South India', in *Epigraphia Indica*, 4 (1896-7), pp. 174-6; C.P.T. Winckworth, 'A New Interpretation of the Pahlavi Cross-Inscriptions of Southern India', *J. T. S.* 30 (1929), pp. 237-44.

[2] A. Mingana, op. cit. p. 508.

It seems almost certain that the second and third immigrations had but one effect, that of strengthening the bonds with the Seleucian patriarchate. Syriac remained throughout the liturgical language of the Indian Syrians, but the new colonists were shortly to be absorbed into the bulk of the already existing Dravidian Christians.[1]

For the rest of the Middle Ages we have but scanty information concerning the relations between Mesopotamia and Malabar. We can only mention the testimony of a copyist, writing in Syriac at Shengala-Cranganore in 1301. He gives the name of Catholicos Yahballaha III (1281-1317) and of the Metropolitan of India, Mar Jacob. The copyist describes himself as the latter's disciple, and signs himself as Zacharias Bar Joseph Bar Zacharias.[2]

Whatever has been written in favour of an early connection between the Church of Malabar and the patriarchate of Antioch and of all the East, there is no historical probability whatsoever, or even the slightest evidence that any Indian group of Christians ever came under the jurisdiction of the Patriarch of Antioch, whether Catholic, Greek dissident or even Jacobite.[3]

NESTORIANISM AND INDIAN CHRISTIANS

It has been asserted, and this with special authority by Fr. Schurhammer,[4] that the Christians of India did not cease to be Catholic. If by this statement it is understood that the Christians, who were poorly instructed in theological controversies, were

[1] G. M. Rae, op. cit. pp. 166, ff.

[2] E. Tisserant, *Specimina Codicum Orientalium*, Rome and Bonn, 1914, ill. 34a; J. S. and E. E. Assemani, *Bibliothecae Apostolicae Vaticanae Codicum Mss Catalogus*, Rome, 1758, Vol. II, pp. 187, ff; G. Levi della Vida, *Ricerche sulla formazione del piu antico fondo di manoscritti orientali della biblioteca Vaticana*, Città del Vaticano, 1939, pp. 176, 187-9.

[3] C. Karalevskij, 'Antioche', in *D. H. G. E.* vol. III, 602-12.

[4] G. Schurhammer, op. cit. pp. 25-42.

not formal heretics : namely that they had always believed one way or another in the primacy of the Roman See, we would not contradict it. However, it cannot be denied that from the time of Catholicos Babai (497-502-3) onwards, the Eastern Syrians and consequently the Mesopotamian bishops ruling over the Christian communities of India and their priests accepted the Nestorian formulas.

Some authors have tried to support the orthodoxy of the Indian Christians of those days by pointing out that for a long time they depended not on Seleucia but on the Metropolitan of Rewardashir in Southern Persia. Mention has already been made of the fact that this section of the Chaldean Church was in a sort of schism from Seleucia from about A.D. 585 till the pontificate of Catholicos Timothy I (780-823). But such opposition seems to have been based on nationalistic rather than on doctrinal motives. Inasmuch as that region existed as a separate entity in the ecclesiatical world, it resented the growing influence of the see of Seleucia. Accordingly it attempted for some time to maintain a kind of 'autocephalous' position. It was perhaps to curb that nationalistic tendency that Timothy recognized the Metropolitan of India; he is also said to have written a letter to the leader of the faithful in India on the primacy of Seleucia.

It does not seem, however, that the Indian Christians were ever greatly concerned with the great Christological disputes of bygone days. Their Nestorianism remained a dead letter in practice, even if their liturgical books contained objectionable formulas. Apart from this, they were living in isolation, and separated from any other Christian community in the midst of an overwhelming majority of Hindus and Mohammedans. Thus one can readily understand that when the Portuguese landed, those Christians regarded themselves as belonging to the same Church Universal. Several years were to pass before divergences came to light through the medium of a closer and deeper acquaintance.

MEDIEVAL CONTACTS WITH THE WEST

In order to complement the scanty data available in eastern documents, it seems useful to gather here the western testimonies about the Christians of India.

The first evidence comes from the Frankish monk, Theodore, who was the witness referred to by St. Gregory of Tours (d. A. D. 593 or 594). This monk visited Mylapore, and saw there a large and richly ornamented church where monks were officiating. This testimony confirms a flourishing community: 'There are a monastery and a church magnificently and carefully adorned and built.'[1]

Later on we find in various English texts brief allusions to the embassy sent by King Alfred the Great to the tomb of St. Thomas in A.D. 883.[2]

In 1122, an Indian prelate, John by name, reached Rome. He made known in the West a strange miracle that occurred in India every year on St. Thomas's Feast. It is not impossible that the so-called prelate was a Christian, or even a cleric, from South India.[3]

After this we are able to record the almost simultaneous visits of the two great travellers at the end of the thirteenth century: Marco Polo on his way back from China in 1293, and John of Montecorvino on his way to China, in the course of the same year.

From the story of Marco Polo[4] we learn only this, that both Mohammedan and Christian pilgrims frequented the sanctuary of the Apostle. Pilgrims eagerly carried away a bit of red mud that was supposed to possess strange properties for

---

[1] S. Gregorii Turonensis, 'In Gloria Martyrum', cc. 31, 32, in *M.G.H. Ser. Rer. Merov.* I, b, pp. 507, ff.

[2] A. E. Medlycott, op. cit. pp. 80-4.

[3] P. Devos s.j., 'Le miracle posthume de S. Thomas l'Apôtre', in *A.B.* 66 (1948), pp. 231-75.

[4] M. Polo, *Il Millione*, Florence, 1928, p. 187; H. Yule and H. Cordier, op. cit. pp, 353-9.

curing sick people; but in the two letters of John of Montecorvino nothing is said about the Christians of India, though
during the thirteen months of his stay he travelled about a
good deal. He wrote: 'I saw the greater part of India' (*De
India majorem partem vidi*). In Mylapore, 'near the church of
St. Thomas the Apostle' (*ad Ecclesiam Sancti Thomae Apostoli*),
he even lost his travelling companion, the Dominican Nicholas
of Pistoia. That undaunted missionary appears to have dealt
very much with non-Christians only; he baptized about a
hundred of them.[1] Nevertheless Friar John could not completely ignore the 'Nestorians' of India. Had he not known
them during his extensive travels from Tauris to the Persian
Gulf, and suffered from their opposition in China during a
stay of five years?[2] So we have good reason to surmise that
John of Montecorvino, in other letters, which cannot be found
at present, had been more explicit concerning Christians in
India. A clue to this hypothesis can be gathered from a document sent to Bartholomew of Santo Concordio by another
Dominican friar, Menetillo of Spoleto.[3] The document
stated that, along the coast, the Mohammedans were in the
majority and that further inland a few Christians were to be
found; moreover these Christians were persecuting a still
smaller minority of Jews.

It was Friar John's conviction that the glad tidings in India
would easily bear fruit. However those in authority were
not able to fall in with his suggestions immediately.
His superiors had first of all to provide for the upkeep of
the Chinese mission. This took precedence over all else; and
God alone knows what difficulties had to be faced, there
in China.

---

[1] A. van den Wyngaert, *Sinica Franciscana*, Quaracchi, 1929, vol. I, p. 345.

[2] Letter of 8 June 1305, in G. Golubovich, *Biblioteca bio-bibliografica
della Terra Santa*, Quaracchi, 1919, vol. III, p. 87; letter of 13 February 1306,
ibid. p. 92.

[3] Ibid. vol. I, p. 307.

Four Franciscan missionaries reached Tauris during the autumn of 1320. They were due to go to the Far East, but their journey was to end with the establishment of a new diocese in India. Among the Dominicans of Tauris there was a staunch man from Rouergue (France), called Jordan Catalani, born at Sévérac.[1] He had come to Persia some years previously and in a short time had become an expert in the Persian language. Tired of an atmosphere that was too quiet for him, Jordan joined the Franciscans and landed with them at the port of Thana on the island of Salsette near the present site of Bombay, at the beginning of 1321. That small city possessed a miniature Nestorian community. These good Christians informed the friars about another similar group left abandoned on the coast of Gujarat. Jordan set out immediately to visit those poor Christians, who, for lack of priests, were in a state of almost total religious ignorance. Meanwhile his companions at Thana had been imprisoned and martyred (9 April 1321).[2]

Jordan had no orders to proceed further to China, so he remained in India and was soon joined by another confrère from Tauris. As John of Montecorvino had foreseen, the apostolate among the Indians was quite an easy one. The people were tolerant; but for the Muslims a good many conversions could have been made. Jordan Catalani was eager that his superiors and the Pope himself should take a personal interest in this land, and he therefore sent them many letters. He was called back to the West, where he composed his *Mirabilia*

[1] F. Balme, 'Un missionaire dominicain en Orient au quatorzième siècle. Le Bx Jourdain de Sévérac, évêque de Coulam, sur la côte de Malabar, aux Indes Orientales, 1318-1336', in *L'Année Dominicaine*, 1886, pp. 4-10, 58-70, 217-25, 255-60, 297-305.

[2] An information recorded by G. Golubovich mentions a Franciscan friary at Thana, which was occupied from 1320 till 1390, ibid. vol. II, p. 166. On the martyrs of Thana, we have two letters of Friar Jordan, 12 October 1321, and 20 January 1342, and a letter of Friar Bartholomew, Guardian of Thana, 21 (29?) May 1321, published by H. Cordier, *Mirabilia Descripta. Les merveilles de l'Asie de Jourdain Catalani de Sévérac*, Paris 1925, pp. 19-20, 22-5, 25-8.

Descripta, probably at Avignon.[1] He left there in 1330 as the consecrated Bishop of Quilon. He was the first western bishop of India, and precisely in that part of India where there were Christians already.

Jordan had given to the Roman Curia an account of the political and religious situation of the country. In order to render his ministry more successful, Pope John XXII (1316-34) gave him several letters of introduction. One of these was addressed to all the Christians of India; another to the Catholic converts from paganism or heresy; and the last one was addressed to the *Nascarini* or the *Nazarene* Christians of Quilon.[2]

Oderic of Pordenone (1324-5) visited the Nestorians of Thana. Somewhere in the peninsula he was received in a house of Friars Minor, and from there he proceeded to Malabar where he heard about quarrels between Christians and Jews. Actually most of the quarrels proved to be to the advantage of the Christians.[3] In the Latin text edited by Marcellino of Civezza,[4] it must be noted that there is no mention of Jews but only of Hindus. It is also stated that next to the church of St. Thomas of Mylapore, there were fifteen houses, full of idols, belonging to the Nestorians, 'who are Christians but the worst heretics.'[5]

The *Chronicon, seu Liber Historiae Plurimae*, attributed by Fr. Golubovich o.f.m. to the Franciscan John Elemosina (1336), mentions the Christians of Middle India. The passage speaks of seven kingdoms and a Nestorian monarch. Some missionaries, probably Dominicans and Franciscans, had instructed the monarch in the true faith.[6]

[1] H. Cordier, op. cit., pp. 125 and xix; on India, cf. text pp. iii, ff. trans. pp. 60 ff.

[2] A. Mercati, *Monumenta Vaticana Veterem Dioecesim Columbensem (Quilon) ... Respicientia*, Rome, 1923, pp. 13, ff, 28, ff.

[3] L. de Backer, *L'Extrême Orient au Moyen Age*, Paris, 1877, pp. 95-102

[4] M. da Civezza, *Storia Universale delle Missioni Francescane*, Rome, 1859, vol. III, p. 753.

[5] Ibid. p. 754.

[6] G Golubovich, op. cit. vol. II, p. 127. Unfortunately it seems that the

The Franciscan John Marignola of Florence spent fourteen months at Quilon, detained there by acute dysentery (April 1348 - August 1349). He then returned to Europe via Mylapore, Ceylon and the Persian Gulf. He maintained that the St. Thomas Christians (this is apparently the first mention of the name in western sources) are much more numerous than the Mohammedans. As papal legate, he had received large gifts from the Christians.[1] At Quilon there was a Latin church, dedicated to St. George (*Ecclesia Georgii Latinorum*), built by Jordan Catalani, and adorned by the good friar with many paintings.

As far as Malabar was concerned, there were now two Christian communities living side by side: the Latin Catholics, recent converts from Hinduism, and the local Christians, supposed to be 'Nestorians'. Their mutual relations were not specified. All the same, the fact that the old Christians paid to the legate some sort of monthly tribute, shows that fairly good relations prevailed between the western missionaries and the local Christian communities.[2]

Nicolas de Conti visited India several times between 1415 and 1438. He saw the Nestorians living close to the sanctuary of St. Thomas and also in other places. He said that there were about a thousand of them at Mylapore, whereas the other Christians were spread here and there all over India, somewhat like the Jews in Europe.[3] Conti was the last traveller to leave any account of Christianity in India before the arrival of the Portuguese.

text of that chapter is not yet published, cf. R. Streit, *Bibliotheca Missionum*, Aachen, 1928, vol. IV, p. 73, n. 287.

[1] G. Schurhammer s.j., op. cit. p. 25.

[2] Cf. his chronicle published by J. Emler, in *Fontes Rerum Bohemicarum*, Prague, 1882, vol. III, pp. 496-507.

[3] Poggio Bracciolini, *Historiae de Varietate Fortunae*, Paris, 1723, p. 129; M. Longhena, *Viaggi in Persia, India e Giava di Nicolo de Conti*, Milan, 1929, p. 130.

LAST GLIMPSE OF MESOPOTAMIA

It may seem quite strange that the Syrian documents mentioned at the beginning of this chapter are singularly silent about India, but when studying the history of the Eastern Syrians, one should never forget that Mesopotamia was devastated by the Mongolian armies in 1263. From then onwards the Nestorian community was brutally condemned to a rapid decadence, so much so that it was scarcely able to hand over its history to posterity.[1] In India the big *auto-da-fé* ordered at Diamper was responsible for the loss of many manuscripts. Their colophons would probably have disclosed many details about the local history of the Malabar Christians.[2]

Nevertheless, a final document, fully cognizant of the affairs of the Christian community of India towards the close of the fifteenth century, is to be found in an anonymous story of a manuscript preserved in the Vatican Library (*Vatic. Syr. 204*). It is an unusual compilation written in Chaldaic script, but containing both Arabic and Syriac texts. It was brought over from the East by Andrew Scandar after his mission during the years 1718-21.[3] Here is the summary of the document. After having been without a bishop for a long time, the Christians of Malabar chose three of their own people and sent them to the Catholicos of Seleucia-Ctesiphon to petition him to restore their hierarchy. One of the three died on the way; the other two reached there safely, and were ordained priests at Gazirah by the catholicos himself. They were then sent to the monastery of Mar Eugene to select their future pastors. Two monks were actually chosen and duly consecrated under

---

[1] E. Tisserant, 'L' Eglise Nestorienne', in *D.T.C.* vol. XI, 213-8.

[2] J. B. Chabot, 'L' autodafé des livres syriaques au Malabar', in *Florilegium ... Melchior de Vogüé*, Paris, 1909, pp. 613-23. It is remarkable that the only Syro-Malabar manuscript previous to 1500 and known to us is the *Vatic. Syr. 22*.

[3] J. S. Assemani, op. cit. vol. II a, pp. 590-9; S. Giamil, op. cit. pp. 586-600.

the names of Mar Thomas and Mar John. They accompanied the delegates back to India, where, on their arrival, they were welcomed enthusiastically. They were soon very busy, ordaining priests and consecrating altars, of which the people were greatly in need.

Soon afterwards Mar Thomas returned to Mesopotamia to report to the catholicos and to bring along the tithes and free offerings of the faithful. These included a negro servant. Simon V, the previous Catholicos, had died, but his successor, Elias V (1502-3), again sought the help of the monks of Mar Eugene. Three of them were ordained bishops: one a metropolitan, under the name of Yahballaha, and two suffragans, Mar Denha (omitted by Giamil) and Mar Jacob. Mar John was also to be one of the prelates for Malabar. Such was the hierarchy of the Malabar Christians when the Portuguese came to India. F. Nau has published the colophon of a psalter copied in 1504 by Mar Jacob.[1]

The account preserved in the *Vatic. Syr. 204* gives a vivid picture of the problem of hierarchy and priesthood in Malabar in connection with Chaldea. There is actually a great similarity between the Syro-Malabar Church and the Christian community of Ethiopia. In both cases either the Patriarch of Alexandria for Ethiopia or the Catholicos of Seulecia-Ctesiphon for Malabar reserved to himself the right to consecrate bishops. Each patriarch selected them from among the monks of his own surroundings instead of creating a real indigenous hierarchy.

The information carried by this solitary document is well warranted by the reports of the Portuguese concerning the above-mentioned prelates. The priest Joseph, who had been one of the envoys on the first mission to Mesopotamia, later on accompanied Don Pedro Cabral to Lisbon in 1501. Then

[1] Paris, Bibliothèque Nationale, *Mss. Syr. 25.* Cf. F. Nau, 'Deux notices relatives au Malabar,' in *R.O.C.* 17 (1912), p. 83, ff.

before returning to India he visited Rome and Venice. In
1518 he was the parish priest of Cranganore.[1]

---

[1] Fr. Schurhammer reprinted the statements made by the priest Joseph
in Italy, op. cit. pp. 26-41, following M. Fracanzono da Montalboddo, *Paesi
novamente retrovati et novo mondo da Alberico Vesputio Florentino*, Vicenze, 1507.

III

THE SYRIAN CHRISTIANS UNDER PORTUGUESE RULE AND THE SYNOD OF DIAMPER

PORTUGUESE DISCOVERIES AND PADROADO

THE PIONEERS of Portuguese activity in the Indies entered by the usual route. Joâo Perez de Covilham, together with Alfonso de Payva, was entrusted by King John II to enquire about the kingdom of *Prester John*. He left Santarem on 7 May 1487, passed Alexandria and reaching Aden, went on alone, following the route usually taken by Arabian sailors. Meanwhile his companion had landed in Ethiopia. Perez de Covilham visited the Malabar coast; then, returning to Africa, he visited the coast from Zeila to Sofala, and finally he also entered Ethiopia.

The Ethiopians adhered to the principle that nobody who had once succeeded in entering their country was allowed to leave it. Joâo Perez de Covilham was still there when Rodriguez de Lima reached it in 1520 as ambassador of the Portuguese king, but he had succeeded somehow in sending information to his sovereign about the route; this information spoke of a passage round the southern-most tip of Africa, which led to the Indies.[1]

Vasco da Gama left Lisbon on 7 June 1497, and landed near Calicut on 14 May 1498. An Arab called Majid was his pilot. Henceforward, every year, a Portuguese fleet left for the East Indies; but the expedition of Pedro Cabral in 1500 fell into an ambush set up at the instigation of the Arabs. The arrival of the Franks and the ambushes laid for them through the enmity of the Muslims, together with the revenge Vasco da Gama took

---

[1] F. Alvarez, 'Viaggio della Ethiopia' in J.B.Ramusio, *Della Navigazioni e Viaggi*, Venice, 1563, vol. I, p. 223.

in 1502, are described vividly in a letter written to the catholicos
in the second half of the year 1504 by the three Chaldean
Bishops, Mar Yahballaha, Mar Denha and Mar Jacob. These
prelates have already been mentioned towards the close of the
previous chapter.[1] The bishops spoke of the Portuguese in the best
of terms, calling them brothers and praising them, for they saw
to it that priests accompanied them on their travels. Just as the
Ethiopians must have welcomed the arrival of new and armed
Christians in 1520, so also the Indian Christian minority,
exposed for centuries to vexation by the Muslims, must have
felt greatly encouraged to see other Christians join them with
military strength capable of impressing the sons of the Prophet.

When the first Portuguese explorers landed on the shores
of India, they did not seem to have cared much about discover-
ing whether the Christians they met with belonged to the great
Catholic Church or not. There was nothing surprising in the
fact that these Christians lived practically without communication with Rome. The envoys of the King of Portugal knew
quite well that they had come to countries which had no regular
contacts with Europe. The Christians were, without a doubt,
subjects of the famous *Prester John*, much talked about for the
last two centuries in the West. Thus the Christians benefitted
from this favourable prejudice. That is why the Chaldean
bishops, who remained with the Portuguese for two and a
half months, were allowed to be present at the Latin liturgical
services and were even invited to celebrate the Holy Mysteries
in the chapels built by some newly arrived Latin priests.[2]

Those who wish to understand the successive changes of
attitude of the Portuguese with regard to the local Christians,
whether in Malabar or in Ethiopia, must never forget the
special character of their expeditions. These were altogether
different from the Dutch and English enterprises which came

[1] J. S. Assemani, *Bibliotheca Orientalis*, vol. IIIa, pp. 595-9; S. Giamil,
Genuinae Relationes . . . , pp. 592-600.
[2] J. S. Assemani, op. cit. p. 594.

later. Whilst the navigators of the Low Countries and of Great Britain were private merchants, trading individually or for chartered companies, the Portuguese explorers were officers of Portugal's Royal Navy. They led the fleet of the king, even when they were travelling for trading purposes. On the other hand, the Portuguese sovereign never forgot that he was the successor of the Grand Masters of the Order of Christ. All the expeditions against the Moors had a double character, military and religious. Moreover, when the Infante Henry the Navigator had taken over the administration of the office of Grand Master, the overseas expeditions had the same aims. The Popes had recognized in numerous documents the worth of Portugal in the matter of evangelization.[1] What is more, they granted to the sovereign of Portugal exceptional privileges of patronage over the Portuguese dioceses in foreign parts, whose endowments were usually taken from the revenues of the Order of Christ. This was the origin of the Padroado, whose influence on the missions was at times profitable, though often questionable.

The first missionaries of the Near East, the famous *peregrinatores Christi*, Dominican and Franciscan friars from France, Italy and Germany, had made more friendly contacts with the dissidents, for they had been helped in this by the local Catholic communities constituted during the Crusades.

Quite different was the situation of the missionaries coming under the protection of the Padroado. When they came in contact with Malabar and later on with Ethiopia, they arrived in the midst of Christian communities of which they knew absolutely nothing, neither language, liturgy, nor history. Moreover, the Christians of Malabar and of Ethiopia were not surrounded by other Christian communities who were heretic or schismatic in the eyes of one another. The Syrian community

---

[1]   Cf. C. M. De Witte, o.s.b., 'Les bulles pontificales et l'expansion portugaise au XVe siècle', in *R.H.E.* 48 (1953), pp. 683-718, 49 (1954), pp. 438-61, 51 (1956), pp. 413-53.

in Malabar and the Monophysites in Ethiopia were the only communities representing Christianity in their regions. It followed therefore that good relations between them and the Portuguese prevailed from the start. The Portuguese were happy to meet Christians in the midst of Hindu or Muslim majorities.

EARLY FRICTIONS AND TENSIONS

Whatever might have been the feelings developed by the first happy relations, the Padroado missionaries very quickly became aware of differences in doctrine.

While the missionaries were already busy converting pagans, neighbouring Christians appeared to them to be holding errors in the faith, divergences in ritual, even following a rather strange, if not unorthodox, liturgy. The newcomers were soon scandalized and considered such divergence intolerable. They wanted unity in the Kingdom of God.

On the other hand, when Vasco da Gama set up the first Portuguese establishments in the Indies on a firm basis, the Syro-Malabar Church had just been reorganized. Her hierarchy comprised a Metropolitan, Mar Yahballaha, and three Suffragan Bishops, Mar Denha, Mar Jacob and lastly Mar John, who had been sent from Mesopotamia two years before the others and was still alive. These four prelates, hailing from Mesopotamia, were strongly attached to the catholicosate of Seleucia-Ctesiphon; yet they did not appear to have been fanatical partisans of Nestorianism. The Christians under their care, according to the letter already quoted, numbered about 30,000 families. They were spread out over some twenty towns and a great number of villages. These lay for the most part in the hills of the South-Western Ghats at a distance of about eight days journey from Cannanore, and Italian documents referred to them as the *Serra*. Distant Mylapore should not be forgotten.[1]

[1] J. S. Assemani, op. cit. p. 594.

In order to escape Muslim vexations, the Syrians had
presented themselves before Vasco da Gama in 1503, and had
requested him to protect them. They did not think that this
step could possibly have any bearing on the life of their Church.
The Portuguese military forces, however, were not concerned
with Christian troubles, but with expeditions aimed at stopping
all traffic between the Indies and Egypt. Egypt was also supplying
spices to Venice at that time; moreover the Portuguese wanted
to eliminate all Arabian trade by sea and to stem the progress
of Turkish armies. So the reduction and strict control of trade
relations in the Persian Gulf had the effect of cutting off the
Indian hierarchy from its connection with the Near East. It is
not surprising, therefore, that the documents did not mention
the arrival of any bishop during the first half of the sixteenth
century.

Of the five known prelates, Mar John was still living in 1503.
He appears to have died shortly afterwards. About Mar
Yahballaha and Mar Denha nothing very definite is known.
They also appear to have died not long after they came to India.
Mar Thomas, who had come back to Malabar and settled there,
took care of the southernmost part of India. For a while he
was suspected of heresy, but he certainly died a Catholic some
time after 1536. Mar Jacob submitted up to a certain point to
the Latin customs and succeeded, though not without trouble,
in keeping his position in spite of the efforts of some very
enterprising missionaries, such as Alvaro Penteado.[1] Later on
he retired to the Franciscan friary of Cochin (1543). His
retirement however may have been a forced one; St. Francis
Xavier found him there in 1549.[2] The Saint brought before
King John III the case of the old bishop 'who has well served

[1] Two letters of Penteado were recently published by Fr. A. da Silva Rego
in Documentação para a Historia das Missões do Padroado Português do Oriente.
India, Lisbon, 1949, vol. II, p. 357-60; 1950, vol. III, p. 543-53.
[2] G. Schurhammer s.j., The Malabar Church and Rome, Trichinopoly,
1934, pp. 1-24.

God and Your Majesty in these countries for forty-five years, for he is a virtuous and saintly old man.' Mar Jacob rightly deserved such praise for his conciliatory policy, which was certainly a boon to the Portuguese. But his main claim to virtue lay in the fact that in 1541 he had helped the Franciscans to open a school at Cranganore, which soon received the children of the best Syro-Malabar families. There were more than a hundred boys there at the time when St. Francis Xavier paid it a visit.[1]

Alfonso de Albuquerque had entrusted the spiritual care of the Syrians of Quilon to a Dominican called Rodriguez. In this he showed but little respect for the rights of the hierarchy from Mesopotamia.[1] In 1515, 1,200 'Nestorians' had renounced their errors. In 1516, other 'conversions' were made at Mylapore.[2]

Fr. Schurhammer gathered many texts that seem to show with what *sans-gêne* the Portuguese clergy tried to impose their customs on the Syrians.[3] St. Francis Xavier was more tactful. In spite of the fact that his ministry had first led him to the poor Christians of the Fishery Coast—who had nothing Christian about them but the name—he did not remain a stranger to the very important group of Christians of the Chaldean rite. Several times he had occasion to visit their principal centres, Quilon, Cochin, Cranganore and Travancore (Thiruvancode). One is even tempted to think (whilst he was preaching in their country, though not to them) that he thought of them when he framed the invocation to Our Lady, 'Holy Mary, Mother of Jesus-Christ, Son of God.' He insisted on this formula when writing to his brethren in Rome, as if he

---

[1] St. Francis Xavier to King John III, Cochin, 26 January 1549, in *Epistolae S. Francisci Xaverii aliaque eius Scripta, Nova Editio*, Ed. G. Schurhammer s.J. and J.Wicki s.J., Rome, 1945, vol. II, 2, pp. 14-15.

[2] A. B. de Bragança Pereira, 'Historia Religiosa de Goa', in *Or. Português*, Lisbon, 1932, fasc. 2-3, pp. 34, ff. (reprint, Bastora, *s.a.*, I, 1).

[3] G. Schurhammer s.J., op. cit. pp. 19-21.

had been afraid to offend the delicate ears of old 'Nestorians' recently 'converted' from their errors.[1]

No indication of any religious controversy between the Portuguese and the Syrian Christians can be discovered during the first half of the century. One should remember however that the newcomers did not know Malayalam, and generally transacted business with the help of the Muslims; hence no occasion arose to discuss religion. However, when a catechism was composed in the vernacular, and when an inquisitor had been posted in Goa, the accuracy of the dogmatic formulas in use among the St. Thomas Christians received somewhat closer attention.

Now opposition was to come first in the matter of jurisdiction. The intention of the Portuguese, as we have said, was to make sure that their country had the monopoly of trade relations between the Indies and Europe. The clergy, who along with them had left the banks of the Tagus, had equally strong ideas of absolutism. Pope Calixtus III, in his Bull *Inter Caetera* of 13 March 1455,[2] had granted to the Grand Master of the *Militia Christi* jurisdiction over the whole of Africa from Cape Bojador onwards, and also over the southern parts of Asia. This was a privilege which, for Asia at least, remained a dead letter for forty-three years. Yet it was never forgotten, for the Portuguese kings took care to renew with each succeeding Pope all their rights on Churches in their overseas possessions. That is why, as early as 1503, a Dominican, Dominic de Souza, is found as Vicar General of the Grand Master for the Indies.[3] It has been mentioned already that the hierarchy was rapidly organized in all countries conquered by the Spaniards, whereas in the Portuguese territories it developed very slowly. So, for

---

[1] St. Francis Xavier to the Roman Jesuits, Cochin, 15 January 1544, in *Epistolae . . .*, Vol. I, 1, p. 164.

[2] *Bullarium Patronatus Portugalliae*, Vol. I, p. 36.

[3] A. Jann o.m.cap., *Die katholische Missionen in Indien, China und Japan*, Paderborn, 1915, p. 62, n. 1.

instance, a commissariat was founded in 1500 for the east coast
of Africa and the Indies. The four commissaries, successively
appointed from 1514 to 1534, made only brief visits. The
bishopric of Goa, whose creation had been decided on principle
as early as 1533, was in fact erected only in 1539, as a suffragan
see of Funchal, a town which lay at too a great distance.[1] In
1558, Goa became at last the metropolitan see of the East,
from the western coast of India to China inclusively.[2]

No sooner had the Bishop of Goa been installed than he got
into trouble with the Syro–Malabar hierarchy. Mar Jacob, as
we have already seen, died at Cochin far away from his flock;
we have no proof of his having committed any fault whatsoever. His letters of 1523 and 1530 show what difficulties he
had in resisting the attempt of missionaries to oust him.[3]
When the Church of Mesopotamia sought formal union with
Rome in 1552, one might have hoped that the affairs of the
Malabar Syrians would follow *pari passu*. When the Chaldean
Catholicos-elect, Sulaqa, went to Rome, he made his profession
of faith before the Pope and was thereafter consecrated, but
he did not forget the far-off Syrian portion of his flock. He
even had the idea of travelling to Lisbon and of meeting the
king regarding these Christians of the Eastern rite and their
needs, but as he had little time at his disposal, he solicited and
obtained testimonials from the Portuguese ambassador to the
Holy See for the Viceroy of the Indies.[4] Unhappily, the reign
of Mar Simon Sulaqa did not last long. In January 1555, the
holy patriarch received the crown of martyrdom. He had
been sacrificed through the jealousy of a rival.[5]

Sulaqa, however, had consecrated many bishops, and union
with Rome continued. Further, the two Maltese Dominicans,

[1] Ibid. pp. 55-63, 83-7.

[2] Ibid. pp. 100-13.

[3] G. Schurhammer, op. cit. pp. 10-19.

[4] G. Beltrami, 'La Chiesa Caldea nel Secolo dell Unione', in *O.C.* 29,
(1933), fasc. 83, p. 16.

[5] Ibid. p. 24.

Bishop Ambrose Buttigeg and Fr. Antoninus Zahara, who had accompanied the late patriarch back to Mesopotamia, saw to it that the Indian communities did not remain outside the union. As soon as the new Chaldean Catholicos, Mar Abdisho, was elected by the united bishops of that rite, the catholicos took measures to send as a visitor to India a metropolitan, called Mar Elias, with instructions to install Mar Joseph, brother of the late patriarch, as Metropolitan of the Indies. In fact, two Dominicans also accompanied these two Chaldean prelates. The latter had in their possession letters that Sulaqa had brought from Rome for the Viceroy of the Indies. After attending the installation of Mar Joseph, the two friars had to go back to Europe via Lisbon. Mgr. Beltrami's supposition that the party comprising Mar Elias, Mar Joseph, Bishop Ambrose Buttigeg o.p. and Fr. Antoninus Zahara o.p. sailed from Ormuz to Mozambique, and thence to Goa, has been confirmed by Fr. Wicki's recent contribution. This route seems rather roundabout and the idea is apparently far-fetched, yet there is no other way of accounting for the signature of the manuscript *Vatic. Syr. 27*, in which Mar Joseph maintains that he finished it in the town of Mozambique on 8 July 1556 (1867 of the Greek era). Their arrival at Goa must be placed near the close of the same year, at the latest in November.[1]

CONFLICTS AND OPPOSITIONS
THE TRIBULATIONS OF MAR JOSEPH

Sulaqa, the deceased Catholicos, was right when he foresaw that difficulties would arise from the local Portuguese

---

[1] Pope Julius III had been requested by Patriarch Sulaqa to provide him with two qualified missionaries. The Maltese Dominicans were chosen by the Pope on account of their knowledge of Semitic languages, cf. E. Tisserant, 'L' Eglise Nestorienne', in *D.T.C.* 11(1), 228-9. On the travel of the friars, cf. J. Wicki, s.j., 'Zur Orientreise des papstlichen Nuntius Ambrosius Buttigeg o.p. (1553-6) in *O.C.P.* 19 (1953), pp. 350-71. On their voyage to Goa, cf. G. Beltrami, op. cit. p. 38 and n. 6.

authorities. The Christian communities in the South-Western Ghats were almost fully outside the influence of the western clergy and the latter were in no wise disposed to let a Mesopotamian bishop visit the Syrians and settle among them.

Neither the letters from Rome, nor even the presence of the faithful Dominicans put a stop to the Goan Inquisition in any way. Thus, while the friars from Malta were obliged to remain in Goa, the Chaldean Bishops, Mar Elias and Mar Joseph, were forcibly sent to the Franciscan monastery of Bassein, and kept there for eighteen months before they were allowed to pursue their journey southwards. The Guardian of the Friary, Fr. Antonio da Porto, fully conscious of the importance of the task entrusted to his care by the Governor, Francis Barreto, found it necessary to write to the King of Portugal on the bishops' behaviour. His letter is most interesting in so far as it provides us with the clearest account of how the Padroado authorities judged the question of the eastern clergy.[1]

The good Franciscan acknowledged the strict orthodoxy and dignity of the two prelates, though they were less acquainted with moral theology than the priests of the West; yet they had the necessary instruction, and knew the doctrines of the eastern writers, which conformed to the teaching of the Fathers. The piety of the Chaldeans was such that they served as models to the Portuguese living in India. Since they belonged to a monastic order, they practised mortification, never touched meat, abstained from wine during Advent and Lent, and spent much time in prayer and contemplation and in the study of the Holy Scriptures, the Fathers of the Church and other authors.

However, in spite of the piety with which Frey Antonio da Porto saw them say Mass in Syriac, he, probably according to orders received, taught them Latin and the Latin ceremonies of Mass. Eventually, he witnessed the fruit of his labours when on Easter Sunday 1557, the bishops performed their liturgical

---

[1] G. Beltrami, ibid. Portuguese text, pp. 40-3, n. 9.

services in the Latin rite, which they have continued to do ever since, if we are to believe the Portuguese account. Such results had not been without labour: the devout Franciscan had got them to say 'Dry Masses' under his watchful eye. Probably they did not pronounce Latin quite in the Portuguese style, but it was possibly no worse than that spoken by Frenchmen or Italians.

After this 'conversion' of his guests to Latin practices, the Guardian of Bassein went on to explain to them that they really had nothing to do in Malabar, and that, moreover, episcopal authority would rightly prevent them from going there. Was not the Bishop of Goa the rightful ruler of Malabar, just as he was the Bishop of all the Indies and of the whole East under Portuguese control? Hence, concluded the good friar, to go and administer the sacraments to the Eastern Christians of Malabar without the leave of the ordinary of Goa would go far to prove that they were the thieves who had entered the fold without passing through the door. Frey Antonio expressed the hope that Mar Elias, the visitor, sick at heart, would soon go back home, and that Mar Joseph, who had been consecrated expressly as Bishop of Malabar, would journey to Lisbon and to Rome, and then on to Mesopotamia. But in the meantime, a truly Nestorian bishop had cunningly escaped from the Portuguese guards and had succeeded in reaching Malabar. Frey Antonio then suggested that Mar Joseph could be used to oppose the intruder, but on condition that a Portuguese Franciscan would accompany him, and that he would perform all pontifical services according to the Latin rite.

This letter from the Guardian of Bassein, naive as it might seem, bespoke clearly enough the deep-rooted mentality of most of the Latin missionaries working in India from the sixteenth century until as late as the establishment of the Syro-Malabar hierarchy in the twentieth century. The few exceptions unhappily confirmed the rule. Until fairly recently such views were still held by many Latin clerics working in the east, even after the memorable Encyclical *Orientalium Dignitas*.[1] They continued to harp on this one point, at least from a practical point of view, that the Latin rite was superior to any Eastern one, an opinion which Rome has always refused to acknowledge.

The resolution of Mar Joseph, who had decided to defend his cause at Lisbon, the entreaties of Bishop Buttigeg, and perhaps also some orders from Portugal, had at last brought about the release from Bassein of the Chaldean bishops in the second half of 1558. And so Mar Elias and Mar Joseph, accompanied by their Maltese advisers, departed for South India. They first halted at Cochin, and later began visiting the Syrian Christians. Bishop Buttigeg died there, and Fr. Antoninus Zahara was left alone to watch over the visitation of all the parishes of the country. This lasted for two whole years. No one among the Syrians, it appeared, opposed the Chaldean bishops, who this time were too obviously united with the Pope. This shows more clearly than ever that any positive 'Nestorianism' was a dream of the past. It should be mentioned also that many non-Christians were baptized in the course of the visit. Already in those remote days, the Syrians of India possessed a genuine missionary spirit, the more so because it was spontaneous. In point of fact they had always made proselytes among their non-Christians neighbours. No wonder, then, that the preaching during those two years provoked conversions more numerous than was usually the case.[2] Unhappily such zeal was to be hampered, if not hidden under a bushel during the following centuries, because the Christians lost their normal independence and, therefore, their religious spontaneity.

By a Brief of 24 January 1561, Pope Pius IV (1559–65) recalled Fr. Antoninus Zahara O.P. The Pontiff hoped that the

---

[1] Pope Leo XIII's Apostolic Letter intended to preserve and foster the rites and disciplines of the Eastern Churches, published in *S.D.N. Leonis Papae Papae XIII Acta*, Bruges, 1898, vol. V, pp. 303-11.

[2] G. Beltrami, op. cit. p. 51.

Dominican might be useful in Egypt, where he had been with Bishop Buttigeg in 1555.[1] The Inquisition of the Indies, always over-zealous in its watchfulness, seized this occasion to get rid of Mar Joseph, and accordingly sent him to the inquisitors of Lisbon.[2] Mar Joseph, Bishop of Malabar, brother of Catholicos Sulaqa the martyr, probably went on board ship full of confidence, for he was convinced that the Portuguese king, no less than the Holy See, would grant him rights over the Syrian see of Angamale; however, he was prevented from going to Rome.

In Lisbon, where he was kept for more than a year, he succeeded in proving his orthodoxy, and from Cardinal Henriques, then Regent of the Realm, he won his case against the Viceroy of the Indies, but it was judged inopportune to allow him to proceed and make his visit *ad limina*. He had to be satisfied with the blessing of Pope Pius IV, sent to him with a Brief of 27 June 1564. In this document he was told to return directly to Malabar, following the Regent's instructions. He was exhorted also to persevere in the Catholic faith, to which, two years earlier, he had made solemn profession before the Patriarch-Catholicos Abdisho. The prohibition against Mar Joseph's visiting the Roman Curia must be connected with the protest made by the Portuguese ambassador at the sixth session of the Council of Trent (17 September 1562) against the title by which Patriarch Abdisho claimed for the Catholicos of the East the jurisdiction over the bishoprics and metropolitan sees of India.[3] Portugal had the avowed intention of keeping under her own control all that was going on in the Indies, but the Pope was in sore need of Portuguese support to ensure the success of the Council, and wished to avoid a possible clash.

Poor Mar Joseph, however, was not near the end of his

[1] Ibid. pp. 34-7.
[2] Ibid. pp. 86 ff.
[3] S. Ehses, 'Concilii Tridentini Actorum Pars V', in *Concilium Tridentinum. Diariorum, Actorum ... Nova Collectio*, Freiburg, i. B. 1919, vol. VIII, p. 959.

troubles. When the Catholic Syrians of Malabar saw him leave for Europe by order of the Inquisition, they hastened to warn the patriarch, and requested him to send a new bishop. The Metropolitan Mar Elias, then back in Mesopotamia, probably seconded their demand. He had been taken with Mar Joseph to the Franciscan convent of Bassein and had had the opportunity of ascertaining for himself, *de visu*, the crying want of the Christians of Malabar for ecclesiastical assistance. There was need for more than just one or two bishops. Patriarch Abdisho chose as bishop a monk who assumed the name of Mar Abraham. The new prelate, remembering the fate of Mar Joseph his predecessor, took great care to avoid Goa. When Mar Joseph came back, Mar Abraham was already peacefully installed in the south, but Mar Joseph was carrying letters which would ensure him the support of the Portuguese authorities, particularly so since he had agreed to the use of unleavened bread and Latin liturgical vestments. This did not signify by any means that the prudent prelate actually carried on a thorough Latinizing policy. Owing to the presence of two prelates of equal status, it would have been impossible for the people not to be divided. Some stood for Mar Joseph, others for Mar Abraham. The latter, however, was soon put under arrest by the Portuguese authorities, and placed on board a ship bound for Lisbon. More cunning than Mar Joseph, Mar Abraham succeeded in eluding his guards, landed at Melinda and made for Mesopotamia. Such rough treatment from the Portuguese was to have great effect on the subsequent relations between them and Mar Abraham.

Patriarch Abdisho, whose promise of obedience to the Holy See was no doubt quite sincere, did not consider himself qualified to settle the controversy, and therefore sent Mar Abraham to Rome. Pius IV did not hesitate: since there were now two bishops and many faithful, the diocese should be divided and one half given to each. The residential sees of the prelates would be fixed by the patriarch. The Pope knew quite well that many difficulties would be raised by the Goan hierarchy; he took care therefore to warn the Archbishop of Goa and the Portuguese Bishop of Cochin by Briefs of 28 February, 1565.[1]

In the meantime, the persecution against Bishop Mar Joseph flared up again. He was even denounced to the Inquisition in Goa and in Lisbon. The Lisbon inquisitors had obtained a Brief from Pius V (1566-72) by which an enquiry was allowed. Mar Joseph, though the brother of the martyred Sulaqa, was again arrested and put on board a ship en route for Portugal and Rome *cum fidis custodibus*.[2] As was expected of him, the Portuguese ambassador in Rome had promised his sovereign to draw up the charge against the unfortunate Chaldean prelate. The Roman judges, however, like the Franciscan Guardian of Bassein previously, felt obliged to give way before the piety of Mar Joseph and to recognize his orthodoxy. Yet the measure of suffering was full, and Mar Joseph received, near the tomb of the Apostles, the crown which he had merited, through his long and slow martyrdom which was perhaps a more painful one than that of his heroic brother. Eighteen Syriac manuscripts, and one Arabic and one Persian manuscript, which he had always carried with him on his travels, were incorporated in the Apostolic Library of the Vatican by right of spoil.[3]

In obedience to Pius IV's prescription, Catholicos Abdisho divided the Syrian diocese of India into two. The see of Angamale was assigned to Mar Abraham, together with a little more than half the diocese as a reward for having journeyed all the way to Rome. As it happened, the partition of the diocese was not a permanent one; for after the death of any one of the bishops, the other was to take charge of the whole eparchy again.

[1] S. Giamil, *Genuinae Relationes . . .*, pp. 69-73.

[2] G. Beltrami, op. cit. p. 92.

[3] G. Levi della Vida, *Ricerche sulla formazione del piu antico fondo dei manuscritti orientali della Biblioteca Vaticana*, Rome, 1939, pp. 179-97, 441, ff.

MAR ABRAHAM, THE PADROADO AND THE JESUITS

When on 24 August 1567, Patriarch Abdisho wrote to the Archbishop of Goa regarding the division of his Indian diocese, Mar Joseph had probably already been removed far from his flock.[1] Portuguese opposition, however, had not died out. When after leaving Rome Mar Abraham reached India, the testimonials he possessed proved to be of no use to him. The Archbishop of Goa, George Temudo o.p., *cum sapientissimis viris*, examined them and declared them to be either false or obtained by subterfuge. Mar Abraham was taken to the Dominican monastery of Goa. He was to await there the arrival of new letters coming directly from Rome. However, the Portuguese forgot that the crafty bishop knew something about escape, and as at Melinda, so now he got away from his confinement in the monastery and reached the hills of the South-Western Ghats, where he was given a glowing reception by the Syrians. Nobody knew whether the feelings of the lucky prelate were more embittered than before, and since the Portuguese soldiers did not venture far inland, Mar Abraham spent a few years in peace.

Being unable to use compulsion to catch the elusive Chaldean, the Archbishop of Goa tried to make him leave his refuge with an invitation to the second Synod of Goa, but Mar Abraham discovered the trick and did not appear. Rather upset after this unsuccessful attempt, the members of the synod passed a decree (1st decree of the third session), in which they requested the Pope that 'for the good of the Christian community of St. Thomas' its bishop might be appointed by the King of Portugal and not by the Chaldean patriarch; or at least, that the Archbishop of Angamale, who was the head of that Christian community, might be forced to join the bishops of the province of Goa, since he had no suffragans of his own and

---

[1] A. Rabbath, *Documents inédits* . . . , Paris and Leipzig, 1910, vol. II, pp. 432-4.

could not easily go to Mesopotamia.[1] Mar Abraham, however, knew his way through the Roman Curia, and as soon as he got to know the contents of the decree, he set to work without delay. Through the intermediary of the King of Cochin, he wrote to the Pope and explained that after having been imprisoned twice, he would not answer any further call from the Portuguese until he possessed a papal safe-conduct.[2] The Pope prudently answered, on 21 December 1576, that being unaware of any vexation to which the Archbishop of Angamale was supposed to have been subjected, he could not possibly settle anything in the case.[3] Mar Abraham, however, was not satisfied to have the Cochin king write on his behalf. In the course of the following year he forwarded a renewed profession of faith to the Holy Father, Gregory XIII (1572-85), and on 3 January 1578, writing from the Jesuit school of Cochin, Mar Abraham assured the Pope that henceforward there would be no more enmity between the Portuguese and himself, and that he would grant full facilities to the Jesuit fathers to exercise their ministry in his diocese.[4]

If, already by 1577, Mar Abraham was bent on closer relations with Rome and accepted the Jesuits so easily, it might have been partly due to the fact that he was again threatened in the exercise of his jurisdiction. A bishop, Mar Simon, had been sent to the Indies by the Nestorian Patriarch of the time, Elias VII (1576-91). The Syrian community was being split up. Though Rome was far away, one had to rely on her to break the efforts of the dissidents. The Jesuits probably favoured recourse to the Holy See, and they wrote to Rome to recommend Mar Abraham and his archdeacon, George. The Pope answered with many letters, extending over a period of two years from October 1578 till 5 March 1580. He addressed himself to the

[1] *Bullarium Patronatus Portugalliae*, Lisbon, 1872, app. I, p. 51.
[2] G. Beltrami, op. cit. p. 55.
[3] G. Beltrami, op. cit. p. 56.
[4] Ibid. pp. 98, ff.

Archbishop of Goa, to Archdeacon George, Bishop-elect of Parur, and to the clergy and faithful of Angamale. Despite the efforts of the King of Cochin, who did not like armed interference in religious matters, the intruder, Mar Simon, was arrested and sent to Goa, thence to Lisbon and Rome. After various investigations at the Curia during the year 1585, it was recognized that Mar Simon was neither a bishop, nor even a priest. The Pope banished him to the Franciscan convent of Lisbon, where he died in 1599.[1] He had, however, left in India a local priest called Jacob, to act as his vicar-general, and so the troubles went on for some ten years more.

The third Synod of Goa had been fixed for 1579.[2] The Pope saw to it that Archbishop Mar Abraham was able to be present. He wrote to him to make him feel at ease (25 November 1578), and recommended him to the Archbishop of Goa, as well as to the Portuguese king (letters of 20 November and 3 December 1578).[3] Since the summonses to the synod were delayed, the Jesuits advised Mar Abraham to hold a diocesan synod in the meanwhile. He did so in October 1583, and told the Pope of the happy results of this initiative in a letter, dated 13 January 1584. At last the Provincial Synod at Goa took place, on 5 June 1585. Mar Abraham betook himself there, not without misgivings, yet encouraged by Fr. Alexander Valignano, the Visitor and Provincial of the Jesuit missions in the Indies.[4] The whole of the synod's third session was

[1] Ibid. pp. 103-7.

[2] *Bullarium Patronatus . . .*, app. I, p. 54.

[3] G. Beltrami, op. cit. pp. 99, ff.

[4] Alessandro Valignano s.j. (1539-1606) was appointed Visitor of the Asian missions of the Society in August 1573. After having visited Goa and other Indian missions, he sailed for the Far East, visited Macao, then reached Japan in July 1579. Though Japan remained the object of his particular care (two further stays, 1590-2 and 1598-1603), he was well acquainted with Indian problems and also with the Christians of St. Thomas whom he visited at least once in 1583, cf. A. Valignano, s.j., *Historia del principio y progresso de la Compañia de Jesus en las Indias Orientales*, (1542-64), Ed. J. Wicki, s. J. Rome, 1944, pp. 45-8 and pp. 336-41.

devoted to the archdiocese of Angamale.[1] The fathers of the council asked for a seminary to be erected in Malabar. This seems a strange request, since only the previous year a seminary was entrusted to the Jesuits at Vaipicotta. Rules were also framed for the admission of candidates to the priesthood, and even for priests coming from other dioceses. These resolutions were wise enough, as were also the recommendations that the practices of simony be done away with; yet others more questionable were added about the liturgy. The synod settled that the Latin breviary and missal be translated into Syriac, together with the more essential parts of the ritual and pontifical. Mar Abraham signed the acts (did he understand all their consequences?), and returned home with the Catalan Jesuit, Fr. Francis Roz, as companion. The synod had decided to appoint Fr. Roz as auxiliary and adviser to Archbishop Mar Abraham.

As Fr. Roz had studied Syriac, it did not take him long to discover that the names of the three Greek doctors, Theodore of Mopsuestia, Diodorus of Tarsus and Nestorius, were written in the liturgical manuscripts used in Malabar, and that in these liturgical manuscripts Mar Abraham appeared as bishop. These books were examined privately by the scholarly Jesuit when visiting the churches; for he was not presented with any of them officially.[2]

Such findings, apparently acknowledged by the archbishop, were in themselves already suspicious; there was all the more reason for suspicion, for Mar Abraham had promised at Goa to correct the liturgical texts. He seemed now to have forgotten all about his promise; further, in 1590, he bluntly refused to ordain the seminarists of Vaipicotta according to the formulas of the Latin pontifical. The Chaldean prelate was more than personal in his dealings with the Portuguese.

---

[1] *Bullarium Patronatus* . . . , ibid. pp. 73-6.
[2] 'Aliorum enim librorum copiam, nec archiepiscopus, nec archidiaconus, nec alii facere mihi volunt', in F. Roz, 'De Erroribus Nestorianorum', Ed. J. Hausherr, s. j. in *O.C.* 11 (1928), fasc. 1, p. 15, n. 3.

Fr. Hausherr S.J., when he published the *De Erroribus Nestorianorum* — a manuscript discovered by Fr. Castets S. J., a missionary at Trichinopoly — did not tell us for whom it was intended. But it aimed at the deposition of Archbishop Mar Abraham, and was probably written at the end of 1586 or the beginning of 1587.[1] How could there be, in such circumstances, any form of collaboration between the archbishop and his adviser and auxiliary, Fr. Roz? The latter, moreover, firmly maintained that he had no esteem whatsoever for the prelate.

The Venerable Abraham George, Jesuit of Maronite descent, in his letters from Vaipicotta to the Jesuit General, Claudio Acquaviva, on 13 October and 15 December 1593, also asserted that the affairs of the St. Thomas Christians had taken a bad turn; that the archbishop openly declared himself a Nestorian, and that he administered the sacraments for money. The zealous Maronite, who died a martyr at Massawah (Ethiopia) a few months later, added a list of various errors to these denunciations. It is difficult to believe that Archbishop Mar Abraham could ever have professed these errors but for the fact that Fr. Abraham George, the author of the denunciations, attested that he had found evidence for them in a letter surreptitiously intercepted.[2] One can understand that on receiving such information, Rome felt uneasy. On 27 January 1595, Clement VIII (1592-1605) entrusted the Archbishop of Goa with the task of enquiring about the life and the faith of Mar Abraham.[3] Whilst this letter was on its way to India, Mar Abraham was at death's door, and he requested the Jesuits to give him the last sacraments.[4] However, he recovered and continued to govern his archdiocese. We do not know the

---

[1] The text of Fr. Roz was found in the Jesuit Archives of Rome, ibid. p. 35.

[2] A. Rabbath, op. cit. vol. I, pp. 321-30, who published two letters of Fr. Abraham George. Their original is found in the Jesuit Archives of Rome, *Goa*, 13, fo. 165-7 and 14, fo. 34-5.

[3] G. Beltrami, op. cit. pp. 248-50 giving the text.

[4] Fr. J. Castets in his preface to F. Roz, op. cit. p. 8.

results of the Goan enquiry, which, in accordance with papal orders, the new Archbishop of Goa, Alexis de Menezes O.E.S.A., had to make immediately after having taken possession of his see. Meanwhile Mar Abraham, without being deposed, died in about February 1597. Alexis de Menezes was then visiting the Latin communities of Malabar.[1]

MAR ABRAHAM'S SUCCESSION AND THE VISITATION OF ARCHBISHOP ALEXIS DE MENEZES

It was to be expected that the succession to Mar Abraham would not be without difficulties. Rome had indeed to give heed to both the Chaldean patriarch and the Portuguese Government; so, to avoid all local competition, Gregory XIII decided that Archdeacon George de Christo would take over the administration of the diocese in the event of a vacancy until a new bishop could be appointed by papal decree. The archdeacon was notified of those arrangements by a Brief given on 3 January 1579.[2] Following these instructions, Mar Abraham, just before he died, recommended all his priests to submit to the archdeacon. Gregory XIII, moreover, had by the brief of 4 March 1580, confirmed the election of the archdeacon to the newly created Indian see of Parur. This election had been engineered by Catholicos Mar Abdisho (1555-71).

---

[1] According to Fr. du Jarric, *Thesaurus Rerum Indicarum*, Cologne, 1635, pp. 614, ff., Mar Abraham died in union with Rome, but according to Portuguese authors and to Fr. Castets, he died a heretic, 'the like of whom had never been seen', cf. G. Beltrami, op. cit. pp. 118, ff. and Fr. Roz, op. cit. p. 8. Such is the interpretation Mgr. Beltrami gave to the texts already mentioned. Still the question could be asked whether Fr. Castets had anything else than the evidence of Fr. du Jarric concerning the illness of Mar Abraham in 1595. Fr. du Jarric expressly speaks of this last event, but he must have been convinced that it carried off Mar Abraham; for, though in his text he does not explicitly state what had happened, yet on the margin the words 'Archiepiscopus moritur' are found. One of the following paragraphs begins thus:' Angamalano igitur episcopo Abraham ... demortuo', Fr. du Jarric, op. cit. p. 617.

[2] G. Beltrami, op. cit. p. 185, giving the text.

Archdeacon George de Christo died before he was consecrated, and he was succeeded by a relative whose name was George de Cruce. We must not confuse the two here.[1] A good opportunity to start an indigenous hierarchy of Eastern rite was lost. These arrangements were made at a time when Mar Abraham enjoyed the full confidence of the Jesuits and the Holy See, and when the struggle with the intruding Nestorian bishop, Mar Simon, was at its height; but after the denunciations made by Fr. Roz and Fr. Abraham George, Clement VIII, by the Briefs of 17 January 1595, and 21 January 1597, had ordered the Archbishop of Goa to appoint a vicar apostolic in case of a vacancy. Mar Abraham, however, had not been notified of the simultaneous abrogation of the Briefs of Gregory XIII. The vicar apostolic, to be chosen by Menezes, was now to have full authority in spiritual and temporal matters. This would continue until such time as the Pope should provide the Syrian archdiocese with some clearer status. In the second Brief two points were asserted: firstly, that this new situation was not to prejudice any previous acts, customs, statutes, etc., and, secondly, that the Pope intended on this occasion—*hac vice specialiter et expresse*—to depart from them.[2]

Alexis de Menezes could hesitate so. And in the course of his visitation of the Latin parishes, he appointed Francis Roz as Vicar Apostolic of Angamale. Since the latter had been associated with Mar Abraham for twelve years, he knew the affairs of the archdiocese better than anybody else. However, when the archbishop went back to Goa, his counsellors remarked that as Archdeacon George de Cruce had already taken hold of the reins of the administration of the archdiocese, it was not fitting to dispossess him. Menezes agreed, and confirmed the archdeacon in his office of administrator; yet he gave him Fr. Roz

---

[1] Ibid. pp. 196-8, giving the text; G. M. Antão, *De Synodi Diamperianae Natura atque Decretis*, Goa, 1952, p. 55, n. 87.
[2] G. Beltrami, op. cit. pp. 252, ff. giving the text.

and the Superior of the Seminary at Vaipicotta as advisers.[1] In their opinion these measures would be sure to satisfy the St. Thomas Christians. However, the archdeacon was not pleased at having advisers imposed upon him, and he, therefore, postponed his profession of faith which was to have signified his taking charge of the administration. Did he do this in the hope that meanwhile a bishop from Mesopotamia would arrive? At all events he convened an assembly of both the clergy and the people, in which it was decided to keep the Syro-Malabar rite and customs at all costs, the 'Law of St. Thomas', *Legem Sancti Thomae*, and to refuse any bishop who had not been approved by the Patriarch of Chaldea, Simon IX Denha (1581-1600), in union with the Holy See.

Faced with such a movement, apparently the symptom of an imminent schism, the Archbishop of Goa resolved to visit the Syrian communities of Malabar himself. This he did from 27 December 1598 onwards despite the general state of high tension then prevalent. His visit lasted several months; we know its details through the account of the Augustinian friar, Antonio de Gouvea, who later on became Titular Bishop of Cyrene.[2]

Gouvea reckoned that there were about 70,000 Syro-Malabar Christians. With genuine skill he described the attitude of the Portuguese missionaries towards the Syrians. Their first feeling was one of admiration for the Christians: these were so few; they were so poor; they were surrounded by a countless

---

[1] Ibid. p. 120.

[2] Gouvea composed his book at the request of his superiors, so that the brilliant action of Menezes might be entered in the glorious records of the Order of the Hermits of St. Augustine. The author, who dated his preface from Goa, 27 September 1603, had not been personally present at the visitation made by Menezes. He however stated that he had consulted those who were continually with the Archbishop of Goa, especially his confessor and confrère, Fr. Bras of St. Mary. Very reliable information came also from Fr. Roz, cf. A. de Gouvea, *Iornada do Arcebispo de Goa, Dom Frey Aleixo de Menezes . . . quando foy as Serras de Malauar*, Coïmbra, 1606, p. 6, and fo. 152.

number of non-Christians. Often too they had been oppressed by local potentates, and their places of worship were miserable compared with the many rich temples of the Hindus. Nevertheless they had the great merit of having kept in its integrity the faith in the Trinity, which is the firm foundation of the Christian religion. Unhappily — though they were not at fault in this — they were ill-instructed Christians, and they fell into heresy because of their hierarchical superiors. The bishops from Mesopotamia were themselves attached to the Nestorian heresy. One could therefore understand that on seeing such a regrettable situation, the Archbishop of Goa and his friend, Fr. Bras of St. Mary, wanted at all costs to help the poor straying sheep, and bring them back into the fold under the one true pastoral staff of Peter's successor, so they made great efforts to succeed in this. Notwithstanding the exhausting climate of South India, Menezes wanted to visit personally the smallest communities before and after the future diocesan synod. With his retinue he devoted a full year to visitation, moving about mostly by boat from one place to another on the *rios*, or backwaters of the area. With undaunted courage he faced all sorts of dangers from obstinate Christians and petty princes who had been induced to believe that the Archbishop of Goa had the intention of fully subjecting all the Christians to the Portuguese, and thus removing them from the authority of their traditional leaders under the pretext of submitting them to the Pope.

The archbishop left Cochin at the beginning of February 1599. His first halt was at Vaipicotta (Chengamangalam) where with the Jesuit fathers he was on safe ground. Three boys of the college-seminary, who belonged to the nobility and were receiving education together with the clerics, made Latin, Syriac and Malayalam speeches during the academic seance arranged for the occasion. In these speeches they requested the archbishop to bring back the true faith to Malabar and to root out the Nestorian heresy for ever. In his answer, given at an inaugural function in the church of Vaipicotta, the archbishop spoke in a general way against those prelates who came from Mesopotamia, without, it seems, making the necessary distinction between Catholic and Nestorian bishops. All of them, since they had secretly come to Malabar, were taken to be the thieves who had not entered the fold by the door, hence they were such men as would lead the faithful to hell.

This theme was then evolved in such a manner as to put the clergy and the faithful on their guard against the arrival of a bishop sent by the Catholicos of Seleucia. For in spite of the watch set up by the Portuguese at Ormuz and Goa, such an event always remained a possibility. Probably Menezes was not unaware of the fact that steps had been taken to obtain a bishop from Seleucia in the traditional way. The archbishop's instruction was completed with a summary of the Catholic doctrine on Purgatory; then Menezes administered the Sacrament of Confirmation.

In point of fact, the question of Confirmation was a delicate one in Malabar. Here, as elsewhere, priests were accustomed to anointing during Baptism, and a few of these unctions probably belonged to the essential rite of Confirmation, but since, in the Eastern Churches, the priests administered Confirmation during the Baptismal rites, one could readily perceive that the priests, who had little education, and the faithful too, could not see the difference between the two sacraments. Even today, though the Holy See has expressly forbidden the administration of Confirmation to Oriental dissidents who have correctly received Baptism according to the full customary rite of their Churches, one still finds Latin priests who have their doubts about the prohibition. Hence the Portuguese priests might be excused if they insisted on giving Confirmation according to the Latin rite.

They had a further and an explicit reason for their opinion that the Syrians of Malabar had not received proper Confirmation. The unctions of Baptism given by the *kattanars* (the local name for priest) were not made with Holy Chrism, which is the obligatory element of Confirmation, but with coconut or palm-oil, which moreover had not received any blessing whatsoever. In Vaipicotta, owing to the great influence of the Jesuits, the faithful came in numbers to receive Confirmation; but, elsewhere, the invitation of the archbishop was given the cold shoulder. Further the refractory element among the clergy began to deny that Confirmation was ever instituted by Our Lord, and so the whole question became a subject of bitter discussion.

The day after his arrival at Vaipicotta and while he was present at the Chaldean service, Menezes noticed that prayers were said for the Patriarch of Babylon, ascribing to him the title of 'Universal Pastor of the Christian Church'. This was an evident encroachment on a title proper to the Pope of Rome alone. Moreover was the patriarch not a Nestorian? No, Simon IX Denha, the third Patriarch since Sulaqa who was the first to be reunited with the Catholic Church, was no doubt a Catholic, and had been confirmed in his office by Rome on 16 June 1581.[1] Was this known in India, or did they pretend to follow the principle that all that came from Mesopotamia was Nestorian? However, the Archbishop of Goa was afraid to offend those who sided with Rome, by attending services in which the name of a heretic was mentioned. So when he attended the Chaldean service a second time, he fulminated an excommunication *latae sententiae* against anyone who dared to mention the Patriarch of Babylon in any church service; the Pope had to be named in his stead. A stir was created! A new theme of discussion now arose and had to be considered over and over again: are there many laws in the Church which can be opposed to one another, in particular the law of St. Peter and the law of St. Thomas? Or is there only one law, that of Christ, which was adopted by all the Apostles?

---

[1] E. Tisserant, 'L'Eglise Nestorienne', in *D.T.C.* vol. XI, 230 and 263.

After Vaipicotta, Archbishop de Menezes proceeded to Parur, Mangate (Alangad), Chegeree (Chewarra), and Canhur (Kanjur). The Archdeacon, George de Cruce, should have accompanied the archbishop, but he retired to his residence at Angamale. He had advised his priests to receive Menezes with due honour, but only as a foreign prelate, just passing through. Since the Syrian metropolitan see had already been vacant for two years and the expected appointment from Rome was not forthcoming, Menezes deemed that the time had come to have an ordination. In the same year (1599) he summoned the future priests to Diamper (Udayamperur) for Saturday in Holy Week. The archdeacon, as administrator of the diocese, was also invited, but the latter, relying on Clement VIII's Brief, strongly objected to this act of jurisdiction which Menezes intended to perform. He maintained that the Pope had not given the archbishop any sort of power over the Syrians, but only over the Latins. Determined to defend his privileges, George de Cruce in his turn excommunicated *latae sententiae* all those who were to be ordained by the Goan prelate. He made clear to them that they would never be admitted among the clergy of Angamale, and even threatened their families with coercive measures. The archbishop took no notice of this and proceeded to ordain thirty-eight priests. He had examined them especially on their knowledge of the Syriac language. Then they made the profession of faith prescribed by Pius IV, took the oath of obedience to the Pope and promised to give up the Nestorian errors as well as obedience to the Patriarch of Babylon.

On the Friday before Palm Sunday, the archbishop reached the big Christian community of Caturte (Kadutturutti), where he had intended to celebrate the Holy Week services. The priests of the village were troubled however when they learned that Menezes intended to hold pontifical services and to administer the sacraments personally. They also anticipated some clear profits from Easter Communion, for it was the custom that all the faithful going to Communion should offer to the celebrant one *fanam* ($\frac{1}{8}$ of a rupee). The priests laid their grievances before the sovereign of the land, Queen Pimenta (Vatakkumkur), and the latter handed an order to Menezes to quit the place within three days. The queen was told that the archbishop would turn her Christian subjects away from her. The archbishop replied that, on the contrary, he was preaching to all to submit to legitimate authority; further, he claimed the liberty to officiate, on the basis of privileges granted by the rulers of the country for over 1,500 years, according to which the St. Thomas Christians had a right to foreign religious heads. If the reply is true, it was rather a witty twist he gave to the privileges. But was Menezes the legitimate foreign head?

In order to impress the people of Kadutturutti still more and to make them appreciate the splendour of the Latin ceremonies, Menezes had also called in a choir from Cochin, and from Wednesday in Holy Week, the services were held in Latin first and then in Syriac in the principal church. The archbishop attended both services so as to show to all that he had jurisdiction over the Syrians as well as over the Latins. After the *Tenebrae* of Wednesday evening, the archbishop gathered the priests together and explained to them the meaning of the Sacred Oils which were to be consecrated the next day in such quantities that all the churches would be provided for. On Maundy Thursday, after the blessing of the Oils and the celebration of the Pontifical Mass, the Blessed Sacrament was placed on a specially prepared and richly adorned altar. The faithful were greatly edified, since they had never before seen such honours given to the Holy Eucharist. In the afternoon, the *Mandatum*, the service of the Washing of the Feet, took place, and Menezes washed the feet of the priests. When the archbishop in full pontificals was seen kneeling before each of the *kattanars* in turn and washing and kissing their feet, a thrill went through the crowd, who were truly touched by such humility. Many of the priests wept. The service on Good

Friday, with the Adoration of the Cross, improved still more the good dispositions of the St. Thomas Christians, who were very devout to the Cross. In the evening the *Tenebrae* were sung; but during the second Nocturn, a priest who had organized the rebellion made his appearance in the church with his followers, all well-armed. Such were the sentiments of the congregation that people and clergy alike, far from being willing to join the hostile manifestation, surrounded the priest and brought him before the archbishop. They tried their very best to persuade the rebel to ask pardon, but the unhappy man was adamant and refused to submit. His action did not prove unprofitable, for once the service was over the nobility and the clergy, all in one body, presented themselves to Menezes and protested their entire submission.

In this way Kadutturutti became the first community to be fully won over. Others followed in the course of the ensuing weeks, Molandurte (Molanthurutti) and Diamper (Udayamperur) being among the most important. It was clear that the pro-Roman party was on the verge of success. Menezes then took the opportunity of making new advances to Archdeacon George de Cruce through the intermediary of a priest whom he fully trusted. The reply was a favourable one. The archbishop at once made haste to inform George in writing of the conditions he was to accept. These were: to renounce the errors of Nestorius, Diodorus of Tarsus and Theodore of Mopsuestia; to acknowledge that there was but one law, that of Christ, and not several arbitrary ones differing one from one or other, for example, that of St. Thomas, of St. Peter, etc.; to make his profession of faith according to the formula sent to him at the time of his nomination as administrator of the archdiocese of Angamale; to proceed with the correction of the liturgical texts; to promise obedience to the Pope; to anathematize the Patriarch of Babylon; to undertake not to accept in his diocese any bishop not appointed by the Pope, and not acceptable to the Portuguese authorities; to acknowledge the authority of the

Archbishop of Goa; to prepare the summoning of a synod and to accompany the Archbishop of Goa during his visitation.

The meeting of Menezes and the archdeacon took place at Vaipicotta. George de Cruce requested as a special favour that he should not be forced to make a public act of submission. He then made the necessary promises, took the oath and signed the document acknowledging the conditions laid down by Menezes. Only the archbishop and Fr. Roz were present. Then it was settled that the synod would take place at Diamper (Udayamperur) and would begin on 20 June, the third Sunday after Pentecost.[1]

THE SYNOD OF DIAMPER [2]

A few days before the synod, Menezes arrived at Diamper to see and check the preparation of its many details. He then received its members and began the opening ceremony as given in the Latin pontifical. He also saw to it that Litanies of the Saints were first sung in Syriac and then in Latin. On 21 June everybody, including the clergy and four lay deputies from each community, made his profession of faith. The archbishop himself, with his hands on the Gospels, started reading the formula of the profession of faith as prescribed by the Council

[1] The story of Menezes' visitation as written by Gouvea is on the whole confirmed by other sources, mainly drawn from Jesuit archives. Yet one cannot help feeling that Gouvea was loud in his praise of the archbishop and that he appeared to be more of a panegyrist than a scholar. It would have been most interesting to read side by side Gouvea's account and the archdeacon's report, if the latter ever existed.

[2] The Acts of the Synod of Diamper were published for the first time at Coïmbra in 1606 under the title *Synodo diocesano da Igrejia e bispado de Angamale dos antigos christãos de Sam Thome das Serras do Malavar das partes da India oriental, celebrado pello Reverendissimo Senhor Dom Fray Aleixo de Menezes ... no terceyro domingo depois de Pentecoste aos 20 dias do mes de iunho da era de 1599. Na igreja de todos os Santos, no lugar et Reyno do Diamper ...* The volume, containing 62 folios is generally bound together with the *Iornada do arcebispo de Goa* printed in the same year. J.F. Raulin, ex-General of the Hermits of St. Augustine, translated the Acts of the synod from Portuguese into Latin. As

of Trent; but several Syrians then protested that since they had always been Christians, they felt offended at being asked to read such a document in public. In a short instruction, however, the archbishop explained the reasons why the Church demanded that profession. Then headed by the archdeacon, they all read their profession according to the Tridentine formula, and completed it with the anathemas against the Nestorian errors. The session lasted seven hours. The priests spoke in Syriac, the lay deputies in Malayalam.

The agenda for the synod mentioned that the following session, or *actio tertia*, would be devoted to fundamental dogmatic questions, but the *kattanars* asked that these questions be treated with a certain reserve and without any interference from the canons of Cochin, or other Portuguese clerics, for they found it hard to see errors in their long-standing beliefs which were now to be discussed in an assembly of strangers. The

---

a sort of introduction to them, he wrote a summary of the *Iornada*, and a short history of Christianity in India, *Historia Ecclesiae Malabaricae cum Diamperitana Synodo* ... , Rome, 1745, fo. 18 and p. 529. The Acts themselves, covering pp. 59-282, were reprinted by J. D. Mansi in the supplement of Coleti's edition of the councils, *Sanctorum conciliorum supplementum*, Lucques, 1772, vol. VI, col. 1-208. It is this edition that was anastaticly reproduced in the new Mansi, *Sacrorum conciliorum nova et amplissima collectio*, Paris, 1902, vol. xxxv, col. 1161-368. The Acts of the synod, in Portuguese and in Latin with Raulin's notes, are to be found also in the *Bullarium patronatus Portugalliae regum*, Lisbon, 1872, appendix I, pp. 147-368. Mathurin Veyssière de La Croze devoted pages 77-328 of his *Histoire du Christianisme aux Indes*, La Haye, 1724, to the visitation of Angamale archdiocese by Alexis de Menezes, and to the Synod of Diamper. The tone of this work is far from being unprejudiced. The librarian of the King of Prussia bears the Portuguese archbishop a grudge for having made away from the Malabar Church everything that could have brought her near the Reformed Church. W. Germann, *Die Kirche der Thomaschristen*, Gütensloh, 1877, pp. 380-94, and 414-28, gives rather a detailed report of the double visit of Menezes, before and after the synod. In 1949, a French summary of the proceedings of Diamper with commentary was published by Fr. C. De Clercq, in 'Conciles des Orientaux Catholiques', *Histoire des Conciles*, Paris, 1949, vol. XI, part I, pp. 33-67. More recently, Fr. G. M. Antâo printed at Goa a Latin dissertation on the Diamper Synod under the title *De Synodi Diamperitanae Natura atque Decretis*, 1952.

archbishop readily assented, and the order of the session was modified. They began, therefore, with the examination of the point which had been reserved for the *actio quarta*, the questions of doctrine and discipline relating to Baptism and Confirmation. The synod sat daily from 7 to 11 a.m. and from 2 to 6 p.m. Anybody was allowed to present his own observations on the article of doctrine or on the schemes of the decrees. The Archbishop usually replied personally.

On 23 June the synod dealt with everything that came under the *actio quinta*, the Sacrament of the Holy Eucharist and the Sacrifice of the Mass. On the 24th the Portuguese went to a rather distant church to celebrate the feast of St. John the Baptist. Meanwhile, Archbishop Alexis de Menezes opened the session with a general exposé of the faith. Then long discussions followed until far into the night, and every single point was cleared up. The priests accepted the formulas proposed by the archbishop without much disagreement. Only on one point did his wishes meet with any resistance; he would have liked the clergy to give up the Chaldean office, on the false assumption that the Nestorian heresy cropped up on nearly every page. It would be replaced by the Roman breviary translated into Syriac. The *kattanars*, however, were attached to their traditional prayers, and in the end a compromise was reached; only corrections would be made. The day's work resulted in the approval by the members of the synod of a decree on faith in fourteen chapters. It was to be used as a summary of the doctrine until a somewhat more elaborate catechism in Malayalam was composed. The principal points dealt with in these chapters were: the Trinity; the Incarnation; the divine Motherhood of Mary; Original Sin; the Guardian Angels; the Church and its organization; the Canon of the Sacred Books.

Next came twenty-two decrees in which problems were dealt with concerning Malabar. First we have Holy Scripture (decrees two and three), because the Canon of the Syro-Malabar Church was incomplete. Esther, Tobias, Wisdom, the Second Epistle of

St. Peter, the Second and Third Epistles of St. John, the Epistle of St. Jude, and the Apocalypse were all omitted. Missing also were the passage on the 'sinful woman', the verse about the 'three heavenly witnesses', and a few other words. As a matter of fact, these defects were not peculiar to Malabar; the Syriac texts of the Bible were the same everywhere, even before Nestorius' time, hence it made no sense to charge the so-called Nestorians with falsifying the Scriptures. For example, they had been satisfied with substituting 'God' by 'Christ' in a few passages, such as Acts. xx, 21, 1 John III, 16. Fr. Roz, qualified as he was by his knowledge of both Holy Writ and the Syriac language, was given the task of seeing that the books of the Syriac Bible conformed to those of the Latin Vulgate.

Further, three decrees warned against non-Christian influence, which was all the more dangerous since it came from an overwhelming majority; moreover, most of the non-Christians in many places were rich and held the monopoly of education. The fourth decree condemned the doctrines on metempsychosis and fatalism. Through the influence of such doctrines some Christians, it seemed, held that the fate of each person's future was irrevocably determined at birth. The same decree also warned the people against indifferentism in matters of religion. In a country where so many cults existed side by side, one could easily be tempted to regard all religions as equally good. The twelfth and thirteenth decrees concerned attendance at school: as far as was feasible, each Christian community was to have its own Christian master. Where this was not possible, the children of Christian parents were to be allowed to attend non-Christian schools, but only in so far as some assurance could be given that they would not have to take part in any act of non-Christian worship. Christian masters could receive non-Christians among their pupils, but they should not tolerate the presence of anything that savoured of non-Christian worship within the school.

However, what was foremost in the mind of the Archbishop

of Goa was to remove for good all Mesopotamian and Nestorian influence in matters of faith and Church organization,
and in liturgical formulas. This was a somewhat delicate proce-
dure, since it endangered that Christian edifice to which, in
spite of all its imperfections, these people had been accustomed
for centuries. Moreover, were they not well worth some sympathy for their ignorance and simplicity? Alexis de Menezes,
born and brought up in the atmosphere of the Counter-Refor-
mation in Europe, was not the man however to yield even an
inch when he thought something to be his duty.

In the fifth decree the question arose of the Crucifixion and
the Passion of Our Lord. The 'Nestorians' preferred to leave
it out entirely on the pretext of giving more respect to Christ;
but at the same time they were depriving themselves of an
essential source of true piety. There sixth decree explained what
was to be held on the virginal Motherhood and the purity of
Mary. The seventh and eighth decrees clarified the organization of the Church. There was to be only one law, that of
Christ; there were not to be two different laws, one of St.
Thomas and the other of St. Peter, as some apparently thought.
If there was only one law, there could be only one Vicar of
Christ; therefore the title of Universal Pastor could not be
applied to the Patriarch of Babylon. This assertion led to a
practical corollary stated in the nineteenth decree: the oath,
taken during the secret meeting held after Mar Abraham's
death, was disapproved of and the members of the synod
promised to obey the Pope and not to accept any bishop but
the one appointed by Rome.

In Mesopotamia, and consequently also in Malabar, the
Eastern Syrian Christians had no knowledge, either theoretical
or practical, of the decisions taken by the Oecumenical Councils
since Ephesus (A.D. 431). In the twentieth decree the Church
of Malabar officially declared her acceptance of all of them,
but above all of those of the Council of Ephesus, in which
Nestorius was condemned. She officially acknowledged the

III.   1. Hindu or Buddhist temple transformed into a Christian church at Thiruvancode, formerly the headquarters of Dhariyaykal Christians and the most southern Christian community of Travancore. Now a Jacobite church.

2. Pre-Portuguese Baptismal Font showing marked Hindu influences, such as lotus flowers on the basin and four lions for the base — Syro — Malabar Church, Edapally.

IV. 1. Carved lintel with crosses and peacocks, motives often found on the Christian monuments of Malabar — Eastern gate, Knanaya Jacobite Church, Kottayam.

2. Ruins of the Portuguese fort, Cranganore.

sanctity of the Papal Legate, St. Cyril of Alexandria. The last Oecumenical Council, that of Trent, the teaching of which was at the time being put into practice all over the Church, was also accepted by the twenty-first decree. Much care was also taken to specify that the Syro-Malabar Church would observe all the provisions of Trent regarding discipline which were already in force throughout the Church and particularly in the neighbouring dioceses that formed part of the ecclesiastical province of Goa. Such an unhappy mixture of Latin customs and those of the Church Universal resulted in the Syrians imitating the Latins for centuries to come.

The reform of the faith had to be carried out in every Christian community through preaching. The seventeenth decree set up rules for the approval of preachers. The eighteenth dealt with retractations. Anyone having previously held erroneous doctrines was to retract them before his congregation. Finally, in order to make sure that all this would not remain a dead letter, all present pledged their word to obey the decisions of the Holy Inquisition of Goa (twenty-second decree). On top of this the tribunal was earnestly requested to appoint two commissaries at Angamale on account of its distance. It was each person's duty to denounce heretics and it was only natural that this should be especially so for the members of the hierarchy (twenty-third decree). Obviously the good Menezes was heretic-hunting.

But the preservation of the faith does not depend on preaching only. Faith can be corrupted by reading bad books; it can be also endangered by incorrect liturgical formulas. Literary works which were branded as dangerous, were all accordingly condemned by name in the fourteenth decree, and as far as most of them was concerned, mention was made of what was most objectionable in them. Some instances may here be given: the apocryphal narration of the childhood of Our Lord, known under the name of the *Protoevangelium Jacobi*; the apocryphal letter on the observance of Sunday; a book—till now unknown

6

—on the procession of the Holy Ghost; the *Book of the Fathers* i.e. a collection of dogmatic testimonies; the treatise on the sacraments by Patriarch Timothy II; the theological encyclopaedia of the Metropolitan of Nisibis, Mar Abdisho, together with his *Paradise of Eden*; some collections of homilies; a commentary of the Gospels following Theodore of Mopsuestia; lives of persons regarded as saints by Nestorians such as the monk Joseph Busnaya, the abbot Isaias, Rabban Hormizd, and the collection of monastic biographies, a kind of *Flos Sanctorum*, which must have been the *Book of Chastity* of Ishodenah, Bishop of Basrah; the *Book of Ordinations*; the hymns of George Warda and those of Qamis bar Qardahe; a compilation of Mesopotamian canon law or *Liber Canonum*; three books pervaded with superstitions: the *Book of Charms*, the *Ring of Solomon* and the *Parisman* or *Medicine of the Persians*.[1]

The question concerning liturgical formulas was a more thorny matter; here the point was not to condemn outright, but to correct. Some expressions endangered faith in the mystery of the Incarnation. Names of personages were to be erased, since they were either formal heretics or suspected of heresy. Certain feasts also were to be abolished (ninth and fifteenth decrees). All the liturgical books were to be brought for correction either to the archbishop in the course of his visit, or to Fr. Roz, or generally speaking to the Jesuits of Vaipicotta (sixteenth decree). Heretical books were to be destroyed forthwith, and in this case a time-limit of two months was granted. This section ended by replacing the titular saint of the cathedral of Angamale, built by Mar Abraham.[2]

---

[1] These various works were identified by J. B. Chabot, 'L'autodafé des livres syriaques du Malabar', in *Florilegium . . . de Vogüé*, Paris, 1909, pp. 615-23.

[2] At present, there are three churches at Angamale. The most eastern one was built by Mar Abraham, and it is now attached to a recently erected convent of Syro-Malabar nuns. Mar Abraham is buried in the sanctuary of this church.

Instead of the monk Hormisdas or Hormizd, Hormisdas the martyr would be henceforward venerated (tenth decree).[1]

The *actio septima* on the Sacraments of Order and Marriage took place on June 25; on the 26th the *actio octava* on the organization of the diocese; on the 27th of the same month the *actio nona* on reform of morals. In this last session twenty-four decrees were promulgated relating to some very important points of social life: regulations about inheritance and adoption; contacts with non-Christians; attendance at mixed, but non-religious meetings; behaviour towards high caste non-Christians, the Namputhiri Brahmins and the Nairs, and towards the Pariahs or Untouchables. Prompted by deeply Christian feelings, Menezes would have liked to get rid of many regulations tending to embody certain age-long customs of the Syrians and savouring of an aristocratic and caste-bound system. One of the worst consequences of such customs turned out to be rather adverse to Christian equality—for unfortunate people, belonging to lower stratas of society, were practically prevented from becoming Christians. On the other hand, it would have been most imprudent to renounce privileges which were enabling the Christians to deal on an equal footing with Brahmins and Nairs. At all events the Syrians present at the council refused to give up their social status.

The synod concluded with its twenty-fifth decree in the same *actio nona*. All the rectors of the churches were enjoined to keep in their archives at least one copy of the Malayalam translation of the acts of synod. This translation was to be the official one, signed by Archdeacon George de Cruce and by the Superior of the College of Vaipicotta. In order that all the faithful might be taught the prescriptions of the synod,

[1] Hormisdas the monk should be identified with Rabban Hormizd, who lived in the seventh century, cf. E.A.W. Budge, *The Book of Governors*, London, 1893, vol. I, pp. CLXVII ff. St. Hormisdas the Persian, who lived in the fourth century, and who is found in the Roman Martyrology for 8 August, was most likely the saint chosen by Menezes and his advisers, cf. *AA.SS.* Paris, 1863, August, vol. II, p. 341.

its Acts were to be read by sections whenever there was no sermon at the services on Sundays and Feast-Days. Two authentic copies, signed by the archbishop, were to be kept, the first at Vaipicotta, the second one at Angamale.

Following this last decree, the list of the seventy-five parishes of the Syrian archdiocese was proclaimed together with the names of the parish priests and their assistants. Some of the priests were put in charge of those chapels ministering to the faithful who were too few to form actual parishes. The priests whose names had been called, came forward and kissed the hand of the archbishop. He gave them an ardent exhortation; in it he followed the 'Monitions' to future priests as laid down in the Roman pontifical.

At the conclusion of all the ceremonies, all, i.e. a total of 153 priests and 660 laymen, put their signatures to the Acts. After that, the archbishop intoned the *Te Deum*, which was sung in procession by the Portuguese in Latin, by the local clergy in Syriac and by the faithful in Malayalam.

Before returning home, each parish priest received from the archbishop an altar-stone, which he had personally consecrated, together with cruets for the Holy Oils, a ritual with the text of the various sacraments translated from Latin into Syriac, a catechism in Malayalam and a surplice for the administration of the sacraments. All the churches and chapels were provided with chalices, altar cloths and vestments. When this was over, Alexis de Menezes, who now felt sure that he would be well received by everybody, resumed the visit of the archdiocese of Angamale.

The account of the second part of the visit following the synod goes from folio 73 to folio 114 in the original edition of the *Iornada*. The daily programme of the archbishop was a heavy one. In each parish he visited, the prelate obviously attended a liturgical service. He also gave Confirmation to all those Christians who had not been previously confirmed. There were often several Baptisms and always at least one instruction during which the main decrees of the synod were read out together with an exhortation to observe them. All the Syriac books, liturgical and others, were brought in, and those already condemned were burnt at once, while the others were duly corrected. Parochial treasurers were appointed, and confessors were approved; but this was not all, for should any non-Christian, attracted by the external grandeur of the ceremonies, set foot in the church, the opportunity was taken at once for catechetical instructions. A few weeks later with the help of God's grace this would develop into an actual conversion. If sick people were brought to the archbishop's notice, he promptly visited them, and he would read over to them a few passages from the Gospels.

In this way the visit went on from the beginning of July till 16 November, on which day the archbishop was back in Goa. Meanwhile Pope Clement VIII had sent a Brief of encouragement[1] to the archbishop which reached Goa almost simultaneously with his return. When, almost at the end of his journey the archbishop received the Brief, it looked to him as if providence was testifying in favour of his work. It seemed to him a pledge, too, of the success of reforms instituted with such difficulty.

AN APPRECIATION OF THE SYNOD OF DIAMPER

The disciplinary measures taken at Diamper will be examined in Appendix I. They have often been subjected to bitter criticism.[2] Many people nowadays are shocked by the tendency to reduce everything to the standard of Roman and Portuguese customs. Was not this tendency the leading principle of Archbishop de Menezes and his collaborators? Doubtless such an

---

[1] Brief of 1 April 1599, in *Bullarium Patronatus*, vol. I, p. 335.

[2] In one of the most recent studies on the synod, Fr. C. De Clercq remarks: 'All the causes of subsequent dissensions ... are provoked by Menezes' excessive reforms and also by doing away with the hierarchy of the rite,' op. cit. p. 67.

attitude was the opposite of those methods which the Holy
See fostered elsewhere, especially in the Near East and even
in Italy. Never did Rome advocate any policy that would
change the Byzantine, the Maronite or even the Chaldean
rite in Mesopotamia into the Latin one; moreover, the Acts
of the Synod of Diamper were never officially approved. Actually they were not in need of approval since a synod that was
only diocesan was not subject by law to Rome's scrutiny.[1]

There are many good reasons for the belief that Fr. Roz,
who became the first Latin prelate of the Syrians, succeeded
in preventing the synod's explicit approval by Rome, although
an attempt to do so was apparently made by Goa.[2]   According
to some of his unpublished letters, Bishop Roz had found that

---

[1] Cf. G. Beltrami who corrected the assertion of Pastor, following Raulin,
Müllbauer and Jann, op. cit. p. 124, ff., n. 84. G. M. Antâo tries to prove that
the synod was implicitly approved by the brief of Clement VIII, *Divinam Dei
Omnipotentis*, 19 May 1601, published in *Corpo Diplomatico Portuguêz*, vol.
XII, pp. 99-102, cf. op. cit. pp. 79-82, 91, 112-8, and appendix, doc. XI and
XIV.

[2] On 7 December 1603, Bishop Roz convened a new synod at Angamale.
All precautions were taken to make it juridically valid as a diocesan synod.
It cancelled several measures taken at Diamper, corrected others and added
new decisions. The reason for holding such a new meeting was that the Synod
of Diamper was regarded by the bishop and his collaborators as invalid.
The legal conditions for such assemblies were not fulfilled, the Indian members
of the synod were not always consulted or at least they did not understand many
of the proceedings, and they had signed only because the then Fr. Roz had
asked them to do so. What was even more serious a defect, Menezes had
tampered with the text of the synod, adding new decrees or correcting some
of the old ones. Besides this, many a decision, particularly as regards local
customs, were unbearable. The new Synod of Angamale was therefore intended to replace Diamper's as the Canon-Law of the Syro-Malabar Christians.
Thus Bishop Roz and his friends tried their level best to prevent any kind of
approval of the text of Diamper, but they wanted Rome to move in favour
of the text of Angamale only. We do not know whether they succeeded in
reaching their second goal, but they did reach the first one. Cf. two letters
of Bishop Roz to Fr. Claude Aquaviva, General of the Society, 20 November
and 26 December 1603; three letters of the same to Fr. John Alvarez,
Assistant of Portugal, 27 December 1603, and in 1605; letter of Fr. J. M.
Campori s. j. to Fr. Aquaviva, 9 January, 1604, to Fr. John Alvarez, 2 January

the archbishop had added various other measures to the already signed text of the synod. This could only have invalidated the text itself written by common consent and would only have angered the Syrians had they come to know of it. As a matter of fact, the text of the synod, a well-written Latin copy, bound with the coat-of-arms of Clement VIII, is still kept in the Roman Archives of the Jesuits.[1] It is probably that very copy which was sent to Rome for approval, but which was never handed over to the Roman Curia, thanks to the efforts of Bishop Roz.

Already then, as now and always, there have been protagonists of the Latin rite. Among them the Catholic apostles of Malabar of the second half of the sixteenth century are probably to be blamed least of all. Actually they were confronted with a Christian community which they thought to be a heretical one, though whether formally or materially is a distinction of no importance here. They really found books which contained undoubtedly erroneous formulas. Spurious liturgical texts were also discovered, and general carelessness in ecclesiastical organization and rather loose morals were prevalent. Why, then, should the idea of applying the Tridentine reform not have risen in their minds? Archbishop de Menezes thought that he had the same mission in the archdiocese of Angamale as had St. Charles Borromeo in the archdiocese of Milan. If Menezes had not the same success, the reason lay in the fact that differences of language and rite complicated things in no small way. He showed both true zeal and genuine devotion.

Moreover, Menezes wanted to be quite sure of the validity of the sacraments which had been conferred. His efforts to latinize the Syro-Malabar liturgical texts sprang from that

1604; letter of the Vice-Provincial A. Laertio to Fr. Aquaviva, 15 January 1604, in *A.R.S.J. Goa*, 15, pp. 155-6; 176-7, 178-9, 182-3, 196-200, 242-3, 246.

[1] Ibid. 62, pp. 1-92.

viewpoint. Instead of destroying the existing Syriac manuscripts, he could have had them corrected, but his method was that of certainty, so that any future heresy could be more easily averted. Such a course of action, arising from the lofty motive of prudence, had also for its basis a real ignorance of matters pertaining to the Eastern rites. As far as the Portuguese clergy and laity were concerned, much ignorance was perhaps entirely due to the geographical situation of Portugal. As the country faced the west, Portuguese sailors and missionaries had very little opportunity to frequent the eastern shores of the Mediterranean. Their caravels sailed across the Atlantic, to the north, south and west. Of all the nations of Europe, Portugal was in the least favourable position for any contact with the Eastern Christians. The Spanish, French or Italian people would have probably acted in a different way.

IV

THE ST. THOMAS CHRISTIANS UNDER THE JURISDICTION OF THE JESUITS AND THE CARMELITES

THE JESUITS IN INDIA AND IN MALABAR

BARELY six years had passed since Ignatius of Loyola and his companions had laid down the first foundations of the Society of Jesus at Montmartre near Paris, and the approbation of the first constitutions of the new Order had not yet been made public when at the beginning of 1540 Simon Rodriguez and Francis Xavier were destined by Paul III for the mission of the East Indies. Simon did not move further than Lisbon, and the two companions, newly allotted to Xavier, fell sick and remained a full year in Mozambique. Yet the man who landed all alone at Goa on 6 May 1542 possessed such gifts of intelligence, energy, administrative ability, and above all, of holiness, that before the close of the sixteenth century, the Jesuit mission in the Indies had reached a high degree of prosperity. Yet the Jesuits were not the only missionaries in those regions: from the time of the first Portuguese expeditions, secular priests and religious missionaries, such as the Trinitarians, the Dominicans and above all the Franciscans, had come in large numbers. The Jesuits had not been the first to busy themselves with the Syrians of Malabar, for the College of Cranganore, founded in 1541 by the Bishop of Goa, John de Albuquerque (1537-53), a Franciscan, had been, in accordance with an agreement made with Mar Jacob, entrusted to the Franciscans. Near the end of his life, the same Mar Jacob was living at the Franciscan convent of Cochin, as we have already seen.[1]

[1] Cf. *supra* pp. 31.

THE ELECTION OF FR. ROZ, THE FIRST LATIN PRELATE
OF THE INDIAN SYRIANS

When Mar Abraham died and the Holy See was resolved
to replace him with a prelate from the West, the choice could
not but fall on a Jesuit. As a matter of fact, as early as 1552,
the Franciscans had given up the College of Cranganore.
Within six years they had succeeded in training fourteen Syrian
priests.

The Franciscans however did not know Syriac and were
not specialists in the teaching profession. On the other hand,
most of the first disciples of St. Ignatius had followed university
courses. Very soon after their arrival they had taken over the
management of the College of St. Paul at Goa, and so they
were the most suitable people to train the Syrian clergy of
Malabar. In 1552 they opened a college at Cochin. In 1581,
they added to their residence at Vaipicotta a seminary for the
Syrian clerics, and at the same time maintained a school for
Syrian boys at Cranganore. So without enjoying any monopoly, it was the religious society which had the closest contact
with the Syro-Malabar community. In 1595 the seminary
already comprised forty-five students, of which twelve were
priests, three were deacons and eighteen had received minor
orders.[1]

This state of affairs explains why Alexis de Menezes appointed Fr. Francis Roz, who was professor of Syriac at the
seminary, as administrator of the archdiocese of Angamale as
soon as he heard of the death of Mar Abraham. This measure
was evidently a temporary one; in fact it was soon cancelled
by the pressure brought to bear upon the archbishop by his
advisers at Goa. Nevertheless Menezes had to propose a final
nominee at Lisbon. We are aware of the archbishop's views
through one of his letters written on 19 December 1597 to
the Titular Patriarch of Jerusalem (Latin), Mgr. Fabio Biondi,

---

[1] P. du Jarric, *Thesaurus Rerum Indicarum*, Cologne, 1615, pp. 365-70.

who had been the Apostolic Collector of Portugal.[1] Breaking
with the long-standing practice of the Roman Church, Menezes insisted on his proposals. The Pope should select a Latin
prelate, preferably Jesuit, in order to prevent the Patriarch of
Alexandria and that of Babylon — the former, Menezes considered to be a heretic and the latter a Nestorian, as was Mar
Abraham — from appointing a prelate of their own. The
newly-chosen prelate was to be made a suffragan of Goa, as
was the neighbouring Bishop of Cochin. Such a proposal is
quite surprising, and Rome must have been genuinely alarmed
to see the Nestorian heresy take firm root in the Indies.
Further, the Curia had had the opportunity of witnessing the
singular orthodoxy of prelates like Sulaqa, Mar Elias and
Mar Joseph.

Such ideas were not entirely new, for even before Alexis
de Menezes expressed them, the Maronite Jesuit the Venerable
Abraham George wrote on 15 December 1593 to the General
of the Jesuits, suggesting that the Christians of St. Thomas be
given a truly Catholic pastor. He should be chosen from outside the Chaldean rite—a priest from Syria if that was possible.
He even proposed by name a certain Moses, a Maronite like
himself, whom he knew personally. Abraham George showed
genuine shrewdness when he pointed out that neither a Jesuit
nor a Portuguese should be appointed as prelate;[2] but how to
escape the obligations of the Padroado if no Portuguese was
selected?

There was a great deal in favour of Fr. Roz. Was he not
already known to the Christians of St. Thomas, and was he

[1] *Subsidium ad Bullarium Patronatus Portugalliae*, Alappey, 1903, pp. 12, ff.
The Apostolic Collector of Portugal was a papal officer, whose duty it was to
receive the taxes, mainly Peter's pence. It originated in the dues levied for
the crusades, cf. M. Michaud, 'Chambre Apostolique', in *D.D.C.* vol. III
pp. 405-7.

[2] A. Rabbath, 'Deux lettres du Vénérable Père Abraham di Giorgio',
in *Documents inédits pour servir à l'histoire du Christianisme en Orient*, Paris,
1905, vol. II p. 326.

not very well acquainted with their affairs? Moreover, he spoke
Syriac and Malayalam equally well. He had one more advantage. As he was born in Catalonia, he was by birth a subject
of King Philip III, who at the time reigned over Spain and
Portugal. Consequently Francis Roz was preconized at the
consistory of 20 December 1599, following Cardinal Gesualdo's report. It is worth mentioning that the see of Angamale,
which had been metropolitan up to now, was to be lowered
to the rank of an ordinary bishopric, suffragan of Goa.[1]

---

[1] 'Referente cardinale Gesualdo providit (Summus Pontifex) Ecclesiae
Angamalensi vacanti per obitum Mar Abraham, de persona Francisci [Ros,
added above the line], fuitque dicta Ecclesia ex metropolitana reducta in epis-
copatum, et constituta suffraganea metropolitanae Ecclesiae Goanae ', *A.V.*,
Acta Consistorialia, Acta Camer. vol. 13, fo. 133, v. The sheet, that contains
Cardinal Gesualdo's proposals, has come down to us in a collection of several
various documents, gathered by Cardinal Santore and kept in the Vatican
Archives. In this document the description of the diocese is given as follows:
'Angamalensis civitas est in Indiis orientalibus in regno Coccini, cuius rex est
gentilis, amicus tamen et tributarius regis Portugalliae, qui civitatem regiam
Coccini possidet. In dicta civitate Angamalensi est ecclesia archiepiscopalis,
quae habet archidiaconatum, et per archidiaconum exerceri consuevit
jurisdictio archiepiscopalis. Adest seminarium, quod regitur a patribus
societatis Jesu, et in eo aluntur quinquaginta vel sexaginta ex christianis
descendentibus ab eis, qui a S. Thoma apostolo ad veram fidem conversi
fuerant, et instruuntur in litteris humanioribus, ac latina et caldea (*sic*)
lingua, necnon in casibus conscientiae, in fidei catholicae rudimentis,
et in ritibus ecclesiasticis, jamque e dicto seminario plures exierunt
satis bene instructi, et ad sacros et presbyteratus ordines promoti. Prope
civitatem sunt duae residentiae seu loca, alterum fratrum praedicatorum,
alterum fransciscanorum; et tam seminarium, quam haec duo loca re-
gularium sumptibus regis Portugalliae sustentantur. Ipsa Angamalensis ecclesia
hactenus habuit praelatos caldaeos (*sic*) schismaticos, qui varios errores pra-
esertim nestorianos sequuti sunt: hos autem ei praeficere consuevit patriarcha
Syriae. In ea cultus divinus lingua et ritu caldaeo (*sic*) persolvitur. Sub dicta
ecclesia tantus est numerus christianorum, qui juxta antiquam traditionem
deseendunt, sicuti dictum est, ab eis qui ad Christi fidem a sancto Thoma
apostolo conversi fuerunt ut sint plus quam ducenti mille, et fere ad 300 mille
ascendunt. Inter quos praelatorum et malorum ministrorum culpa nonnulli
et errores (non tamen gentilitatis) vigent, quibus expellendis opera datur, et
jam illis purgati reperiuntur libri eorum, qua in re promovendus praecipue ela-
boravit. Ampla est eius dioecesis, et magnam regni Coccini partem comple-
ctiur. Nihil aliud de statu ecclesiae ad praesens haberi potuit; in libris Camerae

The statutes of the diocese were reorganized according to the principles used for the creation of the Latin dioceses of the Indies. They formed the subject matter of the Bull *In supremo militantis*, of 4 August 1600.[1] The King of Portugal had to guarantee the new bishop an annual subsidy of 500 crusados, corresponding to 375 ducats *de camera*, and in exchange he was given the right of presentation as a consequence of the Padroado. No sooner did the letters about Fr. Roz's election reach the Indies, than he was consecrated at Goa on 25 January 1601.[2]

BISHOP FRANCIS ROZ AND HIS SUCCESSORS

The leader of the St. Thomas Christians had always been a metropolitan, so the St. Thomas Christians could not possibly be indifferent to the fact that their new shepherd was a mere bishop. The lowering of the title made the subjection to Goa too obvious — it meant submission to the Portuguese. The St. Thomas Christians, their traditions of independence overridden, naturally turned towards the local princes, as they had done at the time of Menezes' visit. Though the Jesuits had had, since 1599, a small residence at Angamale, the new bishop deemed it more prudent to reside regularly at Cranganore, where a Portuguese garrison was located. The town however belonged to the Latin diocese of Cochin, and its bishop protested. It speaks for Paul V's ability that, without any further hesitation, he suppressed the two obstacles that hindered Francis Roz in his ministry. Following the repeated requests of Bishop Roz,[3] the Pope restored to Angamale its

---

non reperitur taxata, quia non est solita provideri per hanc sanctam Sedem', A. V., *Archiv. Consist., Acta Miscellanea*, vol. 53, fo. 227.

[1] *Corpo Diplomatico Portuguez*, Lisbon, 1902, vol. XII, pp. 80-2.

[2] A. Jann, *Die katholischen Missionen in Indien, China und Japan*, Paderborn, 1915, pp. 169, ff.

[3] Between 1601 and 1605, Roz wrote in this connection to the Pope, the King of Portugal, the cardinal, as well as several letters to Fr. Aquaviva and

archiepiscopal dignity on 22 December 1608, and two years
later he confirmed the division of the bishopric of Cochin,
assigning the jurisdiction over Cranganore to the Archbishop
of Angamale.[1] Whereas the latter had to attend the provincial
synods of Goa, he was not subjected any longer to control
from that see.

In spite of the fact that these measures had given some sort of
satisfaction to the faithful, the archdeacon was not too pleased
with them. From time immemorial, this personage occupied a
position no one else possessed in any of the other eparchies
(ecclesiatical circumscriptions) of the Eastern Syrians or
Chaldeans. In the Indies, the metropolitan was always a
foreigner, therefore he could not rule without the help of a
local individual in whom he had full confidence, and through
whose hands all business had necessarily to pass. Was not this
situation, heretofore most favourable to archdeacons, now
greatly altered, perhaps even completely reversed? Bishop Roz
spoke Syriac and Malayalam fluently and for many years he
had been familiar with the affairs of the archdiocese; he therefore
kept George de Cruce, whose orthodoxy he did not altogether
trust, in the background. The latter felt as though he had been
shelved, and could not but strongly resent this action. However the storm did not break out until 1618, when the archdeacon accompanied Fr. Robert de Nobili s.j. to Goa in
order to defend his case before the commissaries of the
Inquisition, before whom he had been summoned on a charge
of heresy.[2] Without warning George, the archbishop appointed the Superior of the Seminary at Vaipicotta as the substitute
of the archdeacon. This was replacing a Syrian by a European,

---

Fr. John Alvarez, already mentioned, Cf. *A.R.S.J. Goa*, 15 and 16, *passim*.
The archdeacon and eleven Syro-Malabar priests wrote also to the cardinals
on 13 December 1602, ibid. 15, fo. 109. Vice-Provincial Laertio in 1604, and
Fr. Stephen de Brito in 1603 also pressed the matter with Fr. Aquaviva,
ibid pp. 1-2, 133-4, 209-10.

[1] *Bullarium patronatus . . .* , vol. II, pp. 8-17.

[2] E. Amann, 'Rites Malabares', in *D.T.C.* vol. IX, 1713

which meant a step forward in submitting the St. Thomas
Christians to foreigners. The archdeacon refused to acknowledge this appointment, which had been published without
his knowledge. It meant nothing to him that Fr. Stephen de
Brito, coadjutor with right of succession to Francis Roz, had
declared himself in his favour. Moreover the old archbishop
remained obstinate. For four years the disagreement dragged
on, and only just before his death did Roz reconcile himself to
George. This was a true reconciliation, for when the see became
vacant on 18 February 1624,[1] the archdeacon peacefully
administered the archdiocese until the arrival of a duplicate of
the Bulls addressed to Fr. de Brito, the first copy of the Bulls
having been lost in a shipwreck.[2]

PRELIMINARY EMBARRASSMENTS

When Fr. Stephen de Brito became Archbishop of Angamale and was consecrated at Goa, George de Cruce prepared a
splendid welcome for the new prelate. George could not help
feeling grateful to the man who had intervened in order to
reinstate him in the good books of his predecessor. There was
hope that peace would reign in the days to come.

In 1628 we see the archdeacon sending a report to the Apostolic Collector of Lisbon, which was a violent attack against the
Jesuits and the archbishop.[3] The occasion for a renewal of the
conflict arose from the arrival in Malabar of a Roman Dominican called Francis Donati. This excellent missionary, who was
to die a martyr in April 1634, arrived at Goa and later at Cochin

---

[1] The slab of Bishop Roz is kept in the old Parur church. A recent but
very unsatisfactory biography of the Catalan prelate was published by A.
Santos S. J., *Francisco Roz s.j., Arzobispo de Cranganor, Primer Obispo Jesuita
de la India*, (1557-1624), Madrid, 1948.

[2] K. Werth, *Das Schisma der Thomas-Christen unter Erzbischof Franz Garzia*,
Limburg a. L., 1937, pp. 25, ff.

[3] The year before, the archdeacon had already intrigued with an Augustinian friar of Cochin to get rid of the Jesuits, cf. *Relatione informatoria . . .*,
A. P. F. Scritt. Refer. (ant.), vol. 191, pp. 508-32.

after many adventures.[1] He made use of the new title 'Apostolic Missionary' received from the Sacred Congregation *de Propaganda Fide* in order to start a school intended for the training of Syrian clerics.[2] He was very successful in this venture, particularly as he taught Syriac, a language of which the archbishop had no knowledge. This hampered the latter's participation in the liturgical functions performed by his own clergy. Stephen de Brito thought that the Society of Jesus must defend her rights. In his mind Fr. Donati O.P. was an intruder, and his school an institution which was in unfair competition with the Seminary of Vaipicotta. The Syrians, on the contrary, felt flattered because Fr. Donati used their liturgical language. Moreover they were somewhat discontented because the archbishop was not in such close touch with them as his predecessor had been. Soon a clique of opponents was formed and the archdeacon's complaint was that the Jesuits prevented other religious from working among the Malabar Christians. Having drawn a parallel between the good works of Fr. Donati and those of the Jesuits, George concluded in these simple terms: in future no Jesuit should be appointed as archbishop of the Syrians; Fr. Donati is to be the coadjutor and successor of Stephen de Brito.[3]

The Collector having gone to Rome, the archdeacon's report was examined in a plenary session of Propaganda on 16 September 1630. Since Fr. Donati was an Italian, there was no hope that the Portuguese king would ever put his name forward, so a resolution was passed for his appointment as

[1] A. M. Alori, 'll P. Francesco Donato O.P. Missionario e Martire nelle Inde', in *Missioni Domenicane*, 13 (1940), pp. 30-1, 34-6.

[2] Fr. Donati settled at Kadutturutti, where the compound of his church and school can still be seen. It is used now as a Christian cemetery.

[3] K. Werth, op. cit., p. 27. According to some of the letters of the archdeacon, there about 250,000 Syrians in Malabar, with 100 priests and clerics divided among 120 churches, cf. letter of 1 Jan. 1629, *A.P.F. Scritt. Origin.* (*Lettere Antiche*), vol. 98, fo. 81; letter of 4 Jan. 1534, ibid. *Scritt. Refer (ant.)*, vol. 194, fo. 142.

bishop *in partibus infidelium*. It was also decided that the Jesuits should no longer oppose the establishment of other religious orders in Malabar. These decisions show the spirit which inspired the young Congregation of Propaganda. It strongly opposed anything which had the slightest tinge of monopoly. None of these resolutions ever materialized. Fr. Donati never became bishop, and in 1646 the Dominican Michael da Cruz Rangel, Bishop of Cochin, still had reason to denounce to Propaganda an ordinance of the Portuguese king in which he forbade any religious other than Jesuits to interfere in the affairs of the Syro-Malabar Church.[1]

Thenceforward, the archdeacon waged an unceasing war. At the close of 1632, he wrote letters to the Portuguese king, and later, during the course of December 1633 and January 1634, to the Holy See railing against the Jesuits and praising the Dominican Donati and his work. There is no need to give details. Let us note however that the local clergy appeared to be kept under strict tutelage, and further, the number of ordinations was so limited that several parishes were in need of priests. Moreover the *kattanars* were not allowed to preach, the triennial synods prescribed at Diamper were not held, and non-Jesuit missionaries were still excluded.[2] On 16 February 1634 Fr. Donati wrote to Propaganda. His statement reproduced in substance that of the archdeacon.[3] On receiving these complaints, the Sacred Congregation forbade under pain of

[1] K. Werth, op. cit. p. 28.

[2] ibid. p. 31, ff. There were other complaints, viz. the non-observance of the ecclesiastical customs of the Syrians, such as consulting the archdeacon before appointing priests or ordaining candidates; the prevention of priests from enjoying church dues and taxes, etc., cf. letter of the archdeacon to the Collector of Portugal, 5 Jan 1634, *A.P.F. Scritt. Refer.* (*ant.*); vol. 194, fo. 142-5. Complaints were lodged also against the Jesuits, who, after having started a congregation of priests at Edapally, dissolved it in 1634, because the priests indulged in intrigues and supported the archdeacon's party, cf. E.R. Hambye s.j., 'The Syrians and the Jesuits', in *Deepika Special Number*, 1952, p. 245.

[3] K. Werth, op. cit. pp. 33, ff.

excommunication *latae sententiae* any non-Jesuit to be prevented from settling and working in Malabar.[1] Before this decision was made known in India, Fr. Donati died, and the archdeacon's death followed soon after in 1637. Thomas de Campo (Parampil Thumi) replaced the latter, and when Stephen de Brito died, Francis Garzia s.j., his coadjutor with right of succession, took peaceful possession of the archiepiscopal see. Again the future appeared secure: the Seminary of Vaipicotta was flourishing and the missionaries were well received in the country. And then the arrival of a bishop from Mesopotamia revived all the old problems.

THE BREACH OF 1653

In the course of the spring of 1652, an eastern monk went begging at the door of the Capuchin monastery in Surat, and was well received there. He then told the fathers that he was a patriarch on his way to the St. Thomas Christians.

The Goan Inquisition was warned but it could only arrest him later, on 3 August, while he was visiting the shrine of Mylapore. He was provisionally interned in the Jesuit College there. From Mylapore he managed to address a letter in Syriac to the archdeacon, in which he told him of his appointment by the Pope as Patriarch of the Syrians of Malabar, and requested him to send some armed men to fetch him.[2] As the

---

[1] Ibid.p.38.

[2] Here is a Latin translation of that letter, found in the Propaganda archives: 'In nomine essentiae eternae omnipotentis. Patriarcha D. Thomae Apostoli; Pax Dei Patris, et benedictio Domini nostri Jesu Christi et incubatio Spiritus Sancti—Ecce ego Ignatius Patriarcha Totius Indiae, et Sinarum, mitto vobis Epistolam per manus Diaconorum, qui huc venerunt ex vestra regione. Cum autem legeritis Epistolam diligenter, mittite ad me duos sacerdotes, et quadraginta viros. Quos quidem si mittere volueritis, caute mittite illos, atque cito et quamprimum. Etenim videntes isti vos, dimittent sine impedimento. Venite, Filii; audite me, et discite a me; quia data est mihi omnis potestas a Domino Papa, scilicet Ignatium omni potestate praeditum esse. Nunc, itaque, ne timeatis, quia veni habens in manibus thesauros multos, et alias magnas divitias, iuxta vestram necessitatem. Quamobrem

Christian communities knew who he was and realized his predicament, they started to act in his favour at once. They had recourse to Archbishop Garzia, but his answer was categorical. He said that even if it were true that the monk Athallah had been sent by the Pope, he could not take possession of the see, since each appointment had to be preceded by the presentation of the Portuguese king. This answer was no doubt quite legitimate, but it was a blow for the poor Syrians, and so, when a few days later they heard that Athallah would come to Cochin by sea, they gathered in large numbers at the gates of the city, and demanded *en masse* that either the prisoner be liberated, or at least that they be given a chance to speak to him and examine his claims. Instead of making a diplomatic excuse the authorities rushed the supposed patriarch to Goa by night. In order to prevent any attack on the town, they spread the less palatable story that the unfortunate prelate had been accidentally drowned.

The Christians were naturally furious. They were completely taken aback by this obvious deception. Almost at once they gathered in front of the church of Mattanchery, tied a long rope to the famous Coonan Cross and swore that they would never be under the Paulists i.e. the Jesuits, and that in future they would never obey Archbishop Garzia. Then the archdeacon, Thomas de Campo, produced a real, or supposed, letter from Athallah authorizing the Syro-Malabar communities to choose a bishop for themselves. The malcontents assembled at Alangad on 22 May 1653, and twelve priests

plurimum satagite, me ad vos adducere; in nomine tamen Dei Genetricis Mariae, tam sacerdotes et diaconi sancti gregis, quam omnes magnates. Et sciatis me ad hanc adventasse urbem Mailpur, quia didici, huc advenire solere plures viros, et sacerdotes, qui me adducere possunt ad vestram regionem Indiarum. Anno 1652, appuli Mailpur mense augusto die 2a. Ad monasterium Jesuitarum, id est...in eodem monasterio dicessor, et ipsi valde mihi favent, eorum merces augeatur hic atque ibi. Pax sit ad illos, et vobiscum, et nobiscum semper. AMEN. (s) Ignatius, Patriarcha totius Indiae et Sinarum, *A.R.F. Scritt. Refer. (orig.)*, vol. 232, fo. 2, 1

imposed hands on the archdeacon and proclaimed him metropolitan as Mar Thomas I. During the ceremony the false
letter of investiture was laid on his head. Henceforward, Mar
Thomas performed pontifical functions, ordained clerics and
gave dispensations in marriage impediments, etc. The secession
spread practically over the whole of the Malabar Church.
In the meantime, Athallah was condemned as a heretic by the
Inquisition of Goa and died at the stake in 1654.[1]

It was only at the close of 1655 that Rome received news of
the defection of the Syro-Malabar communities. As soon as he
could do so, Archbishop Garzia had dispatched to the Curia
his collaborator of old, Fr. Hyacinth de Magistris, an Italian
Jesuit. Meanwhile the four hundred Syrians who still remained
loyal had requested the Carmelites to keep the Holy See
informed of their affairs. Warned already by reports of previous
troubles, Propaganda immediately grasped the consequences of
the situation. Availing itself of the fact that the Carmelites in
India had already established good relations with the St. Thomas
Christians, it decided to send them an Apostolic Commissary,
Fr. Hyacinth of St. Vincent O.C.D. The latter took two compan-
ions with him, Fr. Joseph of St. Mary (Sebastiani) and Fr.
Matthew of St. Joseph, both Italians like himself. It was under-
stood that to avoid any disagreeable reaction on the part of the
Portuguese, the papal mission would pass through Lisbon. The
journey by sea was rather long, hence the Pope decided that FF.
Hyacinth and Matthew would proceed by sea, whereas Fr. Joseph
would take the shortest way, through Syria and Mesopotamia.
The latter set out, accompanied by two German Carmelites,
Marcel of St. Ivo and Vincent-Mary of St. Catherine. When
Fr. Joseph reached the neighbourhood of Goa on board a Dutch
vessel, about the middle of January 1657, he was informed by
a message from his confrères of Goa that his mission would be
opposed by the Portuguese authorities and by the Inquisition.

[1] K.Werth, op. cit. pp. 43–50

Aware, moreover, that Dutch warships were cruising in sight of the town, he refrained from landing. He sent an account of his mission to the inquisitors and proceeded to Edapally, where the rebellious archdeacon resided.

Taking advantage of his mission to the Syrians, Fr. Joseph took great care not to have any dealings with either the Jesuits or the Portuguese. This precaution however did not gain for him the confidence of the rebels. Furthermore, noticing that the negotiations did not make any progress, he sent Fr. Vincent-Mary of St. Catherine to Cochin and Cranganore with the Papal Briefs addressed to the secular authorities and to Archbishop Garzia. Meanwhile the Governors Francisco de Mello and Antonio de Souza Coutinho were deeply concerned with the Dutch threat, and in order to make sure of the help of the Malabar Christians, they paid a visit to Fr. Joseph at Edapally and encouraged him to pursue his peace-making activities. It was much easier now for the Carmelite friar to take action since he had the positive support of the Portuguese and also of Archbishop Garzia who welcomed the order of the Holy See with genuine sincerity and accordingly recommended the commissary to all Catholics. However, despite many discouraging attempts, the zealous Carmelite met with a well-disposed community among the Syrians of Kuravalangad and the nearby churches.

At the end of the year 1657, the Christians of Kuravalangad, Kadutturutti, Muttuchira and Muttam, in the south, and those of Parur, Angamale, Kanjur, etc., in the north, had rallied round Fr. Joseph in large majorities. Meetings continued for several months more, during which time the invalidity of the 'consecration' conferred on the archdeacon and hence of all his faked episcopal actions was discussed. Thomas de Campo, though in all probability personally convinced of his bogus consecration, stubbornly refused to resign, and used every means in his power to defend himself. Still, in spite of the many divisive forces among the Christians, Fr. Joseph of St. Mary continued to win over to his side many priests and communities. In one respect only, however, did he fail completely, viz. nobody was willing under any condition to submit to the jurisdiction of the archbishop.[1]

Towards the end of 1657, it was reported in Malabar that Fr. Hyacinth of St. Vincent had arrived at Goa with the official recommendations for which he had gone to Lisbon. Fr. Joseph could now absent himself, report to Rome on his activities and obtain new instructions. On 15 December he presided over a farewell meeting at which forty-four priests, representing twenty-eight communities, were present. He entrusted Fr. Matthew with temporary powers until the arrival of Fr. Hyacinth, and gave him very detailed instructions. Fr. Joseph left Malabar on 17 January 1658. He met his confrère at Goa, together with Fr. Hyacinth de Magistris s.j. who had just arrived from Europe; then taking a route via Mesopotamia and the Mediterranean Sea, he reached Rome on 22 February 1659.

During his absence, the union made no progress whatsoever. Neither negotiations, nor threats, nor forcible measures used by the Portuguese authorities curbed in any way the resistance of the archdeacon's party. Archbishop Garzia viewed the action of the new commissary rather unfavourably. Just as he was about to die, he chose his confrère, the Provincial of Malabar, Fr. Nunez Barreto s.j., as administrator of the archdiocese, but the latter was wise enough to withdraw when the prelate died, on 21 September 1659.[2] A few months later, on 10 February 1661, Fr. Hyacinth of St. Vincent, worn out by excessive labours, the climate and the failure of an effort he had sustained for a little more than two years, also went to his reward.[3]

[1] Ibid. pp. 79-89. Very good study of the Carmelite's mission.

[2] Ibid. p. 129, no. 47. On Archbishop Garzia's last years and achievements, cf. D. Ferroli s.j., *The Jesuits in Malabar*, Bangalore, 1951, vol. II, pp. 45 ff.

[3] D. Ferroli, op. cit. pp. 100-3

When Propaganda learned through Fr. Joseph of St. Mary (Sebastiani) the real state of affairs in Malabar, it would have willingly replaced the archbishop immediately; but it had first to make sure that the Portuguese Court would offer a suitable candidate. On the one hand, the election of Sebastiani, a non-Portuguese, might ruffle the feelings of the Padroado authorities; on the other hand, it might be possible to appoint an Indian, say Thomas de Campo himself. This would have been a bold step indeed, but it was one that would have satisfied the archdeacon's ambitions and so would have cut the schism at its root. As far as the first proposal was concerned, the critical situation of the Portuguese possessions in India would not make the appointment of a non-Portuguese in any way more palatable.

While the cardinals were hesitating, Pope Alexander VII decided that Fr. Sebastiani should go back to Malabar with the title of Vicar Apostolic and Administrator of the archbishopric of Cranganore. He was to receive episcopal consecration in Rome in the strictest secrecy. Joseph of St. Mary (Sebastiani) was accordingly consecrated as Titular Bishop of Hierapolis on 15 December 1659. The secret was so well kept that during his second journey which began on 7 February 1660, his three companions had not the slightest suspicion of his new dignity. The new vicar apostolic was provided by Propaganda with precise instructions. These were directed towards one aim, the squashing of the schism. For this purpose he was given entire liberty as to the choice of means, and was empowered with the greatest authority. It seems that all eventualities had been foreseen—the life or death of Archbishop Garzia, the co-operation or resistance from the archbishop and the Jesuits, the opposition of local leaders, etc. The vicar apostolic could, if he deemed it opportune, consecrate an Indian bishop, or divide the territory of Cranganore and Angamale so as to form two districts, a southern and a northern one.

He also had the power to choose a successor and to consecrate him.[1]

One thing was likely to give some offence in these instructions: the Sacred Congregation advised that the knowledge of Latin among the young clerics should be cultivated so as to induce them to give up their Syriac rite spontaneously.[2] The fear that heretical propositions were contained in the liturgical formulas was still a real obsession. However, the advice given was so much against the constant tradition of the Holy See that Propaganda sent along with the mission two Maronites, because of their knowledge of Syriac.

THE SYRIANS AND THEIR APOSTOLIC VICARS

Sebastiani set out from Rome on his way to Aleppo. There he contacted Francis Piquet, the ever-obliging French Consul, who was to be the agent of the Sacred Congregation *de Propaganda Fide*, with the task of transmitting messages and funds. While he was at Aleppo, he received news of Garzia's death, and this rendered his mission far more easy, but he heard also that the Dutch had made substantial progress in their war against Portugal. Before long they would be a direct threat to Malabar.

For a century and a half the Dutch were satisfied with carrying on the normal trade in spices north of Lisbon, but after their

---

[1] K.Werth, op. cit. pp. 134-50

[2] Here is the passage relating to the rite: 'Benche non piacirà alla Sacra Congregatione divertire i Popoli da proprii riti, come siano lodevoli, et approvati dalla Chiesa: perche non dimeno l'ignoranza di quei della Serra li rende molto esposti al pericolo d'imbeversi dell' errori de Libri Soriani, che si vanno in volta con l'accettazione di quel rito, che da loro si osserva, e e quest' istesso dà edito (come si e veduto) a Vescovi Scismastici di Babilonia d'insinuarsi per farli ricadere nel Nestorianismo: Percio valendosi dell' instanta che fanno esto medesimi di Maestri che insegnino la lingua latina, procuri onninamente, o comme Vescovo o come Commissario Apostolico, d'introducerla, e stabilircela, e con questa divertirli insensibilmente da quel rito, et indurli al latino.' *A.P.F. Scritt. Refer.* (*orig.*), vol. 233, fo. 29

rebellion against Spain in 1581, they were excluded from the harbour of Lisbon and resolved to oust the Portuguese from the very source of their trade, in the same way as the latter had broken the Arab-Venetian monopoly. Their aim was very similar to that of the Portuguese at the end of the fifteenth century. The Dutch were not satisfied with trading only; they also wanted to establish a monopoly for themselves. Although Ceylon was the centre of all transactions between producers and consumers or traders, its conquest alone would not suffice. Malabar had to be brought under their sway.

Sebastiani, aware of the anti-Catholic tendencies of the Dutch, thought that this would induce the archdeacon to make them some advances. He therefore did not hesitate to break one of his instructions: from Surat he went to Goa to have his title of Apostolic Delegate for Malabar recognized by the Padroado. In order not to cause any alarm among the authorities, he was particularly careful not to reveal to anybody that he had been consecrated bishop. But when he landed at Cochin on 14 May 1661, in possession of adequate recommendations from the civil authorities and from the Inquisition of Goa, he presented himself in his new dignity. At Cochin neither the chapter of the cathedral nor the governor, who was entirely convinced of the Padroado privileges, was inclined to receive a bishop hailing from anywhere other than Lisbon. Yet Sebastiani took possession of the archiepiscopal palace that lay outside the city, and after a few days he had won the battle.

The archdeacon was his first concern, for the Dutch military successes made the suppression of the schism daily more urgent. The Portuguese understood this, and favoured his action. Many communities came over and others were strengthened in their union. Yet Thomas de Campo evaded all the attempts of the civil authorities, who were anxious to take him prisoner. He took refuge in the hilly part of the country and from there maintained his influence.[1]

[1] K.Werth, op. cit. pp. 151-63

In the meantime, after a short defence, Cochin had fallen into the hands of the Dutch (6 January 1663). Though he had remonstrated with General Rickloff, the Dutch Commander, about the purely religious nature of his position, Sebastiani was ordered to quit Malabar forthwith. He obtained, however, a ten days' extension of the order, and summoned a synod at Kadutturutti. All priests in union with Rome as well as many laymen were asked to be present. Sebastiani told them how things stood and that he had powers to give them a bishop. All the members of the synod unanimously proposed a cousin of the archdeacon, parish priest of Kuravalangad, Alexander de Campo (Parampil Chandy), who happened to be Sebastiani's candidate also. On 1 February 1663, the new bishop was consecrated after he had taken the oath to receive anyone coming in the name of the Pope and never to give episcopal consecration to his cousin Thomas without an express order from Rome. A council of five members, chosen from among the most worthy priests, was given to the new prelate. Sebastiani then solemnly launched a major excommunication against the rebellious archdeacon, and left for Cochin on 4 February. He was received with due honour by General Rickloff, to whom he recommended the Catholics and their new bishop. At the same time he insisted that the archdeacon was not to be recognized as bishop by the Dutch authorities, to which proposal Rickloff retorted that he did not hold Thomas de Campo in great esteem, and that his soldiers did not call him archdeacon but 'archdevil'. As a matter of fact the General always flatly refused to give audience to the intruder, while on the other hand he was always ready to receive the new Indian bishop.[1]

On March 5, while passing through Vengurla, a Dutch fortress situated north of Goa, Sebastiani received a letter from the confrères he had sent to the 'Rome of the East.' Before

[1] Eustachio di S. Maria, *Istoria della vita . . . del Ven. Mgr. Fr. Giuseppe di S. Maria de' Sebastiani*, Rome, 1719, pp. 277-83

that date the Viceroy Antonio de Mello Castro, had received instructions from Lisbon to expel the vicar apostolic, and also Fr. Hyacinth of St. Vincent, whose death had not yet been heard about in Europe. Now the Carmelite prelate was invited to visit Goa and settle a quarrel among the members of the clergy. Sebastiani moved at once to Goa and heard there that the new bishop of the Syrians had proved a success. How satisfactory this was after so many trials! When a truce was signed between the Portuguese and the Dutch, he entertained the hope—but only briefly—that he might be allowed to return to the south, but he had to be content with leaving Fr. Matthew of St. Joseph O.C.D. in Malabar as adviser to Alexander de Campo. After a very hard journey, full of incidents and adventures, via Basrah, Baghdad, Mosul, Aleppo and Alexandretta, Sebastiani reached Rome on 6 May 1655, bearer of the most precious data on the position of Christianity in India.[1]

With the support of his advisers, Fr. Matthew of St. Joseph and Fr. Cornelius of Jesus of Nazareth, Bishop Alexander de Campo[2] ruled the Syrian Catholic communities of Malabar very efficiently. He had some 40 parishes under him. He even made a good number of conversions in spite of the regular war which his cousin Thomas relentlessly waged against him and the Latin missionaries. Thomas was stubbornness itself, first in his schism, later on in the Jacobite dissidence to which he ultimately came to adhere, as will be explained below.

Yet in 1674, feeling the burden of advancing years, Alexander sent a request to the Pope for a coadjutor with right of succession. This step was inspired by prudence. Propaganda immediately accepted his views, and on 31 March 1675, four Carmelites left Rome. They carried instructions entitling them

---

[1] K. Werth, op. cit. pp. 294-330; 'Hierarchia Carmelitana, ser. IV, De praesulibus missionis Malabaricae', in *A.O.C.D.* 11 (1936), pp. 188-98

[2] He used to sign himself 'Metropolitan of all India' and, according to the customs of the ancient Chaldean prelates, 'Gate of all India'. cf. D. Ferroli s.J., op. cit. p. 123

to appoint as Bishop of Hadrumeta and coadjutor to Alexander the priest they should judge the most fit: 'either a secular priest or a religious who, however, is a native of the place, not a European'.[1]

Only two of the religious reached Malabar, FF.Bartholomew of the Holy Ghost[2] and Angelo Francis of St. Teresa. On 3 March 1676, they designated, not a Syro-Malabar, but the Vicar General of the Cochin Diocese, a Latin of Portuguese extraction, Raphael de Figueredo Salgado. One cannot imagine a less happy choice. Without any doubt the fathers had good reason not to appoint the nephew of the bishop, Matthew de Campo; but the question might be asked whether the spirit of the Roman instructions had been truly followed. However, Alexander at first refused to consecrate the coadjutor imposed on him. When at last he accepted and the latter was solemnly enthroned at Edapally in 1683, peace was soon disturbed by Salgado's pretensions to rule the diocese by himself, without any regard for the rights of Alexander de Campo. This state of affairs reached a climax, particularly at the time of Alexander's death. The Carmelites thought it necessary to send one of their men to Rome, Fr. Lawrence of St. Mary, to request the appointment of another prelate. The Brahmin Custodio de Pinho,[3] who had become an Oratorian at Goa and was already Vicar Apostolic of Bijapur and Golconda, was appointed Apostolic Visitor of Malabar in January 1684, while Figueredo was suspended from office. Both of them died soon after, Figueredo on 12 October 1695, and Pinho in 1697, without being able to fulfil his mission.[4]

---

[1] 'Hierarchia Carmelitana', ibid. 12 (1937), p. 13

[2] Bartholomew of the Holy Ghost was a Maronite from Aleppo, by name Hanna. Since he knew Syriac well he could help both in the formation of clerics and the return of the dissidents. He was very friendly with the Jesuits of Ambazhakat.

[3] D. Ferroli s.j., op. cit. p. 183 and note.

[4] 'Hierarchia Carmelitana', ibid. pp. 13-16; Anquetil du Perron, *Zend-Avesta*, Paris, 1772, vol. I pp. CLXXX-CLXXXII; M. Müllbauer, *Geschichte*

THE CARMELITES SETTLED IN MALABAR

The Holy See was now faced with an impossible situation. The Syrian communities were divided into three groups, headed by Thomas de Campo, Alexander de Campo and Raphael de Figueredo respectively, and they continued thus after the deaths of these three personages. Moreover the Latin diocese of Cochin and the archdiocese of Cranganore, both of which depended on the Padroado and within whose territories most of the St. Thomas Christians lived, were more often than not without resident bishops.[1]

On the other hand, the Dutch Governors of Cochin neither allowed any interferences from the Goan ecclesiastical authorities in the territories they controlled, nor did they permit any European missionary to enter the territory. As he wanted to reach some solution, cost what it might, Pope Innocent XII addressed himself to the Emperor of Germany, Leopold I, asking him to negotiate with the Netherlands. The Emperor promised to ensure to the Calvinists of Hungary free exercise of their religion, in exchange for which by the Act of 1 April 1698, Belgian, German and Italian Carmelites would be allowed to reside in Malabar and continue their missionary activities.[2]

Following on this agreement, Angelo Francis of St. Theresa, Superior of the Seminary founded by the Carmelites at Verapoly in 1682 for both Syrian and Latin clerics,[3] was, by a Brief of

der katholische Missionen in Ostindien, Freiburg i. B. 1852, pp. 307-10. The manuscript *Syriac 25* supplement 72 of the National Library, Paris, a psalter copied by Mar Jacob, belonged once to Alexander de Campo, and has notes written by him, or about him, for the years 1660-70, cf. H. Zotenberg, *Catalogues des manuscrits syriaques et sabéens (mandaïtes) de la Bibliothèque Nationale*, Paris, 1874, p. 10.

[1] Cranganore till 1701 and Cochin till 1693 were administered by ecclesiastical Governors, cf. D. Ferroli s.j., op. cit. pp. 72-87 and 97-109

[2] 'Hierarchia Carmelitana'. ibid. pp. 17, ff.

[3] During the first decades of its existence, Verapoly Seminary seems to have catered to the needs of the Latin community chiefly. The majority of the Syrian clerics were still being formed by the Jesuits. Their Seminary of Vaipicotta was moved to Ambazhakat in 1662, owing to the capture of

20 February 1700, appointed Vicar Apostolic 'of the land of the Malabars or of St. Thomas', with the dangerous clause 'till the Archbishop of Cranganore and the Bishop of Cochin have personally occupied their respective sees'.[1] When the news of his nomination reached India on 6 December 1700, Fr. Angelo Francis summoned a meeting of all the Syro-Malabar communities which were in union with Rome. They all gave him an enthusiastic reception on 13 February 1701. However he was not able to secure his consecration either from the Bishop of Cochin, Peter Pacheco O.P., who did not reside in his diocese, or from the Archbishop of Goa. Actually the Padroado prelates did not want to acknowledge the fact that Holy See could appoint a bishop in India without the approval of Lisbon. Fortunately for the Carmelites there happened to be in Malabar a certain Mar Simon,[2] a bishop hailing from Mesopotamia, who consented to consecrate the bishop-elect on 22 May 1701, in the church of Alangad. This happened exactly forty-eight years after the pseudo-consecration of the Archdeacon Thomas, who had

Cochin and its environs by the Dutch. Till the destruction of the new house by Tippu Sultan's troops in 1790, the Jesuits trained an average of forty Syrian clerics every three or four years. At Ambazhakat the scholasticate of the Malabar province was established in 1667, of.D. Ferroli s.j., op. cit. pp. 286-97, 550-1. The ruins of the Jesuit College can still be seen a mile or so from the village of Ambazhakat in a place called now *San palur*, i.e. St. Paul's.

[1] 'Hierarchia Carmelitana' ibid. p. 17

[2] The story of Mar Simon is one of the most obscure of a period already abounding in riddles. Thanks to unpublished documents, it can be ascertained that:(1)—he was a Catholic prelate of the Chaldean(East Syrian)rite in communion with Rome; (2)—he hailed from Diarbekir and was titular, or actual Metropolitan of Adana in Asia Minor;(3)—his coming to Malabar should be connected with the reunion of the Chaldeans of Diarbekir, a movement that led to the formation of a new Catholic patriarchate;(4)—he passed through Rome and Lisbon before sailing for India;(5)—he was authorized to go to Malabar in order to foster the reunion of the Jacobites;(6)—after having consecrated Bishop Fr. Angelo Francis c.d. he was rushed forcibly to Pondicherry, where he lived on till his death on 16 August 1720, cf. also Paulinus a S. Bartholomeo, *India Orientalis Christiana*, Rome, 1794, pp. 250-54; E. Tisserant, 'Eglise Nestorienne', *D.T.C.* vol. XI, 238-40.

been at the bottom of all the troubles and discords which had split the communities of Malabar ever since.[1]

The news, however, that a vicar apostolic had been appointed directly by the Holy See soon led the Portuguese Government to take a stand. On 5 December 1701 the Jesuit John Ribeiro (1701-16) was appointed as Archbishop of Cranganore.[2] During the year 1704, in spite of the opposition of the Dutch and of a portion of the clergy, he actually took over the rule of the archdiocese. The Syrians were not all ready to submit to a Jesuit prelate, so on 20 June 1704 a party of priests met at Kadutturutti and framed a resolution to obey only the Carmelite bishop. Though he knew that the Portuguese clergy were all for him, and that he could reckon on Dutch support, the Carmelite bishop thought it was only fair that he should submit to the limiting clause of his nomination Brief, i.e. 'to rule the Syrians till the Archbishop of Cranganore could occupy his see'. On 29 June 1704 he circulated a statement explaining his policy to the communities who were in obedience to him, and this done, he retired to the monastery of Verapoly.[3]

Such divisions could have done nothing but show favour to the party of Thomas de Campo, whose successor had at this time become a Jacobite. Propaganda took in the situation, and accordingly decided on 26 September 1706, that the jurisdiction

---

[1] 'Hierarchia Carmelitana,' ibid. p. 22

[2] Fr. John Ribeiro was the first Jesuit prelate to reside in Malabar since Archbishop Garzia's death on 3 September 1659. All the priests appointed archbishop by Portugal in the meantime either refused, or could not reach Malabar, cf. D. Ferroli s.j., op. cit. pp. 45-87. From the time of Mgr. Ribeiro, the Archbishops of Cranganore used to reside at Puttenchira, in the church of which four of them were buried. Their tombstones can still be seen. One of the companions of Archbishop Ribeiro was Fr. Ernst Hanxleden s.j., a German from Westphalia (1681-1732). He laboured more than thirty years among the people of Malabar. He was a scholar of repute in Sanskrit and in Malayalam. The religious poems he composed in this latter language are still cherished by the Catholics of Kerala, and till recently they were commonly sung at home during Holy Week, ibid. pp. 315-32

[3] 'Hierarchia Carmelitana', ibid. pp. 22-7

of the vicar apostolic had to be maintained. But this decision had no immediate effect, and had to be confirmed later on by a vote in the plenary session of the Congregation on 25 June 1708. Yet the Apostolic Letters of 13 March and 4 May 1709 insist on the rights of the Portuguese prelates, and on the duty of the vicar apostolic to bring the dissidents back to obedience. In view of the attitude of the St. Thomas Christians and that of the Dutch India Company, this was practically an impossible task. Nevertheless Bishop Angelo Francis set out on his visitation of the Christian communities in January 1712 and continued it till the September of the same year. The strain proved too much for him, and he died of exhaustion on 17 October that very year.[1]

In the Apostolic Letters appointing as his successor, Fr. John Baptist Mary of St. Theresa (Morteo), the following restrictive clause was still included: 'for the churches and places of both the dioceses of Cranganore and Cochin, where the ordinaries cannot fully exercise their respective jurisdiction.' Evidently Propaganda could not abolish the Padroado, and such a compromising attitude would prolong competition, as was evident when Innocent XIII (1721-4) ratified the nomination of the Portuguese Jesuits, Antonio Pimentel (1721-52) and Francisco de Vasconcellos (1722-42) to the sees of Cranganore and Cochin in 1721.[2] Trouble dragged on in the Syro-Malabar community. To add to the difficulties, a Nestorian bishop called Gabriel, coming from Azerbaijan, arrived in Malabar and announced himself as a convert to Catholicism.[3] However, after a new instruction issued by Propaganda in 1724,

---

[1] ibid. pp. 27-32

[2] On Dom Manoel Carvalho Pimentel s.j., cf. D. Ferroli s.j., op. cit. p. 91; on Dom Francisco de Vasconcellos s.j., ibid. p. 110

[3] Gabriel was sent by the Nestorian Catholicos Elias XI (1700-22). Elias belonged to the line of Chaldean patriarchs who resided at Rabban Hormizd near Mosul, cf. D. Ferroli s.j., op. cit. p. 330; E. Tisserant 'Eglise Nestorienne', D.T.C. vol. XI, 238-9, 263

the disturbances seemed gradually to subside. The Christian communities were numerous and strong; but the many *chassés-croisés* and conflicts between the Europeans themselves prevented the development of a higher level of Christian life. Further, the Dutch authorities did not allow more than twelve Carmelite missionaries at a time in the mission, and most of the time there were less than the permitted number at work.[1]

When John-Baptist Morteo passed away on 6 April 1750 he left a coadjutor with right of succession, the Pole Nicholas Szostak, Fr. Florentius of Jesus Nazareth. He had been appointed by a Brief of 6 December 1745, but had not yet been consecrated; and so amidst the wars that were raging over India at the time, Fr. Florentius undertook a hard and perilous journey in order to receive his consecration, which he at length obtained on 22 April 1751. In 1764, he had already succeeded, with the approval of Propaganda, in instilling new life into the Seminary of Verapoly, which he rebuilt. Owing to lack of resources the latter had not survived for many years after 1682. The first impression of the Syro-Malabar missal printed in Rome was also due to his efforts. He died on 26 July 1773 after a long period of illness. His death provoked a quarrel between the missionaries and the local clergy, both Latin and Syrian, which nearly ended in a schism. Who should carry the coffin with the remains of the prelate to his last resting place? This was the bone of contention between the opposing parties.[2] The account of the Christians community of Malabar, which was published by Anquetil du Perron, is to be referred to Bishop Florentius's time, more accurately to the year 1758. His account contains the following figures: 50,000 Latins, 100,000 Syro-Malabar Catholics, 50,000 dissidents, with 12 Latin Churches, 84 Syrian Catholic churches and 20 dissident ones.[3]

---

[1] 'Hierarchia Carmelitana', ibid. pp. 217-26.
[2] Ibid. 13 (1938), pp. 17-37.
[3] Anquetil du Perron, op. cit. vol. I a, pp. CLXXXIII-CLXXXIX, and CLVII.

8

The Carmelites had a difficult apostolate, but in all likelihood they used the right method regarding the Syrians, i.e. the training of priests in the Seminary of Verapoly, and frequent and almost continuous visits to the parishes. They gave advice to the priests and corrected them, making up in this way for the deficiencies in their theological and liturgical knowledge.

The chief difficulty arose from the fact that the missionaries were so few in number; to this must be added others — the climate which exhausted them, and the irregular arrival of replacements.

The shortage of recruits from Europe still continued in spite of the wise arrangement made by Propaganda, by which the normal time of missionary activity in Malabar was limited to ten years. In 1770, only one father was able to visit the Syrian parishes.[1] He was the Bavarian, Eustachius Federl, Fr. Francis de Sales of the Mother of Dolours. The end of his term was due in 1772. He did not ask for a prolongation, but instead insisted on being sent back to his province, for he felt exhausted and tired of seeing so many abuses. When on 4 November 1773, after eighteen months' voyage via Macao, Lisbon and Genoa, he reached Rome, he submitted to Cardinal Castelli, Prefect of Propaganda, a memorandum on the state of the missions, to which he added a few remarks on possible reforms. His account pleased the Sacred Congregation so much that, on 21 March 1774, it was decided to send him once more as missionary with Fr. Paulinus of St. Bartholomew. On 8 July of the same year, Fr. Francis de Sales was chosen as Vicar Apostolic of Malabar. It was thought, no doubt, that none would succeed better than he in carrying out a programme he himself had inspired. In this appointment the Sacred Congregation had brushed aside the *terna* (sheet with the names of three candidates) proposed by the vicar provincial, in which *terna* the latter had the boldness to include his own name.

[1] 'Hierarchia Carmelitana', ibid. p. 145

Upon his arrival at Verapoly on 13 October 1775, the new prelate took a daring step in accordance with instructions from higher superiors of the Order. He deposed the vicar provincial, who had held that position for more than twenty-five years. But a rebellion ensued, Italians against Germans. Such dissension among European missionaries led to immediate repercussions among the Syrians. On 15 February 1776, the representatives of thirty-five communities or parishes decided to transfer the residence of the vicar apostolic to Alangad and to refuse the missionaries any further access to their churches. By the middle of February 1777, Propaganda was now acquainted with the troubles in Malabar, and it decided on the 25th of the same month to force the new bishop to resign from his office.[1] While Rome took this decision with unwonted speed, the St. Thomas Christians organized an embassy to the Holy See. This legation was to present their grievances regarding the missionaries. A rather unexpected accusation was made, viz. that the vicar apostolic had prevented the conversion of Mar Thomas VI, a person referred to in documents as *Laicus Mitratus*, the local leader of the Jacobites.[2] This embassy, which arrived at Rome in 1779, did not seem to have made very much of an impression on the Sacred Congregation; but when passing through Lisbon, an *ex-alumnus* of Propaganda who was leading the delegation — a Syro-Malabar priest called Joseph Cariati (Kariatil) — was appointed Archbishop of Cranganore by the Queen of Portugal. Pope Pius VI sanctioned this appointment on 16 December 1782.[3]

It is not our intention to explain here how the Carmelite

[1] Ibid. p. 153

[2] Actually Mar Thomas VI was duly consecrated bishop in 1772, and he took the name of Mar Dionysios I. It seems likely, also, that the Carmelite missionaries did not use much diplomacy in dealing with the reunion of the dissident prelate, cf. Placid of St. Joseph T.O.C.D. 'The Efforts for Reunion in Malankara, South India', in *Unitas*, 5 (1953), pp. 12-15

[3] C. de Nazareth, *Mitras Lusitanas no Oriente*, Nova Goa, 1924, vol. II, p 50

mission in Malabar carried on under the interim government of Fr. Charles of St. Conrad, Vicar Apostolic of the Great Mogul. Yet it is easy to see that the help provided by the local clergy was not very efficacious, at a period when there were missionaries who failed so openly in their duty of edification. Hence it is not surprising that a new crisis was reached. The missionaries were attacked when it became known in Malabar that the Archbishop of Cranganore had reached Bombay on 1 May 1780. Were the St. Thomas Christians to be subjects of Carmelites from Europe always, or were they to get their own native prelates once more? The Syro-Malabar priest who had accompanied Joseph Cariati to Rome warned his people that the delegation had been unduly detained in Europe. Just as a few hotheads were preparing to go to Goa to make sure that the new prelate was not maltreated, the news that he had died on 9 September was broadcast. He had fallen a prey to a malignant fever. Yet the people believed that he had been done away with by the religious from Europe. Agitation reached such a pitch that it put fear into the heart of the Archbishop of Goa. He did not, however, lose his head in this crisis and to calm matters down he made an unexpected move: he appointed a Syro-Malabar priest, Fr. Thomas Paremmakal, the travelling companion of the late archbishop, as administrator (governor) of the diocese. The Syrians were elated, and thought one of their most cherished dreams was to be realized. Thomas would doubtless show himself a metropolitan of their own race. The administrator of Cranganore seemed to be doing his very best to fulfil their hopes. In the presence of his people he supported their belief that Cariati was killed, so as to render the appointment of a Carmelite vicar apostolic all the more difficult; but at the same time he held contrary views before the Portuguese authorities. In fact, the latter were petitioned by the Syrian people to present Thomas' name to the Holy See.[1] At long last the dispute between the missionaries

---

[1] Ibid. p. 56, ff.

and the Syro-Malabar communities was settled by the King of Travancore, as we know from a letter from the Vicar Apostolic Louis Mary of Jesus (Pianazzi) and his four companions to Propaganda on 7 May 1787.[1] One of these four missionaries was the famous Austrian orientalist, already mentioned, Paulinus of St. Bartholomew (Philip Wesdin),[2] who stayed in Malabar from 1775 till 1789. His data on the Syrian communities refer to this period. According to him there were 84 Syrian Catholic and 32 dissident parishes; the Syrian Catholics were still divided between two jurisdictions, Cranganore with 20 and Verapoly with 64 parishes.[3]

THE NINETEENTH CENTURY AND THE STRENGTHENING OF THE SYRIAN CATHOLICS OF MALABAR

In 1787 there remained only four missionaries and the vicar apostolic. Later on there was only one missionary left. The absence of qualified men explains why in 1803 a man of little accomplishment and meagre ability, Fr. Raymond of St. Joseph (Roviglia), had to be selected as bishop. The necessary Briefs for his consecration came as late as 1807, since the first dispatches had been lost. Happily, under British rule, beginning after the fall of Cochin in 1795, the country apparently enjoyed greater peace. The missionaries were no longer exposed to the whims and fancies of the earlier Dutch Governors. Yet, throughout the Napoleonic era, the relations with Europe were by no means easy. All through this period, unfortunate controversies raged between the Carmelites and the Padroado hierarchy of Cranganore and Cochin. They were almost ended by the Brief *Multa praeclara* of 24 April 1838, and only

---

[1] 'Hierarchia Carmelitana', ibid. pp. 214-19

[2] On the learned activities of the famous scholar, cf. D. Ferroli s.j., op. cit., pp. 118-20.

[3] Paulinus a S. Bartholomeo, op. cit. p. 86; *Notitia .. Missionis Malabaricae*, quoted by D. Ferroli s.j., op cit. p. 128

then was the apostolic vicariate of Verapoly officially erected.[1]

No other important fact is to be recorded in the history of the Syro-Malabar Church for this period except the formation of the Congregation of the Carmelite Tertiaries of the Eastern rite. This happy venture took place during the interim government of the apostolic vicariate, held by Fr. Maurilio Stabellini, when a few priests gathered round FF. Thomas Palakal and Thomas Porukara to lead the life of the religious. Yet the Congregation was only really constituted on 8 December 1855, when under the guiding hand of Fr. Bernardinus of St. Theresa (Joseph Bacinelli), the zealous vicar apostolic of the time, they took their first vows. The young Congregation on that day consisted of eleven members under the name of Servants of Mary Immaculate of Mount Carmel. Its development was so satisfactory that on 1 October 1860 it became a regular Third Order of the Carmelites. Their constitutions were approved by the Holy See on 1 January 1885, for six years, and they were given definite and final approval on 12 March 1906.[2] During the past fifty years, the Syrian Carmelites have extended their field of apostolate all over Malabar, as far south as Trivandrum where they are working for the Syro-Malankara archdiocese, and as far north as Tellicherry diocese where they minister to the needs of thousands of Syro-Malabar immigrants. The Congregation has recently been divided into three provinces.

The creation of a regular native clergy was an excellent move. It naturally conduced to the formation of an elite in the Syro-Malabar communities, and in consequence strengthened and increased their Catholic life and endeavours. Yet Mgr. Baccinelli thought, and rightly too, that the future of the Syro-Malabar communities would never be assured until

[1] *Bullarium Pontificum S.C. de Propaganda Fide*, Rome, 1841, vol. V, pp. 164-8

[2] 'Hierarchia Carmelitana', ibid. 14 (1939) pp. 30, ff. *The Carmelite Congregation of Malabar*, Trichinopoly, 1932, pp. 1-47

the training of the secular clergy was satisfactory in all respects. In this, the Carmelites were imitating their predecessors, the Franciscans and the Jesuits, who had made heroic efforts and great strides in this direction. In bygone days several seminaries, at Cranganore, Vaipicotta and Ambazhakat, had trained excellent priests, and more recently Verapoly had done the same. However, these seminaries had never educated more than a very small portion of the clergy. Most priests were given orders after going through a very jejune and elementary training with a priest reputed for his learning, called *Malpan* (from the Syriac *Malpana*, i.e. master, professor). The *Malpan* taught them to read Syriac, gave them a few practical notions about liturgy, together with the elements of dogmatic and moral theology. This kind of formation was all the more elementary, for no printed manuals, in Syriac or Malayalam, were available at the time. As a consequence, the faithful had little instruction beyond what they could obtain from the missions preached by the Carmelites and their local helpers. Moreover the majority of the priests and deacons failed to find a motive in their faith, a motive which would lead to a firm personal conviction, and were therefore easily led astray by any chance and evil influences. Mgr. Baccinelli had the courage to close some twenty local seminaries, where up to then the Syro-Malabar clerics had been initiated to the priesthood. He replaced them by five seminaries: Verapoly for the Latins and Syrians, and four others exclusively for the Syrians at Elturuth, Vazhakulam, Mannanam and Pulincunnu. Thenceforward no priest could be ordained unless he had followed the complete course at one of those institutions. The Seminary of Verapoly was an inter-ritual seminary: besides its three first Latin students, it had received five Syrians from Mannanam. This last mentioned seminary was soon afterwards transferred to Puthenpally. The transfer brought about such a complete change in the running of the seminary that it was in part responsible for the schism of Mar Rokos, as will be explained later. Yet this reform, radical as it at first appears, definitely established the Syro-Malabar Church, and its present prosperity may well be ascribed in the first place to the clear-sightedness as well as to the courage of Mgr. Bacci-nelli. In 1886, the Seminary of Puthenpally became the central seminary for all the Syrian Catholics, and also for the local Latin clergy of the dioceses of Verapoly, Quilon and Manga-lore. In 1922 it contained more than 120 students. Brought over to Alwaye in 1933, it is large enough to house more than 500 seminarists, the majority of whom now belong to the Eastern rite. It is also subject to the jurisdiction of the Sacred Congregation for the Oriental Church. At Trichur, a semi-nary was started in 1927 for the clerics of this important Syro-Malabar diocese; but, for some reason, possibly the problems of a suitable staff and finances, the project was abandoned on the eve of World War II.[1] It should be added that each Syro-Malabar eparchy also possesses a minor seminary, whose aim it is to prepare young clerics to enter upon their philosophical studies by teaching them a kind of *Humaniora*, Latin, general culture, and also Syriac.

Mgr. Joseph Antonio Mellano (Leonard of St. Louis) pub-lished several books in Malayalam for the use of the clergy. They came from the press of the Tertiaries, which was estab-lished at Kunamavu in 1869. The press was transferred in 1880 to Verapoly, and thence to Ernakulam in 1897. During his government, a breviary for the Syro-Malabar clergy was also printed. When in 1877, Mgr. Mellano was given a coadjutor to take special care of the Syro-Malabar Catholics, the choice fell on the Superior of the Seminary at Puthenpally, Fr. Marcel-linus of St. Theresa (Anthony Berardi). He was the author of a great many pious books. His function ceased in 1887, when, with the establishment of the Indian hierarchy, the Syro-Malabar Catholics were taken away from the jurisdiction of the Archbishop of Verapoly.

[1] *Catholic Directory of India*, Madras, 1932, p. 345

V

RELATIONS WITH MESOPOTAMIA AND SCHISMS

MEMORIES OF THE PAST

UNTIL the coming of the Portuguese at the close of the fifteenth century, the only regular hierarchical relations the Christian communities of India had, were with the catholicosate of Seleucia-Ctesiphon. This was a logical consequence of their geographical situation. Communications between the mouth of the great Mesopotamian rivers and the southern end of India were comparatively easy, and the only risks were those concerned with sailing on heavy seas. At times, however, political rivalries interrupted the traffic along the coast of the Persian Gulf; but, as it was in the interest of all not to hamper the trade in spices, this state of unrest never lasted for any appreciable length of time. Hence this much seems certain that the Church of India, so carefully preserved during the centuries by the catholicosate of Seleucia, always enjoyed bishops and priests in an almost uninterrupted succession. No positive documentary evidence of this, however, is available since, as has been noted previously, most of the manuscripts of the Mesopotamian Churches were destroyed in the thirteenth century, and nearly all those of India met with the same fate in the *autos-da-fé* ordered at Diamper. It is noteworthy that the subscription of the only Syro-Malabar manuscript known to us and dating from the Middle Ages contains the name of the metropolitan who was the contemporary of Catholicos Yahballaha III.[1] How much data on the hierarchy must have been preserved in the liturgical manuscripts which Francis Roz was asked to destroy!

[1] Cf. *supra* p. 17

FIDELITY TO THE CATHOLICOS OF THE EAST

The document preserved in the *Vatic. Syr. 204* [1] tells us how the Christians of India obtained their metropolitans and bishops. Mesopotamian monks were consecrated by the catholicos expressly for this purpose and they were themselves forbidden to consecrate prelates chosen from among the local clergy.

As soon as they arrived in India, the Portuguese, under the pretext of suppressing the trade in spices along the route from Ormuz to Basrah, put an end to the regular renewal of the hierarchy in Malabar. The Archbishop of Goa enjoyed a monopoly in jurisdiction, which was created by Rome for the Latin rite and the newly converted Latin Christians; it was widened to include the local or Syro-Malabar rite by mere abuse. Having the support of the civil authority such an uncanonical abuse progressed so far as to prevent the set purpose of the regular ministry of Mesopotamian prelates, who were strongly attached to the See of Peter and had been regularly sent by Rome. The tribulations of Mar Joseph were a paramount example of this autocratic attitude.

But to change the customs of a people, especially where religion is concerned, is not easy. It is not difficult to understand therefore, that at each new arrival of a bishop from Mesopotamia, real or fake — Catholic, Nestorian or even Jacobite — the Christians of St. Thomas quivered with emotion. Many examples of this have already been described. The greatest tragedy arose from the disruptions caused by the appearance of the monk Athallah with his false pretence of having been appointed patriarch by Rome. Further on we shall see what success a Jacobite prelate achieved. He was able to change the theological tenets, current among the dissidents of Thomas de Campo's party, and he enforced the Jacobite teachings. Several other personages, coming in the name of the Catholicos of the East, only succeeded in disturbing the local hierarchy.

[1] Cf. *supra* pp. 24-5.

Two more astonishing adventures have to be narrated here: those of Mar Rokos and Mar Mellus, both Catholic bishops from Chaldea, who, in spite of Rome's opposition, endeavoured to bring the Syro-Malabar Catholics back again under the jurisdiction of the Patriarch of Babylon.

RENEWED CONTACTS

Before those last two attempts, the Syro-Malabar Christians had already thought several times of appealing to Mesopotamia to keep the Latin missionaries in check. When in 1787 they decided to send a petition to obtain the appointment of Fr. Thomas Paremmakal, the administrator of Cranganore, as their archbishop, a preliminary letter was circulated among the communities. It mentioned the possibility of recourse to the Chaldean Patriarch, Joseph IV (1757-81 d. 1791), should the Queen of Portugal refuse to appoint their candidate. As a matter of fact, when Propaganda turned a deaf ear to their request, the Syrians of Malabar wrote a letter to Joseph IV, which was received by John Hormez, Metropolitan of Mosul.[1] He was a recent convert from Nestorianism, and was temporary administrator of the catholicosate while Joseph IV was in Rome. On receipt of this letter he immediately wrote to Rome asking for instructions. After sixteen months of waiting he thought it reasonable to consecrate an obscure person from Puthenchira, one Paul Pandari.[2] Paul Pandari

[1] Already, since 1728, a movement of reunion with Rome had been going on in the town and the region of Mosul. After 1750, the Dominicans settled at Mosul, and helped a great deal in strengthening the unionist tendencies. John Hormez was re-united in 1778; but, owing to petty competitions, he became a patriarch only in 1830. He died on 16 August 1838, cf. E. Tisserant, 'Eglise Nestorienne', D. T. C. vol. XI, 243-4

[2] Pandari was a Syro-Malabar priest. He actually reached his country under the auspicious name of Mar Abraham. He seems to have been accompanied by a delegate of the patriarch, called Hormisdas. Both are mentioned in the Act of union accepted by Mar Dionysios I (Mar Thomas VI) on 20 May 1799. Before the death of Fr. Thomas Paremmakal, Mar Abraham was not allowed

was accordingly consecrated for the Malabar diocese which was described to Joseph IV as 'deeply perturbed'. This action did not please Rome. Yet when it was learned that Hormez had acted in good faith, Rome felt so inclined towards a compromise that the plenary session of the Congregation of Propaganda of 27 September 1801 decided to send to Malabar Mare John Guriel, Bishop of Salmas, an old student of Propaganda College. This decision was approved by the Pope on 8 November, but the Sacred Congregation had scruples about the formula which had been first drafted. So, instead of the title ' Visitor in the name of the Administrator of the Chaldean Patriarchate', Guriel was called in the decree of 28 August 1802, 'Apostolic Visitor *ad beneplacitum Sanctae Sedis.*' The Carmelite missionaries were invited to collaborate sincerely with Mar Guriel towards pacifying the Syrian communities. Yet the visit, for some unknown reason, did not take place.

This unsuccessful interference of Mesopotamia in the affairs of Malabar had no doubt provoked some disappointment in both countries; but Propaganda could not bring herself to reject all suspicions regarding John Hormez, though these were brought forward by the party which opposed him. One can therefore understand why Propaganda hesitated to bring about peace in Malabar by means of prelates belonging to a Church that was in a state of crisis. This also explains why, when in 1830 the administrator of the apostolic vicariate of Malabar, Maurilio Stabellini, asked for a priest capable of revising the Syro-Malabar liturgy, Propaganda first approached Michael Gjarweh, Patriarch of the Syrian Catholics of the Antiochian rite;[1] and though on 2 January 1831, a letter

to perform any episcopal function, cf. Placid of St. Joseph T. O. C. D., 'The Efforts for Reunion in Malankara, South India', in *Unitas*, 5 (1953), p. 91, and note 11.

[1] Michael Gjarweh was the first Catholic Patriarch of the Syrians to stabilize the union with Rome. He was born in 1731, became Catholic in 1760,

was also dispatched to Mesopotamia, that letter was forwarded to the Latin Archbishop of Baghdad. It was evident that Propaganda did not recognize implicitly any claim of the Chaldean Patriarch to jurisdiction over the Syro-Malabar Church.

DIRECT ACTION

Great was their surprise, when, in 1850, they received in Rome a letter written by the newly appointed Chaldean Patriarch, Joseph VI, dated 24 December 1849. It contained two petitions, forwarded through the Jacobite Bishop of Cochin. Their purpose was to obtain for Malabar a bishop chosen from among the Mesopotamian clergy. This initiative, as was made clear by the Vicar Apostolic of Verapoly, Louis of St. Teresa, had its origin among some Syrians who refused to submit to the Brief *Multa Praeclare*, and clung to the Padroado. They were led by the administrator, or episcopal governor, of the dioceses of Cranganore and Cochin, Manuel de San Joachim das Neves.[1] This extremely inconspicuous group assumed a veneer of importance, since many false signatures had been added to the authentic ones. These letters were sent on to Rome but evoked no immediate answer. However, on 28 January 1852, the Syro-Malabar Christians returned to the attack: they requested from the patriarch a metropolitan and two masters (*malpan*) to teach them Syriac, or at least two masters, if the Pope did not wish to send them a prelate. They also complained that the priests who had signed the first petition had been suspended by the vicar apostolic. They threatened to become Jacobites and gave the address of three priests or dignitaries of their group. Thirty-nine

---

was recognized as patriarch in 1783, and died in 1800, cf. G. Graf, 'Garweh' in *L. F. T. K.* vol. IV, 290-1

[1] C. de Nazareth, *Mitras Lusitanas no Oriente*, Nova Goa, vol. II, pp. 58 and 119-29

priests had signed, but only with their surnames; this was an insignificant number for a total of 648 priests and deacons.

CHALDEAN ATTENTIONS

To be sure, the defects which had been shown up in Malabar were only too real. Communities were left without any instruction whatever, priests had little zeal, there was much moral laxity, and very few Carmelite missionaries could be considered as more than mediocre. On the other hand what spiritual advantage would there have been if Malabar had come under Chaldean jurisdiction? For the Chaldean Church no longer possessed good priests or suitable candidates for the episcopacy. While this state of affairs was under consideration and suitable remedies were being investigated, Propaganda received a direct petition on 1 June 1853, bearing the signatures of thirty priests. Several of the opinions expressed were correct: for instance, it was mentioned that there was no bishop of the Syro-Malabar rite, though the faithful of that rite numbered more than 200,000 while the small number of Latin Christians had three vicars apostolic to care for them at Verapoly, Quilon and Mangalore; moreover the attention of Propaganda was drawn to the fact that the ruling prelates did not know their liturgical language.

By the time this petition had been addressed to Rome, Mesopotamian interference had already been active for at least six months. A priest, Denha Bar-Yona, was touring the communities of Malabar, stirring up the desire for a superior of their own rite, preferably a Mesopotamian. Bar-Yona was helped in this by two convinced *kattanars* and *malpans*, both called Anthony. The documents originating from the Latin mission call them Anthony the Founder and Anthony Thondanatta. The former tried to persuade Rome to appoint a visitor knowing Syriac. This petition was heartily supported by Patriarch Joseph VI Audo as early as 1855, when he reminded

Propaganda of the words of *Etsi Pastoralis* which insisted on respect for the Oriental rites.[1] As he little expected to be allowed to consecrate a bishop for Malabar, Audo proposed, on 7 November 1856, another measure: Propaganda should choose two non-Carmelite visitors, whilst he would select two others, one of whom would be an ex-alumnus of the Propaganda College. All four would examine the situation in Malabar.

In the meantime the change mentioned above had come about in Malabar.[2] The vicar apostolic had created diocesan seminaries and declared that he would no longer ordain clerics who had only undergone training by the *malpans*. In the course of the year 1858, Mgr. Baccinelli refused to ordain the fifteen candidates presented by Anthony Thondanatta. The latter then betook himself to Mesopotamia accompanied by two priests and twelve of his students; there he remained for some months. Several of his pupils died and the Patriarch, Joseph VI Audo, did not dare to do anything in the matter. Anthony came back to India, where he was placed under censure. However there was a frequent exchange of letters between the Chaldean patriarch, or his assistants, and Malabar. They were advised to send numerous petitions to Rome, begging that the St. Thomas Christians might be reunited once more with the see which had cared for them before the coming of the Portuguese. Feeling in Malabar, however, had begun to run high. When writing to Propaganda on 12 December 1859, Joseph VI threatened to resign if the Holy See did not allow him to consecrate a bishop for Malabar, as such a refusal in his

---

[1] *Etsi Pastoralis* are the first words of a Bull of Pope Benedict XIV, published on 26 May 1742, and dealing with the preservation, the defence, and the improvement of the doctrines, rites, and customs of the Italo-Greek Catholics of the Byzantine rite. It was a document of such importance for the future of the Eastern rites at large, that it soon became the pattern of the relations between Latin and Oriental Catholics, cf. text in *Acta et Decreta S. Conciliorum Recentiorum*. Freiburg i. B. 1876, vol. II, pp. 507-22

[2] Cf. *supra* pp. 99-100

eyes would mean an intolerable infringement on the rights
of his Church.

MAR ROKOS AND HIS INDIAN ADVENTURE

During the spring of 1860 Rome answered, side-stepping
the main problem and requesting the patriarch and the Chaldean bishops not to interfere in the affairs of Malabar; but
Mosul remained stubborn, and notwithstanding the express
documents presented to the patriarch by the Apostolic Delegate,
Mgr. Amanton, a bishop was elected for Malabar on 12 September 1860, and was consecrated on the 30th of the same month
under the name of Mar Rokos, and the title of Perath d'Maisan
(Basrah). He was an old servant of the patriarchate, promoted
to sacred orders without any serious preparation. Already
two years previously, when the patriarch was thinking of him
for another see, Propaganda had expressed serious doubts
regarding his fitness.[1]

Mgr. Amanton forbade the newly consecrated bishop any
exercise of pontifical prerogatives, and as early as 4 October
that same year, Rokos was forbidden to leave Mosul under
pain of major excommunication *latae sententiae.* On the eve
of that day, Anthony Thondanatta, who had again come to
Mesopotamia, wrote to his countrymen telling them of the
imminent arrival of Mar Rokos and proposing to them that
they receive him with all honour. But the condemnation,
uttered by the delegate, cooled down the enthusiasm of the
Chaldean hierarchy and of the people of Mesopotamia; they
were running head-on into a schism which nobody wanted.
Moreover it induced the British Consul at Baghdad to prevent
Mar Rokos embarking for India. He was not able to start
until after 17 January 1861, when the patriarch, who had
received a letter calling him to Rome, had succeeded in inter-
preting it as an approval of his policy. The patriarch had

[1] C. Korolevskij, 'Joseph Audo', in *D. H. G. E.* vol. V, 326-32

1. View of the forane church, now the cathedral of Palai, showing the tower which is often found above the sanctuary of the old Syro-Malabar churches.

2. Interior of the church, showing many features introduced under the influence of the Portuguese Baroque style, such as pulpit, carved altar-pieces, decorated sanctuary vault, etc., but keeping the usual divisions of the Chaldean churches.

VI. 1. Parish house of the old seminary church, which once belonged to the Jesuits — Syro-Malabar Church, Vaipicotta.

2. The 18th century forane church of Our Lady of Dolours at Trichur, which was till late 19th century the Syro-Malabar Catholic parish of the town, since becoming the centre of the Mellusian party and more recently of the neo-Nestorian community of Malabar.

written to his priests at Baghdad telling them that all their present doubts would be swept away and their wishes granted; and that he was invited to Rome with two bishops in order that an agreement might be arrived at more easily without intermediaries. Encouraged by this letter, Rokos could claim to be in good faith when he sailed for India, but on landing at Cochin on Ascension Day, he was taken by the *kattanar* Anthony to the Jacobite bishop who was residing there.

Rokos was relying on the support of the British authorities. On 13 May he signed himself in a letter to the Governor of the East India Company, 'Mar Thomas, Metropolitan and Commissary of the Romano - Chaldeo - Catholic Syrians in Malabar'.[1] He also tried to persuade the Catholics of the legitimacy of his mission, by saying that the patriarch had been asked by the Holy See to consecrate him for their communities. In the meantime, he was forced to wait at Cochin, since he did not know which parishes were ready to receive him. Taking advantage of this respite, the vicar apostolic sent the best priests of the young Third Order Regular everywhere, in order to put the clergy and the faithful on their guard against the intruder and to make them sign a profession of fidelity to the Holy See. The success of the new pastor was probably slight if we are to judge by the terms of the circular letter which he addressed to all the Syro-Malabar Catholics on 13 August. He complained bitterly against the Tertiaries and repeated that his consecration was performed according to Papal Bulls. The testimonial letters that Audo had given him, or at least the copies which Mar Rokos had circulated among the Catholics, testified to the authority of the Holy See. Here was reason enough to disturb the faithful. Happily, the Tertiaries opposed a compact united front, which, though not very large, was safe and reliable. Rokos attempted to win over their superior, Fr. Cyriac Elias Chavara, by offering him episcopal consecration, but the humble religious eluded the

[1] 'Hierarchia Carmelitana', in *A. O. C. D.* 14 (1939), p. 32

temptation. An order of the Vicar Apostolic, Mgr. Bernardinus of St. Teresa, was necessary before Fr. C. Chavara would accept the title of Vicar General. Moreover, the vicar apostolic would have gladly promoted him to the episcopal dignity.

In the meantime the Prior of the Tertiaries took upon himself to send a petition to Pope Pius IX, in which he asked for a document which would serve as a guide for the Syro-Malabar Catholics. The answer to this was a Brief of 5 September 1891.[1] All those who had signed the petitions were put on their guard against the intruder. By a second Brief of the same day, the vicar apostolic was ordered to excommunicate Mar Rokos if he did not leave Malabar immediately. Two days later, Patriarch Audo, who had reached Rome several weeks earlier, sent Mar Rokos the order to return to Mosul; this was one of the conditions imposed by the Pope before granting an audience to Audo. After the usual warnings, Mar Rokos was excommunicated on 30 November, but he did not leave Malabar until March 1862. He then took the *kattanar* Anthony with him. The latter carried a letter written by a group of rebels in which they asked that Anthony be consecrated bishop, either by Audo, or by his predecessor, Nicholas Isaias, who had resigned, or, what was worse, by the Nestorian Patriarch, Simon XVII Abraham. During his first few months at Mosul, the unfortunate Mar Rokos, with the patriarch's consent, behaved as though he had not incurred any censure whatever. Nothing less than the Brief *Nuper nobis* of 26 September 1862,[2] was necessary for the patriarch to admit the facts as they were, and Mgr. Amanton had to wait till 22 April 1863 before he could absolve the old servant who had been consecrated by abuse, and who still at that time maintained he had never acted against the orders of the Holy See.

Nevertheless, for all its brevity, the sojourn of Mar Rokos

[1] R. de Martinis. *Jus Pontificium de Propaganda Fide*. Rome. 1894, vol. VI a, pp. 335, ff.
[2] Ibid. pp. 383, ff.

in Malabar had several disagreeable consequences. There were disturbances among the communities, and a number of clerics lacking in the formation or qualities required for the priesthood had been ordained. Anthony Thondanatta returned to Malabar after his consecration by the Nestorian Catholicos, Simon. About that time, a new concordat had been signed between Portugal and the Holy See (21 February 1857),[1] which ended the long-drawn-out dispute between Padroado and Propaganda clergy in India. This state of peace meant for Bishop Anthony the loss of support from those very people who had driven him to disobedience. After having vegetated for a while in the midst of a small rebellious group, he asked for absolution from all the censures he had incurred. This was given in 1865. He then retired, living as an ordinary priest in the Carmelite monastery (Syrian) of Mannanam. Nobody knew at the time if his timely conversion was sincere. Was it a mere subterfuge? At any rate it was not to be long before Anthony interfered again, and this time he had a hand in a much more dangerous movement.

THE FORERUNNERS OF A SCHISM

One might have hoped that the era of Mesopotamian intervention had at last come to an end, but there was only a truce of sorts. When Patriarch Audo was invited to Rome with all the bishops of the world for the Vatican Council, he set out with a firm resolution to reclaim all the ancient privileges of his patriarchate, including jurisdiction over Malabar. He did not succeed, and it was probably because of this failure that he threw in his lot with the minority on the question of papal infallibility. The minority was not a little flattered to have a patriarch on its side. Joseph Audo signed the definition only on 29 July 1872, protesting the while before his own

[1] M. D'Sa, *History of the Catholic Church in India*, Bombay, 1922, vol. II, pp. 179-87, giving the English translation.

people that by signing at so late a date he really intended not
to part with any of his patriarchal prerogatives.[1]

While submitting so reluctantly, he was already secretly
preparing agents for a new campaign in Malabar; for it would
be rather difficult to believe, judging from the patriarch's later
actions, that Audo's only intention was to restore an historical
tradition, and to save souls. It seemed that the financial aspect
of the question was to be a very important factor in the whole
Malabar question, both in the eyes of the patriarch and even
much more so in the eyes of his councillors—the crafty Bishop
Mar Elias Mellus and the Superior of the monks of Alkosh,[2]
Eliseus Dehok. The Chaldeans of Mesopotamia were at the
time little more than 35,000 strong and most of them lived in
the dreary hills of Kurdistan. What were the tithes of these
poor people compared to the contributions and free gifts of
a community nearly ten times more numerous? As a matter
of fact, the reconquest of Malabar began when two monks of
Alkosh came to make collections in India. One of them, Fr.
Philip Aziz, was an old student of Propaganda College. The
Chaldeans had not forgotten the good acquaintances they had
made among the Padroado clergy during the previous visits.
Consequently it was the Padroado parochial house of Trichur
which Fr. Aziz used as his headquarters.

As before in the affair of Mar Rokos, so also now there was
a notable exchange of letters between Malabar and Mesopotamia. Mosul led the operations; the alms-collecting monks
gathered signatures. As soon as Patriarch Audo had secured

[1] Concerning the minority at the Vatican Council, consult the recent and
remarkable work of Fr. R. Aubert, *Pie IX*, Paris, 1952, pp. 327-9.

[2] Alkosh, with the monastery of Our Lady of the Seeds, is situated forty
miles north of Mosul. On the origins of the Catholic establishment there, cf.
S. Bello, 'La Congrégation de S. Hormisdas et l'Eglise Chaldéenne dans la
première moitié du XIXe siècle', in *O. C. A.* no. 122, Rome, 1939. On the
present conditions of the monastic life among the Catholic Chaldeans, cf.
K. J. Mortimer, 'The Monks of St. Hormisdas', in *E.C.Q.* 7 (1948), pp.
477-82.

a certain number of signatures in the spring of 1873, he wrote two letters to Propaganda requesting Rome for permission to consecrate one or two bishops for Malabar; at the same time he also urged that collections be authorized in Europe. Both his requests were refused. On 30 September 1873, the Sacred Congregation categorically declared that any further discussions on the Malabar question would be useless. When this letter reached Mesopotamia, where no apostolic delegate had been residing since the death of Mgr. Castells on 7 September, the patriarch retired to the monastery of Alkosh. There he felt more free, for he was outside the sphere of influence and control exercised by the Dominican missionaries. For a time he resigned himself to doing nothing against the will of Rome; however, on learning in the course of the next spring that the combined efforts of the Holy See and of the French embassy at Constantinople had not succeeded in preventing the *Sublime Porte* from declaring herself in favour of the new Armenian schism,[1] he threw off the mask.

Elias Mellus was dissatisfied with the diocese of Aqra, for which he had been consecrated, and whose revenues he judged to be insufficient. The superior of the monks encouraged the patriarch in his determination to turn a deaf ear to Rome's warnings. Elias Mellus and the superior were his assistants during a ceremony in which he consecrated two new bishops on 24 May 1874; Rome had not been informed. Mellus received Malabar as a reward for his obliging attitude. On 2 July the patriarch entrusted him with a letter addressed to the Christians of Malabar, and on the 4th with another to the British Consul at Baghdad, who was asked to recommend Mellus to the British authorities in India. At

[1] The Armenian schism followed on the Bull *Reversurus*, by which Pope Pius IX changed the electoral system of the Armenian patriarchate, particularly curtailing the lay interferences in the election of the patriarch. Such a measure provoked the division of the Catholic Armenians into two opposite factions since 1869, and this situation dragged on almost till after World War I, cf. F. Tournebize, 'Arménie', in *D. H. G. E.* vol. IV, 338-42.

about the same time, Aziz the monk, wrote to the vicar apostolic of Verapoly telling him that if he wanted to stop Mesopotamian bishops coming to India, he was immediately to restore permission to move among the Christian communities under his jurisdiction and to make collections.

MAR MELLUS AND HIS DEALINGS

In October of that year or perhaps even before, Mar Mellus was already residing at Trichur, although instructions from Rome to forestall him had reached India in advance. Pius IX had always acted towards Patriarch Joseph Audo with extreme condescension. Moreover the support which the Ottoman Government extended to the new Armenian schismatics required tact and prudence; for, if a split occurred, there was no doubt that the Government officials would be in favour of it. The consequence of such an attitude would have proved particularly dangerous in the Vilayets (administrative divisions), such as Mosul and Baghdad, since even the most arbitrary acts could occur in places far away from the central power. Grave reasons therefore prevented the patriarch from being formally condemned. Yet by the Brief *Speculatores super* of 1 August 1874,[1] the intruding bishop and his companions, who had already been suspended in Mesopotamia, were to be excommunicated *maiori excommunicatione*, if after the usual warnings they should refuse to leave India at once.

In his letters of 2 and 4 July 1874, the patriarch had mentioned that the aim and scope of Mar Mellus' mission was the suppression of the Carmelite jurisdiction. In a circular letter issued at Trichur on 30 October Mellus advised all the Syro-Malabar communities to obey the patriarch and to withdraw from the jurisdiction of the Latin hierarchy. Moreover he pledged himself to produce a document in which Pope Pius IX acknowledged the authority of the Chaldean patriarch over

[1] R. de Martinis, op. cit. vol. VI b, pp. 243-7

Malabar; and accordingly he sent a new circular on 7 February 1875, which gave a Malayalam translation of a supposed Brief bearing the date 20 August 1872. The cunning prelate must have been inspired by the tricks of Athallah in 1652! Yet few Christians went over to Mar Mellus' side, and most of these belonged to the communities which were still under Padroado jurisdiction. When the need arose, Aziz did not hesitate to gain hold on a church by using violence. On the whole, the Christians under the jurisdiction of Verapoly remained steadfast; during the summer however four communities were more or less completely won over to the schism. Yet nowhere was the movement a general one. Even at Trichur the Catholics had a chapel which was under the care of the Carmelite Tertiaries. The chief trouble was the fact that Mar Mellus, abusing his powers, had ordained a great number of men who were unfit for the priesthood; in March he had promoted twenty men to sacred orders in the north and in June about thirty in the south. Mellus' hopes ran so high that, in January 1875, he asked the patriarch to consecrate a second bishop for Malabar. A certain monk, Abraham by name, was consecrated on 25 July under the title of Mar Philipos Jacob Uraha. In December he was excommunicated by Mgr. Mellano.

The Mesopotamians were especially aided by the double jurisdiction which the agreement between the Holy See and Portugal had not yet removed. Some of the Syrians were still dependent on the archdiocese of Cranganore, which was ruled by an episcopal governor, Benedict de Rosario Gomez. It appeared that his action against Mellus was lacking in vigour, and the Padroado clergy had not given up all hope of seeing its jurisdiction extend over the whole Syrian community once more. This was clearly proved when the new Archbishop of Goa, Mgr. Ayres d'Ornellas de Vasconcellos, after obtaining special powers from Rome, volunteered to visit and bring peace to Malabar. The Vicar Apostolic of Bombay, Mgr.

Leo Meurin s.j., had to beg him not to do anything of the kind. Let us try to realize the confusion that would have resulted from such an action. Had certain priests of the Mellus party offered to submit to Rome on condition of dependence on Goan jurisdiction, a third party would have been created in Malabar. In the same locality there would have been people dependent on the Carmelites, others on the Padroado, whilst a third group would have been 'Mellusian'.

Rome however did not accept the situation with folded arms. On 27 January 1875, Pius IX sent the Brief *Perlegentes* to the Christians of Malabar congratulating them on their resistance.[1] Several plans to oppose the activities of the intruding bishop were considered. On the other hand, complaints against the Carmelites were not wanting, and some of these seemed to be well-founded. All in all, the conclusion was arrived at that new information was needed and that it should be gathered by persons not implicated in the quarrel. An apostolic visitation was decided upon, and the Vicar Apostolic of Bombay, Mgr. Meurin, was chosen as visitor; his instructions are to be found in the Brief *Oportet* of 24 March 1876.[2] Then on 8 May the prelate made his mission known to all the Syrian churches, after paying a visit to the Archbishop of Goa and the Vicar Apostolic of Verapoly. On the 9th, he published a statement against Mar Mellus. On the 10th, he summoned a meeting of all the priests and some laymen from every parish, to be held on the 23rd of the same month at Mannanam. At this meeting the grievances and wishes of the Syrians were to be manifested. All the priests were invited, viz. all those who had remained faithful, all those who had fallen into schism and even those who had been ordained illicitly by the intruder. Mgr. Meurin's opinion was that the wishes of the Syro-Malabar Catholics must be met with, at least half-way. He was all for the idea of dividing the apostolic vicariate of Verapoly into

[1] Ibid. p. 256.
[2] Ibid. pp. 292-4.

two circumscriptions, one for the Latins and the other for the Syrians. The latter should have a prelate of their own, a European, who would be authorized to celebrate in Syriac. If the Carmelites could not provide the required personnel, the Jesuit province of Lyons to which the College of Gazirah in the Lebanon belonged, would supply the new vicar apostolic with some ten fathers who would learn both Malayalam and Syriac. There should be no difficulty about consecrating the most worthy men among the *kattanars* as officiating bishops, but as bishops who were to have no jurisdiction. One should not overlook the fact, the visitor added, that the Syrian Catholics, though constituting the big majority of the St. Thomas Christians, never had any pontifical service of their own rite, whereas the Jacobites had several bishops. This state of affairs was a real handicap. Mgr. Mellano, who had always worked exclusively for the Latins and had little sympathy for the Syrians, opposed the views of the visitor. Mar Mellus knew of this and spoke about it with contempt. This disagreement between the Carmelites and the visitor prevented any good results the visit might have had.

In order to clear up the whole situation, Propaganda, early in 1877, sent Mgr. Ignatius Persico to make inquiries. At that time the followers of Mellus numbered about 24,000. This number included all the *kattanars* subject to Goa and also four or five belonging to Verapoly. On the other side there were 170,000 faithful Catholics. Mgr. Persico brought with him to India a copy of the Encyclical *Quae in Patriarchatu* published on 16 November 1876.[1] In it Pius IX had summarized the history of all the questions which had brought about Chaldean patriarch's opposition to the activity of the Holy See, either in Mesopotamia or in Malabar. The translation of that important document into Malayalam and its diffusion in all the Syro-Malabar communities brought great relief. It was a joy to know that the scheming patriarch had been sus-

[1] Ibid. pp. 306-10.

pended, and some even wanted him to be excommunicated, but in spite of this the Mellusians were not downcast. The news of Joseph VI's submission which he made on 1 March 1877,[1] reached India during the hot months of that year. Yet in spite of the orders of the old patriarch, neither Mar Mellus nor Mar Philipos Jacob Abraham had any intention of leaving.

FAILURE AND SCHISM

In the course of the following year, Jacob Abraham left Malabar and retired to Bombay. For the past few months the schism had lain stagnant, and hopes of a bright future were smothered. Mar Mellus however did not make up his mind to leave India before the beginning of 1882, when he heard that his companion, Mar Abraham, had become Bishop of Gazirah Ibn Omar (February 1882). Even then, he had not sincerely resolved to submit; for, before his departure, in order to swell his pockets, he ordained to the priesthood quite an appreciable number of candidates between eighteen and twenty years of age, in return for cash payments. Moreover, before embarking on 5 March, he installed as vicars with powers to bless Holy Oils and confer minor orders, Augustine, a monk from Alkosh, who was one of the alms-collectors of 1872, and the unfortunate Anthony Thondanatta. The latter had been consecrated by the Nestorian Catholicos because, as it will be

[1] There is little doubt that all through his stormy career, Joseph VI remained deeply attached to the Holy See. In his consistorial allocution of 28 February 1879, Pope Leo XIII spoke of the patriarch as 'a prelate endowed with an extraordinary sense of piety and religion'. Actually, it was not mere oratorical praise, but the expression of the truth. Joseph Audo was a deeply religious man. His mistakes, even his opposition to Rome, should be explained as inspired by some kind of nationalism, by a strong sense of historical rights (in which he was not always entirely wrong), and by the bad advice given by unscrupulous counsellors, who deceived him, regarding the real intentions of Rome. 'His memory is still cherished by the Chaldean people, who want to remember his virtues only. Leo XIII did not act otherwise,' C. Korolevskij, 'Joseph Audo', in *D.H.G.E.* vol. *V*, 350.

remembered, he had been refused by the Catholic patriarchs. After his reconciliation with the Catholic Church, he had lived for several years as a simple priest, but this temptation to mix with the schismatics proved too strong for him, and he soon followed their fate.

Mar Mellus's arrival was eagerly awaited in Mesopotamia when he landed at Basrah on 13 April. Some people at Mosul had not approved of the submission of Patriarch Audo and opposed his successor Elias Abul-Yonan. They counted on the refractory bishop to be their leader. However, it seems that the latter quickly became wise to the folly of such a project, and so gradually the idea of definitely submitting to the Holy See took hold of him. In December 1883, when a batch of young clerics reached Mosul from Malabar to receive from his hands the diaconate and the priesthood, he refused point-blank to ordain them. But in spite of this, he still corresponded with his partisans and exhorted them 'to remain faithful to Thondanatta the Bishop, and to Augustine the Chorepiscopus' (1887). He also promised either to return to India or to send a bishop whom he himself had consecrated. Not until 1889 did he make his final submission. In 1893 he was assigned to the see of Mardin, where he died on 16 February 1908.

The Mellusians, who throughout had their centre in the church of Our Lady of Dolours at Trichur,[1] were reduced to just over 8,000 in number, when in 1907-8 they submitted to the Nestorian Patriarch, Simon XIX Benjamin, who gave them as bishop, Mar Timothy Abimelech (1878-1945), a Mesopotamian. This prelate introduced Nestorianism, the marriage of priests, and the old East Syrian rite in place of the Latinized one. On account of these changes a split occurred

---

[1] This church was of course the forane church of the Catholics built, it seems, in the eighteenth century. It was wrested from the Catholics by means of forged documents, which were accepted at their face value by the civil court which decided in favour of the schismatics. Fairly recently, a statue of Our Lady of Dolours was desecrated and burned to ashes, and what kind of iconoclastic fury was responsible for this outrage, God only knows.

among the schismatics. Most of those who belonged to the party of the 'Independents', reverted to Catholicism. Today the Nestorian community or 'Surayis' do not exceed 5,000 members, with one bishop, eight priests and six deacons, and about four or five churches and chapels.[1]

It should also be mentioned that in 1895, petitions, mostly spontaneous, were still being forwarded to the Chaldean Catholicos, Abdisho V Khayyath, asking him to see to it that the Syro-Malabar community be attached to the patriarchate of Babylon. This affair was brought before the Holy See. Rome however, acted wisely and well in deciding that the St. Thomas Christians were to remain directly dependent on the Holy See. Since that time the progress of the Syro-Malabar Church, which now possesses a hierarchy of its own, has been so remarkable that no further support from Mesopotamia is needed. On the contrary, Malabar could be asked to develop the Church in the Middle-East. As early as 1876, some well-intentioned priests and religious of Malabar, aware of the difficulties of the Catholics living in the eastern provinces of the Ottoman Empire, volunteered to go and help them. Moreover, the Oriental Congregation in recent times studied the possibility of sending Syro-Malabar priests to Iraq and Persia. They could minister to the Chaldeans and speed up the reunion of the last tiny groups of Nestorians.

---

[1] After the death of Mar Timothy in 1945, they remained without a bishop till 2 June 1952. Then they received a new prelate, Mar Thoma, styled 'Metropolitan of Malabar and of India'. He was sent by the Nestorian Patriarch, Mar Simon XXI, who nowadays resides in the U.S.A. The Nestorians of Trichur practise the Nestorian rite, but with some latinizations, remnants of the recent past. Their doctrinal teaching is not exempt from Protestant influences. The vernacular is only used for the readings in the liturgy. In reality, the laity is all-powerful, and what is most remarkable, is that, in spite of their small numbers, they are in good financial circumstances. The continuation of such a state of affairs is mainly due to social reasons. All the same, their number tends to decrease, owing principally to inter-marriages with the Catholic Syrians, who at Trichur alone number more than 15,000. Cf. J. C. Panjikaran, 'Christianity in Malabar', in O.C. 6 (1926), no. 23, pp. 113, ff. Present data are taken from the personal notes of the translator.

VI

THE INDIAN CATHOLIC HIERARCHY

GLIMPSES FROM THE PAST

THE solemn acts by which Pope Pius XI decided to erect indigenous hierarchies in the Far East and in Africa confirmed and reaffirmed the unquestionable principle that all Christian nations have a right to be governed by their own prelates.

Many felt indignant about the past, as if the lack of Indian, Chinese and Japanese bishops had been the consequence of a strange aberration on the part of the Latin missionaries. However, there had never been any Indian bishops in Malabar before the coming of the Portuguese, and no indigenous prelates in Ethiopia before 1929; and even today, certain dioceses of the dissident churches in the Near East are regularly governed by Greek hierarchies, though they are almost exclusively constituted of Arab-speaking communities. Independently of any Roman influence, the Patriarch of Alexandria, as well as the Catholicos of Seleucia-Ctesiphon, regularly chose persons of their own entourage to govern the remote dioceses of their rite in Ethiopia and in India, even adding the prohibition against the consecration of any local candidate.

The first Syro-Malabar bishop, it should be recalled, was elected and consecrated under extraordinary circumstances, when the Dutch conquered Cochin and expelled the Apostolic Visitor Joseph of St. Mary Sebastiani overnight.[1] The fact that Sebastiani before his departure from Rome had been allowed, in case of need, to consecrate one or even two bishops chosen from the ranks of the local clergy, clearly pleads in

[1] Cf. *supra* pp. 86-7.

favour of the broad-mindedness of Propaganda. Already, then, Rome acknowledged that principle, which has definitely come to stay, as the last thirty years testify. Moreover the experiment proved a successful one. Parambil Chandi (Alexander de Campo) not only succeeded in protecting the faithful committed to his care against the machinations of his ambitious cousin, Thomas de Campo; but he even made conversions. When in his old age he asked for a coadjutor, the four Carmelite commissaries who were sent by Propaganda received the order to select a Syrian.

How a disagreement between them and the old bishop as to who was the right candidate, interrupted the succession, which showed all the signs of a hopeful future, is not easy to discover. How many quarrels and schisms might have been avoided! But the Syrians of Malabar had such an inveterate habit of receiving their bishops from Mesopotamia, that during the following centuries, whenever they had any difficulty in obeying Latin missionaries, they turned towards the Near East. Only once, after the sudden death of Joseph Cariati, who had been appointed by the Queen of Portugal to the see of Cranganore, did they try to obtain the nomination by Lisbon or the consecration by the Chaldean Patriarch, of Thomas Paremmakal who, though a priest of the Syro-Malabar rite, was the administrator of a Padroado diocese like Cranganore; but the adventures of Mar Rokos and Mar Elias Mellus proved the persistence of the Mesopotamian tradition, however humiliating this may have been.

THE DAWN OF BETTER DAYS

Yet from the early nineteenth century the desire for an Indian bishop was always alive. In 1865, the Carmelites, oddly enough, requested Rome to condemn certain writings of the 'would-be bishop' of bygone days, Thomas Paremmakal, which were circulated among the Syro-Malabar communities.

These tracts kept alive those hopes which had been aroused by the arrival of Archbishop Cariati in 1786.

Mention must be made, moreover, of the great perspicacity of a Jesuit of the Madura mission, Fr. Puccinelli, who as early as 1852 recommended that the Vicar Apostolic of Verapoly be given a coadjutor 'for the Syrians', without any right of succession, but who would hold pontifical services in their own rite. He would ordain their priests, and have the ordinary prerogatives of a vicar general in his relations with them.

But it was only after the adventure of Mar Rokos and the conversion of the *kattanar* Anthony Thondanatta, who had been consecrated by the Nestorian patriarch, that Propaganda took the first step. It decided that now was the time to apply to Malabar the dispositions of canon 9 of the IVth Lateran Council for the benefit of the diocese, composed of faithful of differing rites and languages: 'After careful consideration the bishop of the place will choose as his vicar a Catholic prelate who conforms to the usages of those nations; in everything the vicars will obey and submit to him'.[1] Therefore in accordance with Fr. Puccinelli's advice, the Sacred Congregation decided that a vicar general could be consecrated; but when the Vicar Apostolic Mgr. Baccinelli, who had been consulted as to the opportuneness of such a measure, interviewed his missionaries, the latter stoutly opposed any promotion of Indian priests or even of religious. The appointment of a Syro-Malabar vicar general, even though he might not be an actual bishop, would have meant a return to the ancient custom of the metropolitan see of Angamale, where the local archdeacon used to be the perpetual auxiliary of the Chaldean metropolitan and the real ruler of the Syrians. Yet, small though their number was in comparison with the large community

[1] 'Pontifex loci catholicum praesulem nationibus istis conformem provida deliberatione constituat sibi vicarium in praedictis, qui ei per omnia sit obediens et subjectum', quoted by Hefelé-Leclercq, *Histoire des Conciles*, Paris, 1913, vol. V, pp. 1339-40.

they were expected to care for, the Carmelites intended to keep full authority. Mgr. Mellano did not even want to designate one of his confrères as vicar general for the Syrians, though this measure would have eased the tense atmosphere then prevalent. Such tension was the offspring of his personal harshness.

FALSE STEPS

The coming of Mar Elias Mellus revived the whole question once again. It was clear that the consecration of a local bishop would have put an end to the intrusion of the Mesopotamians. To the less unprejudiced mind this was clear. But only too often vested interests succeeded in befogging the issue. Discussions became more and more frequent, though the details do not matter much here. The most drastic solution would have been the division of the vicariate of Verapoly into two circumscriptions, each with its own prelate, one for the Syrians, the other for the Latins. These circumscriptions would have overlapped to a certain extent owing to the fact that the faithful of both rites lived intermingled in many places. A less extreme solution would have been to keep the vicariate within the present limits and to appoint a bishop for the Syrians. This new prelate could have been either a vicar general, or a mere bishop *in pontificalibus* without any jurisdiction and entrusted with the ordinations and other services of his rite. There was no real reason, of course, against having an Indian as an auxiliary bishop of this type. All the various combinations arising from these possibilities had their enthusiastic supporters, and the various solutions were all examined in Rome. A decision, however, was not reached until 1877. On 17 August Fr. Marcellinus of St. Teresa (Anthony Berardi), Superior of the Seminary of Puthenpally, an inter-ritual institution, became the coadjutor of Mgr. Mellano, with right of succession, and the special care of the Syrians was entrusted to him.[1]

[1] 'Hierarchia Carmelitana', in *A.O.C.D.* 14 (1939), pp. 45-8.

The choice was not a happy one. The new bishop-elect was intimately connected with the vicar apostolic, and since he knew that some day he would rule the Latins of the vicariate, he made little effort to win over the affection of the Syrian faithful who had been committed to his special care. What is more, he omitted to carry out one of the conditions laid down by Propaganda at the time of his appointment. He never nominated a vicar general and the four Syro-Malabar counsellors who were to assist him. Thus the intentions of the Holy See were once more to a great extent frustrated.

THE EVE OF MORE AUSPICIOUS DAYS

After the conclusion of a concordat with Portugal on 23 June 1886, and the establishment of the hierarchy in India on 1 September of the same year by the Bull *Humanae salutis auctor*,[1] the problem of the Syrians in Malabar had to be tackled once more.

The Holy See had already endeavoured to withdraw the Syro-Malabar communities as far as was possible from the jurisdiction of the Padroado. Yet was there not a possibility that these Syrians, who had just left this jurisdiction, would simply come under the jurisdiction of the Carmelites once again? Against such a measure very good reasons could have been brought forward. There were the documents on the training of the local clergy from the Brief *Onerosa pastoralis* of Innocent XI (1 April 1680),[2] apart from a whole series of Roman decisions which were being issued including the instruction of Propaganda on 23 November 1845. This last document stated: 'The indigenous clerics are to be educated in all necessary knowledge and piety; they must also be carefully trained for the sacred ministry; and in such a way that, in accordance with the repeated wishes of the Apostolic See, they may be able to

---

[1] *Leonis XIII Pontificis Maximi Acta*, Rome, 1887, vol. VI, pp. 164-79.
[2] *A.V.*, *Archivio dei Brevi*, vol. 1644, fo. 49

exercise any ecclesiastical charges and even the direction of missions, and that may also be worthy of the episcopal character'.[1]

At that time the Syrians were at least 200,000 strong with 360 priests; they possessed four seminaries run by the Syrian Carmelites, who numbered some 59 religious; yet they had no bishop of their own. This was an awkward, if not unjust situation, compared with that of the Armenian Catholics, who were barely 80,000 in number, and yet had a patriarch, eighteen resident bishops and many titular ones. The Chaldeans themselves, though less numerous, had their patriarch and twelve bishops. The establishment of the hierarchy in India where many dioceses numbered less than 10,000 people, made the situation still more humiliating. But the Carmelites said that the mission of Verapoly was a Carmelite one and ought to remain so for ever. Moreover, numerous European missionaries in various parts of India were afraid that if Syrians had access to the episcopate, the Indians of their own missions would begin agitating to obtain bishops of their own blood. Needless to say, several well-balanced persons, keenly aware of the state of affairs, did not fail to remark that this was false prudence, and maintained that Indians of the Syrian or Latin rites in any part of India were worthy of the episcopate.

Yet, since the experiment of 1877 did not yield the expected results, a new solution had to be attempted. The Syrians of the archdiocese of Verapoly were removed from the jurisdiction of the Carmelites and grouped together under the two new vicariates of Trichur and Kottayam. Even then, such was the weight of prejudice that nobody dared to appoint Syro-Malabar prelates immediately. The vicars apostolic nominated on 20 May 1887 were Mgr. Adolf E. Medlycott, for Trichur, and the French Jesuit, Père Charles Lavigne, for Kottayam.

---

[1] *Collectanea S. C. de Propaganda Fide*, Rome, 1907, vol. I, p. 544.

THE WORK OF BISHOP LAVIGNE AND OF BISHOP MEDLYCOTT[1]

Mgr. Charles Lavigne (1840-1913) was a French Jesuit belonging to the Toulouse province. For four years before his nomination, he had been private secretary to the Very Reverend Fr. P. Beckx, General of the Society of Jesus, who died on 4 March 1887. On 13 November 1887, he received the episcopal consecration at Marvejols (Lozère), as Titular Bishop of Milevis and Vicar Apostolic of Kottayam.

On 31 April 1888, he had reached Mannanam, the monastery of the Carmelite Tertiaries and one of the main religious centres of the country. There he was officially greeted by the clergy and the faithful. About 30,000 persons attended the reception. On Ascension Day, 10 May, Mgr. Lavigne entered Kottayam, his episcopal town.

In the new vicariate, there were in those days some 152 churches and chapels, 107,066 Catholics, and 271 priests. The Christians were divided into two communities, the Nordists with about 90,000, and the Suddists with about 10,000 members. As soon as he could, Mgr. Lavigne began carrying out the orders of the Holy See and he appointed four priests as his counsellors. One of them, Fr. Emmanuel Nidiry, was soon

---

[1] Our summary of Bishop Lavigne's activities is mainly based on the following printed sources: (1) — twenty-seven letters, or extracts from letters, written by the prelate, and published in the Jesuit periodical *Lettres d'Uclès*, 1888-94; (2) — one letter of the same, published in *Missions Catholiques*, 1889, p. 87-8; (3) — six letters, or extracts from letters, written by Fr. L. Ricards. J., secretary to Mgr. Lavigne, and published in *Lettres d'Uclès*, 1888-9; (4) — twenty-five letters, or extracts from letters, written by Fr. C. Bonnel s. J., the other companion of the bishop, and published in the Jesuit periodical *Lettres de Jersey*, vol. XII-XV (1893-6). We are also indebted to H. E. Mar Matthew Kawugatt, archbishop of Changanacherry, for several precious data. As regards the apostolate of Bishop A. E. Medlycott in Trichur, we mainly draw our account from excellent notes, which were sent to us by the present Bishop of Trichur, H.E. Mar George Alapatt. We also made use of Bishop Medlycott's necrology published in the *Catholic Herald of India* (Calcutta), 1918, p. 365. By consulting *The Madras Catholic Directory*, 1887-96, we could gather many significant statistics on the progress made by the Syrians of Malabar under the leadership of the two prelates.

made the vicar general of the diocese, with the privileges of administering the Sacrament of Confirmation, and singing Pontifical High Mass. In 1892, Fr. Matthew Makil became the vicar general of the Suddists and was granted the same privileges. Fr. Nidiry remained vicar general for the Nordists till he was succeeded in his office by Fr. Joseph Thayil.

When Mgr. Lavigne reviewed the situation of his flock, he soon realized the difficulties he had to meet with. There was the basic problem of learning the language, Malayalam. Whereas his two Jesuit companions, Fr. L. Ricard, his secretary, and Fr. C. Bonnel, attained some proficiency in that tongue, Mgr. Lavigne never mastered it. Many other problems called for his attention, and he had to be satisfied with using English and with acting through interpreters.

In spite of this serious drawback, Mgr. Lavigne gave himself wholeheartedly to his task. It was a rather forbidding one. His diocese needed to be organized. The old guard of the Mellusian party was still active, and its sympathizers were numerous among both the clergy and the laity. Schools, convents and charitable institutions were lacking everywhere. The Protestants were far better established, especially in the educational field.

Let us briefly summarize the main achievements of Mgr. Lavigne. First of all, he succeeded to a large extent in winning the confidence of his priests; he uprooted the last shoots of the Mellusian schism; he paved the way for a better training of the clergy by creating a new seminary at Changanacherry in 1888. Later on he fostered the reorganization of the major Seminary of Puthenpally (1893), which became the central Seminary for both Syrians and Latins of Malabar. Right from the beginning, he understood what services could be rendered to his diocese by the Carmelite Tertiaries (T.O.C.D.). He gave them all the support they needed for their then existing Seminaries of Mannanam and Mutholy, for their schools, and for their apostolate among the low castes. He sent the first Carmelite scholastics to the Seminary of Mangalore in 1890.

During his days in Malabar, Mgr. Lavigne had several opportunities to encourage the development of religious life among women. He helped the Carmelite Tertiaries to open new convents and schools at Mutholy, Changanacherry, Arakuzha, and Vaicom. He founded a congregation of Tertiaries of St. Francis of Assisi at Palai, and afterwards at Changanacherry. An orphanage was attached to this latter convent. He was very keen on this foundation, and even went as far as to teach needlework to the young sisters. Mgr. Lavigne opened a convent of the Visitation—Third Order Regular—at Kaipuzha (24 June 1892), for the Suddist community. One of his diocesan counsellors, Fr. Louis Pareparambil, the future vicar apostolic of Ernakulam, was appointed superior general of all the nuns of the diocese. Meanwhile, Mgr. Lavigne had moved his headquarters to Changanacherry (21 March 1891). Kottayam was not a Catholic centre, whereas Changanacherry, with its strong Catholic community, was much more suitable for an episcopal residence. At Changanacherry, the bishop started an English school, named after St. John Berchmans, in the premises of the cathedral. Fr. L. Ricard became its headmaster, and also fulfilled the duties of director of all the diocesan schools. Further, Mgr. Lavigne built his episcopal house, which was completed by the end of 1894. For lack of space the ground floor of the house was occupied by more than one hundred boarders of the English school, which had been raised to a fully recognized high school. At Baramangalam, a high school for the Suddists was organized. Finally, Mgr. Lavigne urged the clergy to set up schools in each parish.

Mgr. Lavigne had not come to Malabar for mere administrative reasons. He had made up his mind to launch a large movement of conversions among the low castes, and among the Jacobites. In the former, he was aided by Fr. Ricard. As far as possible, they opened catechumenates in many places, particularly in the hilly districts of the diocese. From 1888 until 1894, more than twenty such centres were established. Mgr. Lavigne spurred on the Carmelite fathers who were already working at Mannanam, Mutholy, and Chettipuzha. He encouraged many a priest to go ahead with his missionary activities.

The reunion of the Jacobites became also one of the main objects of Mgr. Lavigne's activity. During the years 1890 and 1891, there was some hope of receiving many dissidents into the Church. Mgr. Lavigne favoured very much the approaches made by Fr. Emmanuel Nidiry and Fr. Louis Pareparambil. In his personal contacts with the Jacobites, the bishop displayed a great sense of adaptation, and genuine tact. Five Jacobite priests were reunited, together with one deacon who was a nephew of Mar Dionysios, the Metropolitan of the Orthodox Jacobites. Some families followed. The Suddist Jacobites, numbering some 6,000 Christians and ten priests, were moving fast towards reunion, and Fr. Matthew Makil, who became the successor of Mgr. Lavigne, had a meeting with their leaders (19 June 1891). Unfortunately, many of the reunited priests did not persevere in their efforts, and the expected move of the Suddists was stopped. The reunited priests were allowed to retain their Antiochian rite.

Mgr. Lavigne was no longer a young man when he came to India. His frequent visits to his diocese, which reached the most remote places, could not but affect his health, all the more so as the visits were carried out despite a difficult climate. His anxieties, his many cares, and the real poverty he endured, proved too much for a physical constitution otherwise strong and healthy. He had already been taken ill in August 1893, and in the course of the following year, he was obliged to rest for six months in a cooler climate. In 1895, he left for Europe for his visit *ad limina*, but also to recover his health, and to collect more funds for the High School of Changanacherry.

He had dreamed of raising it to a complete first grade University College, and his dream was realized by his successors. Meanwhile, petitions were sent to Rome, asking for an indigenous prelate. Fr. L. Ricard, who was acting as administrator during Mgr. Lavigne's absence, was therefore recalled to Europe in May 1897, and died soon after his return at Sarlat. Mgr. Lavigne never returned to Malabar. He was appointed coadjutor to Mgr. Cazet s. j., Vicar Apostolic of Northern Madagascar, and soon afterward this nomination was changed. He was made Bishop of the diocese of Trincomalee in Ceylon on 27 August 1898.

The work of Mgr. Medlycott in the northern parts of Malabar followed a somewhat similar course. Mgr. Adolf Medlycott was a priest of the Calcutta archdiocese, and he was born at Chittagong in 1835. After he had completed his studies at Propaganda College in Rome, he was for a while employed there as the librarian of the college. He then returned to India, and laboured in various places inside and outside Calcutta. He was military chaplain at Fyzabad when, on 13 September 1887, he was elected by the Holy See as Titular Bishop of Tricomia, and Vicar Apostolic of Trichur. He was consecrated by Mgr. Ajuti, Apostolic Delegate to the East Indies (11 December 1887), and took possession of the vicariate on the following Sunday, 18 December 1887. He ruled the diocese for nine years, until his secretary, Fr. John Menacherry, took over on 11 August 1896.

At that time the vicariate of Trichur was in an extremely sorry state. It was the centre of the Mellusian schism. The church, which ought to have been the cathedral of the new vicariate, was in the hands of the schismatics. Years of internal feuds had shaken the whole fabric of the Church there. From the very outset Mgr. Medlycott had been bent on a double task, the rooting out of the schism and the reorganization of his diocese.

His exemplary life and firmness, his personal charm and

prudence, won for him the hearts of Catholics and schismatics alike. The latter returned to the fold in a such growing numbers (five important parishes were recovered within the two or three first years) that Trichur remained the only place where the schismatics were still strong. The bishop left no stone unturned until he had converted a good number of the dissidents in his episcopal town. He filed a suit in order to get back the parish church of Trichur, Our Lady of Dolours. After many a delay, he lost the case. It was only a material defeat however; for, from then on the lost church was attended by a congregation of schismatics which continued to dwindle in number.

In his fight against the schism, Mgr. Medlycott received considerable help from a group of zealous priests and the Syrian Carmelites (T.O.C.D.) of Elthuruth monastery, near Trichur. The former were by the wishes of Rome members of the diocesan council. Fr. George Mampully became the vicar general, and he filled that office long after Mgr. Medlycott had left Trichur. Elthuruth, founded in 1852, was to the north what Mannanam was to the south, the fortress of Orthodoxy, and the nursery of indefatigable missionaries. It was at Elthuruth that Mgr. Medlycott's appointment was first made known. It was also there that the new prelate was solemnly and cordially received by the clergy.

Mgr. Medlycott wanted to place his diocese on firm foundations. The first thing he did towards achieving his purpose was to organize a network of Catholic schools. After this, it was of major importance to give an impetus to English education. He took immediate steps to do this, and new institutions were erected in many places. The University College of St. Thomas, at Trichur, owes its origin to Mgr. Medlycott. When he arrived at Trichur there was only a seminary at Elthuruth, which was soon to be suppressed and amalgamated with the central Seminary of Puthenpally. St. Thomas' College was a clerical institution for some years and became an English high school. When the bishop left in

1896 he could be rightly proud of the fruits of his labours. There were the St. Thomas' College, the English middle school of Elthuruth, an English middle school for girls at Kunamavu, fourteen English parish schools and some 191 Malayalam parish schools.

When Mgr. Medlycott arrived in the centre of the diocese, he had not even a place to lay his head, So he acquired an extensive piece of land, and there he began building the beautiful house we find to-day, which was completed by his successor. The site of Thope, where now stand the minor seminary, the diocesan hospital, the orphanage, and also a health home for priests, was the result of his farsightedness.

Both Mgr. Lavigne and Mgr. Medlycott endeared themselves to their flock. They loved the people and worked selflessly for their spiritual and material uplift. The Catholics in their turn loved and respected them. The two prelates were exceptionally zealous missionaries; they could adapt themselves to any circumstances, and they made full use of their qualities to benefit a land which for many years had been utterly neglected. Although they were men nurtured in a culture foreign to the Orient, yet they were the men who laid the foundation stone on which the mighty structure of the modern Syro-Malabar Church now stands.

After leaving Trichur, Mgr. Medlycott acted for a while as auxiliary bishop of the Cardinal of Westminster in England. After the death of Cardinal Vaughan on 19 June 1903, he returned to Calcutta. During his retirement, he made full use of his gifts as a scholar and a writer. Impressed as he had been by the traditions of the Syrian Catholics of Malabar, he studied their origins, and his contributions on St. Thomas the Apostle are still regarded as the first serious essays on the subject. On the occasion of his episcopal silver jubilee, in 1912, a deputation of Trichur went all the way to Calcutta in order to offer him the congratulations of his grateful children. Mgr. Medlycott died at Bangalore on 4 May 1918.

In perennial and grateful remembrance for his services, his remains were removed to Trichur on 4 May 1945, and they were later entombed in the crypt of the new cathedral there.

THE FULFILMENT

In the meantime, petitions in favour of the appointment of bishops from their own land were being voiced among the Syrians. The Holy See deemed that the time had now come to crown the work already begun. Three vicariates instead of two were created, the respective sees being Trichur, Ernakulam and Changanacherry. As a matter of fact this latter city had been the residence of Mgr. Lavigne since 1891.

The three new Indian prelates, elected on 11 August 1896, were Syrian. Mar Louis Pareparambil and Mar John Menacherry, for Ernakulam and Trichur respectively, were the general secretaries of the previous vicariates of Kottayam and Trichur. Mar Matthew Makil, nominated for Changanacherry, was Vicar General of Kottayam for the Suddist community. Since, however, the vicariate of Changanacherry consisted mainly of Nordists, it became necessary to divide it in order to satisfy the claims of the Suddist and Nordist communities. Thus in 1911 Kottayam became once more the centre of a vicariate, this time composed entirely of Suddists. It united under a personal jurisdiction all the churches belonging to the group in the two vicariates of Ernakulam and Changanacherry. Mar Makil was then transferred to Kottayam and replaced at Changanacherry by an ex-alumnus of Propaganda College, Mar Thomas Kurialacherry.

Only one step remained before the Syro-Malabar Church was to be definitely established. This step was taken at the consistory of 20 December 1923, on the eve of St. Thomas' feast (according to the Roman calendar), when Pope Pius XI created the Syro-Malabar ecclesiastical province with

Ernakulam as the metropolitan see and the three suffragan eparchies (dioceses) of Trichur, Kottayam and Changanacherry.[1] A little more than three centuries previously, in 1599, on the eve of the day on which the Roman Church celebrates the feast of their Holy Patron, the Christians of St. Thomas were placed under the jurisdiction of western prelates.

On 24 July 1950, the diocese of Changanacherry was divided and the new see of Patai created.[2] The sixth Syro-Malabar eparchy was erected at the end of 1953.[3] Its limits coincide with the then political district of North Malabar in Madras State; and Tellicherry, a small harbour of the Malabar coast, has become the episcopal see. This new diocese copes with the spiritual needs of a daily growing population of the faithful of this rite. These people are recent colonists who left their homeland in search of better land prospects. It is the first time since the sixteenth century that the Syro-Malabar Church has extended its jurisdiction outside the former States of Cochin and Travancore.

Most recent measures have been taken by the Holy See to foster the welfare and missionary activities of the Syro-Malabar Church. Four decrees of the Sacred Oriental Congregation, dated 25 April 1955, and made public on 25 July 1955, considerably extended the jurisdiction of several Syro-Malabar bishops. Thus, the diocese of Changanacherry was enlarged to cover the whole of the former State of Travancore down to Cape Comorin. The diocese of Trichur was made to include the whole territory of the neighbouring diocese of Coimbatore. The diocese of Tellicherry now covers the entire territory of the two Latin dioceses of Mysore and Mangalore. The Bishop of Kottayam, whose duty is to look after the spiritual

[1] 'Bull (Constitution) of Pius XI, *Romani Pontifices*', in *A. A. S.* 16 (1923), pp. 257-62.

[2] 'Bull (Constitution) of Pius XII, *Quo Ecclesiarum*', ibid. 43 (1951), pp. 147-50.

[3] 'Bull (Constitution) of Pius XII, *Ad Christi Ecclesiam*', 31 December 1953, ibid. 46 (1954), pp. 385-7.

welfare of the Suddist community, was given jurisdiction over his subjects who were found all over the newly enlarged ecclesiastical province. Finally, at the beginning of August 1956, the new Syro-Malabar diocese of Kothamangalam was created out of the former territory of the archdiocese of Ernakulam, and the diocese of Changanacherry was raised to the status of an archdiocese. The present situation of the Syro-Malabar Church is as follows: there is the archdiocese of Ernakulam with the suffragan dioceses of Kothamangalam, Tellicherry and Trichur; there is also the archdiocese of Changanacherry with the suffragan dioceses of Kottayam and Palai.

WONDERFUL PROGRESS

While the ecclesiatical units continued to multiply and become organized, religious life also grew rapidly in Malabar. The Carmelite Tertiaries (T.O.C.D.) had had their constitutions approved for six years by a Brief of 1 January 1885, and then permanently in 1906. At first they depended directly on the vicar apostolic, and later, on the apostolic delegate (decree of 15 December 1887). In 1893, with the renewal of the temporary approbation of their constitutions they became autonomous, a step justified by their growing numbers. Their first prior general to reside in Malabar was a European, Fr. Bernard of Jesus O.C.D. (Philip Arguinzoniz), but when he became the coadjutor of Mgr. Mellano, he entrusted the government of the congregation almost entirely to his first assistant who became his vicar delegate. When Fr. Bernard retired in 1902, he readily proposed that the prior general be chosen from among the members of the congregation. The choice fell on Fr. Alexander of St. Joseph (senior), apostolic missionary, and one of the first eleven professed fathers. When the centenary of the foundation was held in 1931, the Congregation of the Syrian Carmelites, now entirely separated from their

Latin brethren, comprised 135 priests, 120 scholastics, 25 novices, 53 lay-brothers and 77 candidates, all this personnel being spread over 16 houses. Ever since then, their number has been on the increase. In September 1942, the new house of the prior general and his definitors (assistants) was inaugurated at Ernakulam. In 1942, the Syrian Carmelites had 247 priests, 86 scholastics, 76 lay-brothers, 19 novices, 11 postulants and 21 aspirants. They maintained 13 priorates, 5 vicariates, 10 missions, 3 scholasticates, 2 novitiates; besides this, they conducted 16 schools of various kinds, 8 boarding houses, 2 industrial schools, 2 commercial schools and 4 printing presses editing three different papers. Since the end of the war, their number has greatly increased and their activity has spread to new fields, such as the University College of the Sacred Heart at Thevara, a suburb of Ernakulam.[1] During the last two years, the Syrian Carmelites have opened two more University Colleges, one at Iranjilakuda, in the diocese of Trichur, and the other near Calicut, in the diocese of Tellicherry. Besides, they are building a large house at Bangalore for their philosophers and theologians, which will be ready in 1957.

A special congregation of priests and brothers, called the Oblates of the Sacred Heart, was started within the last thirty years for the Suddists of the diocese of Kottayam. New constitutions were recently promulgated for them. At about the same time, the Sons of St. Vincent de Paul opened a branch of the Syro-Malabar rite in the archdiocese of Ernakulam, at Angamale.[2] This foundation was recently strengthened, but continues to be of diocesan status.[3]

---

[1] *The Carmelite Congregation of Malabar*, 1831-1951, Trichinopoly, 1932; *The Carmelite Congregation of Malabar*, Mannanam, 1942, ff.

[2] *Statistica con cenni storici della gierarchia dei fedeli di rito orientale*, Rome, 1932, p. 380.

[3] Many congregations for women have sprung up since 1865. The Carmelite Tertiaries had 38 convents and about 630 nuns in 1931 and, in 1953, 1,237 religious and 210 novices. They work in the dioceses of Ernakulam, Changanacherry, Trichur, and Palai. Besides, there are Franciscan Tertiaries,

Since the establishment of the Syrian hierarchy the Syro-Malabar Church has made considerable progress. Does it not justify the trust with which Leo XIII and Pius XI have honoured them? Both secular and regular clergy receive a careful training, many of them have secular and ecclesiastical degrees. The Syrian Catholic life is expressed by an increasing number of charitable works, confraternities, youth associations, etc. There are at least half a dozen monthly and weekly periodicals, and two Catholic dailies, one published at Kottayam by the Syrian Carmelites, the other at Ernakulam by the archdiocese. As well as this the Syrians exercise great influence over the non-Catholic press.

The prosperity of the Syrian Church in India caused the reunion of the great majority of the followers of Mellus. It was also the result of the continued efforts of the late Bishop John Menacherry of the diocese of Trichur and his successors. The tremendous development of Syro-Malabar Christianity also encouraged the Jacobites to look forward to a union. In recent times, a very zealous and learned priest of the then vicariate apostolic of Kottayam, Fr. Emmanuel Nidiry, worked under the direction of Bishop Lavigne for the reunion of the Jacobites. He was followed by a more intensified approach made by the late Mar Louis Pareparambil and the late Metropolitan, Mar Augustine Kandathil of the Ernakulam

also called Sisters of St. Clare, who had 20 houses and 240 nuns in 1931, and, in 1953, 539 religious and 316 novices, in the dioceses of Ernakulam, Changanacherry, Trichur, and Palai. The Nuns of the Visitation (Suddist-Kottayam) possessed 6 houses with 40 nuns in 1931, and, in 1953, 122 religious and 13 novices. The Sisters of St. Joseph (Suddist-Kottayam), started recently, had 16 religious and 2 novices in 1953. The Sisters of the Adoration of the Blessed Sacrament, started by Mar Kurialacherry, had 11 houses and 180 religious in 1931, and, in 1953, 273 nuns and 228 novices, in the dioceses of Ernakulam and Changanacherry. The Sisters of the Holy Family were 42 in number in 1931, distributed among 4 houses. In 1953, they numbered 169 religious and 72 novices. They belong to the dioceses of Trichur, Changanacherry, and Palai. There are also three Congregations of Sisters of Charity, or Medical Sisters, and some smaller groups.

archdiocese. In Changanacherry the late Mar Thomas Kurialacherry did similar work. The remarkable zeal of the late Mar
Alexander Chulaparambil resulted in the launching of a new
mission in 1921 for the re-union of the Suddist party of the
Jacobites in Kottayam. Besides this, the Syrian Carmelites
worked unsparingly for the reunion of the dissidents. All
these efforts definitely contributed to the creation of the Syro-
Malankara community, an event of considerable importance
for the future of the Church in India. For more details, we
refer to the following chapter.

In 1876 the total of the Syro-Malabar faithful was estimated
at 200,000, of which 180,000 were under the jurisdiction of
Verapoly, the others falling under the Padroado. They possessed 420 priests, 215 churches and chapels, 125 seminarists and
6 houses of the Syrian Carmelites.

In 1931, there were 532,351 Syrian Catholics, 635 diocesan
priests, 591 churches and chapels, 220 religious men, 1,052
nuns, 617 Catholic schools, 2,784 teachers of both sexes, and
78,149 pupils.

For 1954, we reckon 1,088, 962 Syro-Malabar Christians,
and the approximate figures of 720 diocesan priests, 700
churches and chapels, 250 religious priests, 4,300 nuns, 713
Catholic schools, and 234,000 pupils.

According to the last Catholic Directory of India, issued in
1956 there are now 1,171,235 Syro-Malabar faithful, 892
diocesan priests, 439 seminarians; 1,026 churches and chapels,
925 schools with 251,251 pupils. We have not been able to
check the number of religious, both men and women.

VII

THE JACOBITES IN INDIA AND THE CREATION OF THE CATHOLIC COMMUNITY OF THE ANTIOCHIAN RITE

SYRIA, MESOPOTAMIA AND INDIA

Most of the Catholics of Mesopotamia became Nestorians at the time of Catholicos Babai (A.D. 496-503), but it would be wrong to think that all of them did so. There were Monophysites among them, and these constituted a rather important group. This is demonstrated by the fact that they were ruled by a prelate of higher dignity than an ordinary metropolitan, 'the Maphrian of the East'.[1]

Commercial relations between the 'land of the two rivers' and India were always so flourishing that one can surmise that during the Middle-Ages there might have been in India some Christian traders professing the Jacobite creed living either separated or in small groups.[2]

[1] The Maphrian was the head of the Jacobites of the Persian empire; his first titular seems to have been Maruta (565-649), cf. I. Ziade, 'Eglise Syrienne', in *D.T.C.* vol. XIV, 3072.

[2] In the twelfth century, Nilus Doxopatres still maintained, in his 'Notitia Thronorum Patriarchalium,' *P.G.* 132, 1088, that the jurisdiction of the Greek Patriarch of Antioch embraced the whole of Asia, including India, whither he was sending a catholicos till his own time. But, India cannot any more be comprised within the limits of the catholicosate. Its centre, called Romagyris, is not to be found at Nishabur in Khorassan (Persia), in spite of C. Karalevskij's assertion in the article 'Antioch', *D.H.G.E.* vol. III, 612, quoting a letter of Patriarch Peter III to Dominic of Grado (*P. G.* 120, 760). Thanks to the history of Christophorus (d. 967), Melkite (Greek) Patriarch of Antioch, published by Habib Zayat in *Proche-Orient Chrétien*, 2 (1952), pp. 11-38, Fr. Néophyte Edelbi was led to write in the same journal (ibid. pp. 39-40) a *Note sur le catholicosat de Romagyris*. He makes clear that Romagyris was situated in Transoxiana, in the region of Tashkent, perhaps in one section of this city. At Romagyris (Rumagird in Arabic) dwelt the Melkites,

Yet the Malabar Christian community formed one block when the Portuguese first came to India. There were no sections among them. They all depended on the Chaldean hierarchy. It is then surely a remarkable thing that, in such circumstances, the group that separated much later from Rome because of its opposition to Archbishop Garzia went over to the jurisdiction of the Jacobite Patriarch of Antioch so readily. For the Monophysite doctrine was far more opposed than Catholic teaching to their supposed and entirely forgotten 'Nestorianism'. Their adventure clearly shows how foreign to the real patrimony of Christian ideas is the notion of autocephaly, which in the last centuries has been so strongly advocated by the Greek Orthodox Churches.

EARLY JACOBITE INFLUENCES

We have been told above[1] how Alexander de Campo received the episcopal consecration in 1663, with the mission to prevent the Syro-Malabar community from passing over to the rule of his cousin the Archdeacon Thomas. The success that followed his administration of the archdiocese of Angamale was such that one could reasonably hope for a general return of the dissidents at the death of the pseudo-Bishop Mar Thomas I. This would have materialized, if during the interval the sect had not already joined a fully organized Church. After his 'consecration' by twelve *kattanars*, Thomas de Campo had practically always acted as bishop. Yet it appears that he continued to entertain some doubts about the validity of his episcopal character, for when his cousin received the consecration, on which no possible doubt could be cast, he felt even more acutely the false position he was in. This tends to explain his

---

who had been expelled from Ctesiphon, when al-Mansur destroyed the old capital of the Sassanides, following his decision to build Baghdad. Anyhow all the texts mentioned here refer to the Melkites, or the faithful depending on the Greek patriarchs, and never to the Jacobites.

[1] Cf. *supra* p. 86.

request to the Jacobite patriarch that one of his bishops be sent to Malabar. No watch was kept now at Ormuz by the Portuguese. In 1665 the Metropolitan of Jerusalem, Mar Gregorios, arrived in India; however Thomas did not receive, it seems, the episcopal character he had been desiring for so long.[1]

Gregorios did not introduce Jacobite tenets immediately, but he succeeded at least in obliging his party to anathematize Nestorius, profess Monophysism of the Severian variety, deny the double *processio* of the Holy Ghost and the dogma about Purgatory. These were the dogmas few in number, which, according to tradition, were at that time imposed on the followers of Mar Thomas. Gregorios declared himself an enemy of the Pope, and this declaration was the point on which the dissident Christians of Malabar and the Jacobite prelate agreed. He also advocated a return to several ancient customs: Eastern liturgical vestments, leavened bread, traditional length of Lent, etc. On the other hand he was forced to adapt himself in many respects to the Latinized Syro-Chaldaic rite of the Catholic Syrians—so strong was the attachment of the new dissidents to their traditions.[2]

Mar Gregorios died in 1672, at Parur Patuna (North Parur), and Thomas de Campo the following year.[3] A brother of Thomas died in 1674, eight days after his election by the *kattanars*; one of his relatives became Mar Thomas II, who ruled until 1686, and he was replaced by his nephew, a mere layman, who was ordained with the title of Mar Thomas III.[4]

[1] Placid of St. Joseph, T.O.C.D., 'The Efforts for Reunion in Malankara, South India', in *Unitas*, 5 (1953), p. 9.

[2] Ibid. pp. 8-9. Since that time, the Syrians, who separated from the Church, were locally called *Puthenkur Syrians*, i.e. *The Syrians of the New Party*, in opposition to the Catholics nicknamed *Pazhayakur Syrians*, i.e. *The Syrians of the Old Party*.

[3] W. Germann, *Die Kirche der Thomas Christen*, Gütersloh, 1877, pp. 525-7.

[4] None of these Mar Thomases seems to have received valid consecration, although Jacobite prelates from abroad continued to come to Malabar after the death of Mar Gregorios, cf. Placid of St. Joseph, T.O.C.D. op. cit. p. 9.

An ordinary priest, who, on the strength of a false papal document, pretended to be a patriarch, created some trouble in the communities at that time; however he was drowned in 1682 or 1683.[1]

We must wait however till January 1685 to find two genuine Jacobite bishops coming to India, Mar Basilios and Mar John. They were monks from the monastery of Mar Mattai, near Mosul. One of them was supposed to have been the Maphrian himself, and was according to Germann, John,[2] and according to a Jacobite document of 1821, published by F. Nau, Basilios. These prelates, if we are to believe the second document, eliminated the last remnants of Latinism preserved until then by the Malabar Jacobites: 'They freed us from the customs of the Franks and brought us back to the usages of our first fathers. From that time till now, we have not subtracted nor added anything.'[3] It is most unlikely however that any evenutal and definite switchover to the pure Antiochian rite was effected before the nineteenth century.

Since their wish to have a Syrian prelate residing with them had not yet been gratified, the Jacobite community, totalling about thirty parishes, attempted a reunion with the Syrian Catholics. Their proposal was that the vicar apostolic and the local prelate should rule Malabar in common. Hence no positive antipathy against the Holy See was to be found among the Jacobites.[4] This can also be gathered from the following incident: a Nestorian bishop, Mar Gabriel, Metropolitan of Azerbaijan, in order to make himself acceptable to the Jacobites of India, produced a document from Propaganda. As a matter

[1] W. Germann, op. cit. pp. 527, ff.

[2] Ibid. p. 528.

[3] 'Deux notices relatives au Malabar', in R.O.C. 17, (1912), pp. 77, ff. trans. p. 81.

[4] Mar Thomas IV sent in 1704 a petition to the Holy See in the name of twenty-nine parishes under him. The petition was forwarded to Rome by a Carmelite missionary, Augustine by name. But nothing came of it, cf. Placid of St. Joseph, T.O.C.D., op. cit. p. 9.

of fact, this document was a letter, in which he was asked to send a more explicit profession of faith, following on his request to be admitted into the bosom of the Catholic Church.[1] And so for many years up to his death late in 1730 or early in 1731, he tried to have a say in the government of the Jacobite community and had controversies with Mar Thomas V.[2]

In 1751, three prelates, sent by the Jacobite patriarch, came to Malabar. Actually their mission had been greatly helped by the Dutch authorities at the special request of Mar Thomas V. One of the Jacobites, Basilios Shukrallah, had received the title of Metropolitan of Malabar, whereas of the other two, one was a metropolitan, Mar Gregorios, and the other a simple bishop, Mar John. They should have consecrated Mar Thomas V, but there arose some disagreement about the payment of 4,000 Rupees that had been promised by Mar Thomas for the journey of the prelates. Mar Thomas V died in 1765, without having received episcopal consecration, and he was succeeded by a nephew, who assumed the title of Mar Thomas VI.[3] Since the dispute over the payment of the money had reached a deadlock, Mar Gregorios consecrated in 1770 a man by the name of Rabban (monk) Kattumangatt, who was an enemy of Mar Thomas VI. Kattumangatt took the title of Mar Kurillos. Mar Kurillos however did not succeed in ousting Mar Thomas VI, so he erected his see at the northern end of the kingdom of Cochin, at Thozhiur. This new autocephalous diocese is still alive to-day, because its bishop takes care, as

[1] W. Germann, op. cit. pp. 532-4.

[2] F. Nau, op. cit. p. 78, trans. p. 81. Many details on those internal feuds are found in W. Germann, op. cit. pp. 533-62, mainly drawn from the correspondence of the Syriologist Charles Schaaf, and the Protestant German missionaries of Tranquebar.

[3] In 1748, Mar Thomas V tried to be reunited with Rome. Till about 1757, some hope was entertained that it would be realized at last. The arrival of the Jacobite prelates foiled the whole attempt, cf. Placid of St. Joseph, T.O.C.D., op. cit. pp. 9-12.

soon as he is elected, to choose and consecrate a successor.[1] Finally under pressure from the civil authorities, Mar Gregorios and Mar John were forced to consecrate Mar Thomas VI, who took the name of Mar Dionysios I.[2]

PROTESTANTISM VERSUS JACOBITE ORTHODOXY

From this period onwards the influence of Protestant missionaries began to increase, and it menaced the authority of the Jacobite prelates from the Near East. The evangelists of the Danish Factory of Tranquebar, whose mission was founded in 1706 by the Saxon Bartholomew Ziegenbalg, had but little dealings with the St. Thomas Christians; yet they did not ignore them, and their accounts awoke in Protestant circles of the eighteenth century that interest for the Syrians, to which the *Histoire du Christianisme des Indes* written by Mathurin

---

[1] Such was often the case. Yet some of the bishops did not receive consecration before their predecessor's death. They were therefore obliged to beg for the same from the Mar Thomite prelates, with whom they have always been in friendly terms. The other Jacobites would not hear of consecrating any of the Thozhiur prelates. Since the Mar Thomite orders are very doubtful, even in the eyes of the Jacobites, it is very likely that the present Thozhiur bishops are not validly consecrated. This small dissident community comprises some 3,000 members. They style themselves the 'Malabar Independent Syrian Church'.

[2] From 1771 onwards Mar Thomas VI (Mar Dionysios I) applied several times to Rome for reunion, even after having received a valid episcopal consecration, cf. Placid of St. Joseph T.O.C.D., op. cit. pp. 12-13. For various reasons—hesitations of the prelate, mistrust of the Carmelites, difficulty of communicating with Rome, conditions put by Propaganda — his first approaches did not succeed. The whole question was taken up again by Fr. Joseph Cariati and his companion, Fr. Thomas Paremmakal in 1778, ibid. pp. 14-15. Cf. also the relation of the efforts made by Mar Dionysios for an eventual reunion entered in *A.P.F. Atti*, vol. CLXIV, ff. 519-25, 526-44, for 18 July 1794. After many talks and postponements, the prelate finally accepted to come over to the Catholic Church on 21 June 1799. But, because he was uncertain of his position in the Catholic Church, he reverted to schism six months later. He then entered in relations with some Anglican missionaries, even before the time of Munro, but without reaching any particular agreement with them, Placid of St. Joseph T.O.C.D., op. cit. pp. 89-92.

Veyssière de La Croze, librarian and antiquary of the King of Prussia, testifies. We must, however, wait till the early nineteenth century to see the Jacobites being taken care of by Protestant missionaries.

After a visit of Dr. Claudius Buchanan, chaplain to the East India Company,[1] Colonel Munro, British Resident at the courts of Travancore and Cochin, obtained, in 1816-19, four missionaries of the Church Missionary Society. Following the methods employed by that zealous Franciscan, Fr. Vincent de Lagos, who even before 1545 had opened a seminary at Cranganore, the newcomers intended first of all to remedy the great 'ignorance' and 'abuses' of the Jacobite *kattanars*. They meant of course to reform the clergy in the Protestant sense. They founded a college-seminary at Kottayam. Next they did their best to bring the Holy Scriptures within the reach of the faithful through a Malayalam translation (published in 1811, 1818 and 1830), and through scriptural classes imparted in the various schools started by the missionaries. These institutions were the vernacular schools of each parish, a grammar school, and even the college-seminary, which admitted lay pupils. Malayalam services were introduced according to the Anglican Book of Common Prayer. Catechisms of the English Church were also translated into Malayalam and published for the benefit of the Jacobites.

For a little over ten years, perfect agreement reigned between the Jacobite clergy and the missionaries. The latter preached often on the reform of beliefs and practices which were not in accordance with the Gospel, i.e. which were not Protestant. They expected that their influence on the future priests would bring about the required pruning of faith and divine service.[2]

[1] Cf. Buchanan's journals, *Christian Researches in Asia*, London, 1819, pp. 128-31.

[2] Between 1818 and 1820, the Protestant missionaries induced some forty priests out of 150 to get married, cf. Placid of St. Joseph T.O.C.D., op. cit., p. 93. Besides they clearly intended to do away with the seven sacraments and the Sacrifice of the Mass.

Mar Dionysios III (Punnathra Mar Dionysios), who supported the work of the C.M.S. padres, died in 1825, and was succeeded by Mar Dionysios IV (Cheppat Mar Dionysios), The new prelate showed his dislike of the missionaries right from the beginning, and he sought the help of the Jacobite Patriarch of Antioch against them. Unfortunately, the Jacobite bishop, who came from Syria, Mar Athanasios, wanted above all to establish on firm grounds the jurisdiction of the patriarch, so he deposed Mar Dionysios and the Bishop of Thozhiur, Mar Philoxenos. The powerful intervention however, of the Protestant missionaries restored the two deposed prelates to their former positions, and Mar Athanasios was exiled from India. Such mediation in his favour improved for a while the relations between Mar Dionysios and the missionaries. However the metropolitan soon found an opportunity to reveal his real feelings. Following a visit of Bishop Daniel Wilson of Calcutta (Anglican Church), Mar Dionysios agreed to call a synod. This was held in January 1836. Instead of bringing in the reforms as desired by Bishop Wilson and the C.M.S. missionaries, the synod showed no sympathy at all for such proposals, and severed all further relations with the Protestants. Properties owned in common by both Jacobites and Protestants were divided.[1]

THE ORIGINS OF THE MAR THOMITES

Nevertheless, a hard core of Protestant sympathizers remained within the Jacobite community. Although they were

[1] G. M. Rae, *The Syrian Church in India*, London, 1892, pp. 281-303; W. Germann, op. cit. pp. 609-705; G. B. Howard, *The Christians of St. Thomas and their Liturgies*, Oxford London, 1864, pp. 56-113; M. B. Sherring, *The History of the Protestant Missions in India*, London, 1884, pp. 286-96; P. Cheriyan, *The Malabar Syrians and the Church Missionary Society*: 1816-40, Kottayam, 1935. We are indebted to Fr. Lucas T.O.C.D. for a very good synthesis of the Protestant influences on the formation of the Mar Thomite community in his unpublished dissertation *The Sacrifice and Priesthood in the Mar-Thomite Church*.

defeated at the synod, they were soon to obtain their revenge. This party was led by four Jacobite priests, the most prominent of whom was Abraham Malpan of Maramon. He was the soul of the reformatory section, and is still regarded by the Mar Thomites as their reformer. Shortly after the split between the missionaries and the Indian Jacobites, Abraham Malpan started to correct the Syrian liturgy, re-writing it along the lines of Protestant teaching, viz. liturgy in the vernacular, suppression of the prayers for the dead and of the invocation of the saints, etc. He managed however to keep intact the externals of the Syrian Mass and of the other liturgical services.

Mar Dionysios IV felt very uneasy about the activities of Abraham and his followers, who were now firmly established at Maramon. He excommunicated the whole party. This was a death-dealing blow for the reformers. The only way out was to get a bishop of their own. Accordingly, Abraham Malpan sent one of his nephews, Matthew, to the Jacobite Patriarch, Ignatios Mar Elias II. Matthew, it seems, was only a *lector* in the Jacobite Church, but he fully sympathized with his uncle's views, particularly so since he had been sent to Madras for further studies in the C.M.S. institution there. Matthew was well received in the monastery of Deir as-Zafaran near Mardin, where the patriarch was residing. After having undergone some sort of training, he duly received the various orders, and was eventually consecrated Metropolitan of Malankara (Malabar) on 2 February 1842. He was known henceforward as Matthew Mar Athanasios. By March 1843 the new bishop was back in Malabar and took possession of his see. Abraham Malpan died three years later.

In his testimonial letters, the patriarch congratulated himself on having found at last, after so many petitions (from 1825 until 1842), an ideal candidate for this very important position. The local Metropolitan, Mar Dionysios IV however, did not hold the same views. He could not very well receive the new patriarchal envoy, whatever the validity of the mission

Mar Athanasios prided himself on possessing. Mar Athanasios had been acknowledged by the King of Travancore as the religious leader of the Jacobites. On the other hand the consecration of Mar Dionysios was doubtful, whilst Matthew Mar Athanasios had been duly consecrated by the patriarch himself. A split in the community was inevitable, and recourse was had to the patriarch. The latter sent one of his metropolitans, Mar Kurillos, to India to bring about a reconciliation.

Since this new bishop had received papers from his master signed in blank, he did not hesitate to fill in the document (*systatikos*) himself, by which he was appointed Metropolitan of Malankara. Moreover he had been clever enough to secure a document by which Mar Dionysios had been persuaded to resign his see. This forgery added to the confusion. An appeal to the civil courts was necessary; Mar Kurillos' craftiness was exposed, and a royal proclamation in favour of Mathew Mar Athanasios was issued (1852).[1]

In the meanwhile another metropolitan, Mar Stephanos, came from the Near East with a letter addressed to Mar Dionysios IV. Something of a government in common was proposed in that letter. As the Anglicans were on the side of Mar Athanasios, the Travancore Government supported him; thus before the arrival of Mar Stephanos, Mar Kurillos was ordered to quit Travancore and Cochin, while Mar Dionysios IV was soon forgotten. Mar Stephanos appealed to the Anglican authorities in England and obtained a decision to the effect that the Anglican missionaries were not to interfere in the affairs of the Syrians of Malabar. Anyway, the British Resident succeeded in getting rid of Mar Stephanos in 1857,[2] whereas Mar Kurillos had already reappeared. The Travancore Government allowed those, who so desired, to follow

[1] Latin translation according to the Travancore Royal Court Judgement in Placid of St. Joseph T.O.C.D., *Fontes Juris Canonici Syro-Malankarensium,* Città del Vaticano, 1940, vol. II, pp. 26, ff.

[2] Ibid. p. 27.

him. Mar Kurillos and his followers had to carry on law-suits in order to recover the churches which were in the possession of Matthew Mar Athanasios. It was this Mar Kurillos who completely replaced the Chaldean rite by the West Syrian rite of Antioch, and introduced West Syrian script among the dissidents of Malabar.[1]

In 1865 another pretender appeared on the scene. He laid claim to the metropolitan see as a member of the Pakalomattam family. It is true that until 1813 this well-known family had enjoyed the privilege of providing all the archdeacons. The new competitor was called Joseph Mar Dionysios V, and he also received consecration from the patriarchal hands. The plot became more and more involved. Joseph Mar Diony-sios had not been able so far to secure any support from the British authorities.

In fact, Matthew Mar Athananios was keen on remaining as the head of the whole Jacobite community of Malabar. Although he had Protestant leanings, he did not make any attempt to carry out the programme of reforms which had been planned by his uncle Abraham Malpan. He was successful in continuing at the helm of the Jacobite Church till 1875, and he was regarded officially as its metropolitan, but, knowing of the growing support given to Mar Dionysios by the Jacobite patriarch, he made haste to ensure his succession. Assisted by the bishop of the small Jacobite sect of Tozhiur he gave the episcopal character to one of his cousins, called Thomas (1868), and declared the new prelate his own successor, under the name of Thomas Mar Athanasios.[2] However, such separatist action could not fail to impress the Jacobite Patriarch, Ignatios Mar Peter IV, who was wholeheartedly in favour of Joseph Mar Dionysios. The patriarch, fearful of the Protestant influences working behind the scene, took the trouble to go to London in 1874, in order to voice his

[1] Id. 'The Efforts for Reunion. . .', p. 93.
[2] Thomas was a son of Abraham Malpan, the founder of the Mar Thomites.

claims and to diminish the activities of the Protestants in Malabar; he then decided to visit Malabar at as early a time as possible.

THE PATRIARCH'S DEALINGS

Mar Peter IV reached India in 1875. In spite of the presence of their hierarchical superior, the great majority of the priests and the faithful as well as the C.M.S. missionaries stood by Matthew Mar Athanasios. The patriarch duly excommunicated the daring metropolitan, and he was supported in this by the royal court of Travancore. The schism, however, continued.[1]

The Jacobite patriarch seemed to have been a farsighted and able man. He wanted to make his long stay in India a means of strengthening his authority for the years ahead. Thus, when he realized that the civil authorities attached great importance to his decisions, he thought that these should be endorsed by civil guarantees. At the Synod of Mulanthurutty held in 1876, the patriarch made it obligatory for all parish communities to sign a promise of absolute obedience to any order coming from Antioch, and this was also to be recognized by government. The original document was to be preserved in the parish archives, and an authentic duplicate forwarded to the patriarchate.[2]

Judging from previous experience an impartial observer could not but rejoice at this important move. For this consolidation of the supreme authority had two purposes: it aimed firstly, at warding off any possible discussions or quarrels that might arise regarding the legitimacy of the bishops; and secondly, at establishing the financial system of the patriarchate in India on solid foundations. Concerning the second

[1] Id. *Fontes. . .*, pp. 28, ff.
[2] Ibid.

point, regulations were enacted for the collection of the *canonicos*.[1]

To aim too high, however, is often risky. By virtue of his spiritual authority, the patriarch divided the Jacobite community into seven eparchies (dioceses), and accordingly he consecrated six more metropolitans, anong whom Joseph Mar Dionysios V became only a *primus inter pares*.[2] His next step was to obtain control over all temporal possessions. When Matthew Mar Athanasios died in 1877, his cousin Thomas automatically succeeded him, became the head of the Mar Thomites and even a sort of superintendent of the properties of all the Jacobites. Such a situation was intolerable in the eyes of the patriarch. Soon a lawsuit arose between the 'reformed party' and the followers of the patriarch. The case lasted ten years, 1879-89, and went through the successive courts of the Travancore Judiciary.[3] The reformers were finally obliged to relinquish every church they had previously possessed.

Still the reformers did not give up hope. Under the leadership of Thomas Mar Athanasios they organized their party into a separate Church, and built new churches in those places where they had been forced to leave the old buildings to the Jacobites. From that time onward they became known before the civil authorities as the *Navikarannakar*, i.e., the 'Reformed Party'[4].

[1] The *canonicos* is the annual tax to be levied on each church and any ecclesiastical property in favour of the patriarch. It is the equivalent of the *cathedraticum* of the Latin Canon-Law.

[2] G. M. Rae, op. cit. pp. 304-26.

[3] Ibid. pp. 327-52, 380-2. There are several juridical texts related to controversy to be found in Placid of St. Joseph, T.O.C.D., *Fontes...*, pp. 30-4.

[4] In 1956 the reformed party, known as the Mar Thomite Church, comprised about 250,000 members under the leadership of one metropolitan and four suffragan bishops. The community is well organized socially and financialcially. They are in close comradeship with the Protestants, and they co-operate with them, even in mere religious matters.

Some Syrians had gone still further on the path of Reform. They joined the C.M.S. missionaries, and thus formed the nucleus of an Anglican community in Malabar. The Anglican diocese of Travancore with headquarters at Kottayam was erected in 1879. After the last war, it merged into the newly-formed Church of South India.[1]

NEW DISCUSSIONS AND INTERNAL RIFTS

After this last struggle, the section of the Jacobite community faithful to Antioch lived unmolested for many years. Nevertheless, owing to the seeds of internal dissension already sown by previous disputes, this euphoria could not last.

In 1906, the Turkish Government deposed the Jacobite Patriarch, Abd-ul-Massih. His successor, Mar Ignatios Abdallah Sattuf, came to Malabar in 1909, and when visiting the Jacobites there, he soon became involved in conflicts with the Metropolitan of Malankara, George Mar Dionysios VI. Of course the patriarch was received with all the honour due to his dignity, but the metroplitan, a man of strong character, stubbornly refused to let him examine the finances. The patriarch did not hesitate to excommunicate Mar Dionysios immediately, and went so far as to appoint on the spot a new metropolitan under the name of Mar Kurillos. This was an action with far-reaching consequences, for the Jacobites of Malabar have been suffering from the effects of this discord to this day.

This move of the patriarch was immediately followed by a division. Two parties were formed of nearly equal strength. They were, and still are called the patriarch's party and the metropolitan's party (metran's party, catholicos' party or Syrian Orthodox).

Faced with a situation which amounted to a stalemate, Mar Dionysios did not lose his head, but had recourse to

[1] E. Chatterton, *A History of the Church of England in India*, London, 1924, pp. 269-81.

Abd-ul-Massih, the former Jacobite patriarch. As the unlucky prelate had never acknowledged the Sultan's decision, he had reason to believe that his jurisdiction had not been taken away, at least in India where the Sultan had no power. In 1912, when invited by Mar Dionysios to come to India, the deposed patriarch gladly accepted the invitation. There is no doubt that the arrival of the ex-patriarch helped to strengthen the new party a great deal.

In the course of 1910 both parties had already defined their positions, the patriarchists in a synod held at Alwaye, and the metran's party at their stronghold at Kottayam. So far the split had but widened. Abd-ul-Massih was induced to give to the Metropolitan of Malankara the title of Catholicos, and although for some time the two offices were held separately, in recent years the catholicos had assumed both the title and the responsibilities of the metropolitan.[1] This means that the present Catholicos, Mar Basilios III, is the hierarchical head in both spiritual and temporal matters.

In the early thirties a new Jacobite patriarch tried to heal the breach, visited Malabar, and died there. The head of the catholicos party was also welcomed at Homs, the residence, of the Jacobite patriarch, but all to no avail.

Both parties are organized as follows: the patriarch's party consisting of an Indian metropolitan, a delegate of the patriarch, who collects and forwards the money, four bishops, and 250,000 followers; and the catholicos' party, made up of the Metropolitan of Malankara (who is himself the catholicos) nine bishops and 450,000 adherents. It is interesting to note that all the Suddists belong to the patriarch's party and have their own bishop residing near Kottayam. Except for this small community, the patriarch's party is particularly strong in the ex-Cochin State and in the northern districts of the

---

[1] J. C. Panjikaran, 'Christianity in Malabar', in *O.C.* VI (1926), no. 23, pp. 122-6. Placid of St. Joseph T.O.C.D., *Fontes...*, pp. 34-40, provides several texts concerning the organization of the two parties.

former Travancore State, whereas the catholicos' party occupies central Travancore. For this reason, the see of the catholicos to-day is at Kottayam.

There have been some attempts made — probably under Anglican High-Church influences—at reviving religious life in the Jacobite Church, but almost entirely within the catholicos' jurisdiction. The most conspicuous and successful have been the congregations of the Fathers and Sisters of Bethany. Others, such as the Servants of the Cross, are pious confraternities. Between the two wars the latter carried on a very encouraging work of conversion among the low caste people: they claim to have christianized more than 15,000 of them.

Outside Kerala, the Jacobites have some centres formed mainly by their own settlers, in such big cities as Madras, Bombay, Calcutta, New Delhi, Poona and Hyderabad. They have a bishop in charge of this *diaspora*, and priests are sent regularly to those various centres. They have recently built their own church in Bombay and, in other towns, they usually borrow the Anglican church for their services.

REUNION MOVEMENTS

The struggle that had dragged on for some many years between the 'Reformed Syrians' and the Jacobites who were faithful to the Patriarch of Antioch, had definitely awakened a certain nostalgia for Catholic unity.

Following the attempts made towards a reunion with Rome in the last years of the eighteenth century and the first years of the nineteenth, a new movement was started by Mar Dionysios V with Fr. Emmanuel Nidiri, a Catholic priest of the Syro-Malabar rite, under the auspices of a joint association called *Jathiaikiasangham*. The then Apostolic Delegate, Mgr. Ajuti, was approached, but the attempt failed. We have already seen how, through the efforts of some prominent

Syro-Malabar priests, a few Jacobite priests and some faithful became Catholic during the times of Bishop Lavigne.[1]

When in 1896 Syro-Malabar vicars apostolic were appointed, they immediately turned their attention towards their Jacobite brethren. They opened several mission stations in Jacobite centres of their respective dioceses.[2] Mgr. Benziger O.C.D., the well-known Latin Bishop of Quilon, did likewise. He was helped by some Syro-Malabar priests, and the work steadily progressed. The converts, both lay and ecclesiastical, were received into the Chaldean rite of the Syro-Malabar Church.

This undoubtedly caused great inconvenience to the reunited Jacobite clergymen. A proposal was then forwarded by some leaders of the patriarch's party, stating that they and their bishops would negotiate for reunion if they were allowed to retain the West Syrian rite of Antioch. The Syro-Malabar prelates proposed to the Holy See that the Antiochian rite be kept. They received a favourable reply in 1921.[3] Thereafter the Syro-Malabar bishops accepted all reunited priests into the West Syrian rite, and they were provided with the liturgical books published by Propaganda. In the diocese of Quilon, however, all continued to be received into the Chaldean rite.

[1] Cf. *supra* p. 130.

[2] In Ernakulam, a congregation of men was founded in 1931 for the reunion of the Jacobites. In the diocese of Changanacherry, several churches were built for the reunited, and later on they were ceded to the diocese of Tiruvalla. In 1921, the Bishop of Kottayam launched a new mission for the reunion of the Jacobite Suddists. Theirconverts, however, remain still under the jurisdiction of the same prelate, but they keep their own rite, cf. T. Arayathinal, ' The missionary enterprise of the Syrian Catholics of Malabar', in *E.C.Q.* 7 (1947), pp. 41-2.

[3] The answer of the S. Oriental Congregation, dated 5 July reads as follows: 'The Sacred Congregation, after maturely examining the matter, has decded to allow the Jacobite priests, who return to the Catholic Church, to preserve their own rite, provided nothing is found therein contrary to the integrity of faith, and any superstitious practices do not result therefrom. In accepting the said priests, the Most Reverend Ordinaries should make an accurate inquiry in order to satisfy themselves that the sacraments, especially Baptism and Sacred Ordination, have been validly administered to them', quoted by Placid of St. Joseph T.O.C.D., 'The Efforts for Reunion. . . .', p. 95.

VII. His Eminence Cardinal Eugene Tisserant blessing the congregation in the traditional Antiochian way at the reception given in his honour at Trivandrum in November 1953.

VIII. 1. The late Mar Severios, Syro-Malankara bishop of Tiruvalla, singing the Gospel of the Nativity during the ceremony of the blessing of the shepherds' fire, Christmas 1953 — Cathedral ground, Tiruvalla.

2. At the interdenominational meeting at Kottayam in December 1952 in honour of St. Thomas the Apostle, His Lordship Mar Thomas Tharayil, Syro-Malabar Suddist Bishop of Kottayam, addressing the audience.

The split that took place within the Jacobite Church in 1912 had a more lasting influence as far as the possibilities of a reunion were concerned. Since many of them became independent of the Patriarch of Antioch, the more intelligent and pious members of the metran's party soon understood their juridical situation. They could no longer claim any status in the Church Universal without depending on some patriarchate or other. As Antioch was out of the question, Rome was the only other alternative. Moreover, the aged Patriarch Abd-ul-Massih, the very author of the last secession, had himself left the Jacobite community, and had become reconciled with Rome after his return from India (3 May 1913). The good old man was still full of his experiences in Malabar and, during the short span of life that still remained to him—he died on 6 March 1914—he frequently talked about the Christian communities of India with the learned and zealous Syrian Catholic Patriarch, Mar Ignatios Ephrem II Rahmani.

These conversations raised an interest in the reunion of the Indian Jacobites, and Patriarch Rahmani tried to contact their hierarchy. He presented them with copies of the liturgical books, the texts of which he had corrected in such a scholarly fashion with the best manuscripts available. Years before, Mar Dionysios V had taken pride in possessing for his personal use the Syrian *Book of Anaphoras* published in 1843 by Propaganda. The beautiful editions published by Patriarch Rahmani at Sharfe, his major seminary, could not but make a favourable impression.

THE ORIGINS OF THE SYRO-MALANKARA CATHOLICS

In 1923, George Mar Dionysios visited the Jacobite patriarch at Homs, and tried in vain to obtain a compromise between the two parties. There he met the Syrian Catholic Metropolitan of Baghdad who urged him to reunite with Rome. Two letters from the Syrian Catholic Patriarch of Antioch did the same. The prelates of the metran's party then decided to deal

12

directly with the Holy See, and at a meeting in 1926 they choose Mar Ivanios of Bethany to open correspondence with Rome. Since mention is made here of Mar Ivanios, we find it necessary to give a short account of his spiritual pilgrimage to the Catholic Church.

Father P. T. Geevargheese (George Thomas Panickerveetil) who belonged to an ancient Syrian family of Mavelikara (Travancore), was the first Malayalee priest of any denomination to take an M.A. in Economics at the Madras University (1907). Soon afterwards he became an influence among his fellow countrymen. After having been Principal of the Jacobite Seminary of Kottayam, he was asked at the beginning of World War I to teach Economics and Syriac at the Protestant College—interdenominational—of Serampore near Calcutta. He also became warden of a hostel which was reserved for Malayalee Christians. Under his influence the atmosphere of the hostel grew deeply religious. There he received many young men and clerics of the Jacobite community who afterwards became important leaders of their Church. In 1919, he laid the foundations of a religious order in Malabar under the patronage of St. Basil, St. Benedict and St. Francis of Assisi. Its first members were taken from his old pupils of Serampore. A congregation of nuns was also started, and its first recruits were trained in Bengal by some Anglican Sisters. To both these congregations Fr. Geevargheese gave the name of 'Order of the Imitation of Christ'.

Between 1919 and 1925, the Brothers and Sisters of Bethany (the name of the first house in Malabar) established their communities in five of the seven Jacobite eparchies. They were to become centres of exemplary Christian life. The synod of the metran's party allowed Mar Ivanios to rule these convents (ashrams) as parishes. All lay interference, so common in the Jacobite Church, was excluded. In 1925, Mar Basilios II consecrated him as Mar Ivanios of Bethany, with exclusive jurisdiction over the monasteries of Bethany. In 1928 the new

Catholicos, Mar Basilios III, made him a metropolitan and gave him Mar Theophilos, a monk of Bethany and former pupil as suffragan at Tiruvalla.

Mar Ivanios was an old friend of Mar Dionysios VI (George Vattacheril), and his confrères in the episcopate held him in high esteem for his knowledge, his piety and the influence he enjoyed in his community. It was not surprising, therefore, that Mar Ivanios was chosen to open correspondence with Rome. In a document written by Mar Ivanios himself, he and two other bishops declared themselves ready to become Catholic. After mature consideration and sufficient inquiries, the Holy See asked Mar Ivanios to meet every prelate of his party individually, and to ask him what he was prepared to do in the matter of reunion. Eventually the new Catholicos Basilios III (Basilios II died in 1929) and all the other Jacobite bishops of his party, except Mar Theophilos, were reluctant to take any decisive step.

On 20 September 1930, Mar Ivanios, together with Mar Theophilos (James Abraham Karapurakal) signed their profession of adhesion to the Catholic Church before Mgr. Benziger O.C.D., Latin Bishop of Quilon, who was deputed for the purpose by the Apostolic Delegate, Archbishop Mooney. Mar Jacob Kalacherry, Syro-Malabar Bishop of Changanacherry, and Mgr. Lawrence Pereira, Latin Bishop-elect of Kottar, were present on that occasion.[1] Before the close of the year thirteen priests and one deacon with thirty-five families totalling 180 persons had followed the two prelates. By

[1] The epoch-making document, by which the S. Oriental Congregation answered favourably to the request of Mar Ivanios in 1930, begins thus: 'In a plenary session of 4 July this year, the Eminent Cardinals, making up this Congregation, undertook an examination of the wishes expressed by the Jacobite bishops of Malabar belonging to the metran's party, namely those of the Most Reverend Mar Ivanios, Metropolitan of Bethany, and of Mar Theophilos, his suffragan, regarding their union with the Catholic Church. Taking into account the opinion of the five bishops forming the metran's party, Mar Ivanios, who drew up the memorandum of November 1926, had remained faithful to the desire, which he had expressed at that time in the name of two other bishops also; and considering that both Mar Ivanios and his suffragan,

December 1931 the bishops had reunited most of the Fathers of Bethany and the whole Bethany Sisterhood, thirty-five secular priests[1] with two rabbans (Antonite monks who are ordinarily candidate-bishops), six seminarists and 4,700 followers. In 1932 a new hierarchy was created for them, with Mar Ivanios as Metropolitan of Trivandrum and Mar Theophilos as Suffragan Bishop of Tiruvalla.[2] The reunited community was given the name of 'Syro-Malankara' (*Syro-Malankarenses Ritus Antiocheni*) to distinguish them from the old Catholic Syrians who are generally known as Syro-Malabar. Actually the new appellation is derived from *Malankara* which is a term synonymous for Malabar.

Since 1932 two more Jacobite bishops have joined the ranks of the new community, Mar Severios of the metran's party in 1937, and Mar Dioscoros of the patriarch's party in 1939.

Mar Theophilos (who had joined the former in subscribing to the same proposals and wishes), from the information imparted to us, manifested themselves as worthy persons, sincere, of exceptional character and highly esteemed...'. The S. Congregation resolved then to receive the two prelates into the Catholic Church, 'with the assurance that the pure Syro-Antiochian rite shall be preserved, and that it will not thus be confused with the Syro-Malabars, whose rite is of Syro-Chaldaic origin; and with the assurance, furthermore, that—the validity of the Baptism, the Sacred Ordination, and the consecration of the above-mentioned bishops having been certified—they will be maintained in their respective office and jurisdiction in such wise that Mar Ivanios will remain Bishop of Bethany with the title of Metropolitan Archbishop *ad personam*, and Mar Theophilos as Bishop of Tiruvalla... *in praesentibus rerum adjunctis*, they will depend immediately on the Holy See, without any dependence on the Syrian Patriarch of Antioch...', document quoted in the original Italian by Placid of St. Joseph T.O.C.D., 'The Efforts for Reunion...', pp. 96-7.

[1] About the married clergy, the S. Oriental Congregation decided thus: 'In the matter of celibacy, no candidate shall be admitted in future to Sacred Orders, who does not promise to remain celibate. For the present, however, married priests, who are converts, will be welcomed, and permitted to function, and deacons, who are married, may be advanced to the priesthood', Ibid. p. 98, with the Italian original text in Placid of St. Joseph, 'The Efforts for Reunion...', op. cit. pp. 95.

[2] Bull (Constitution) of Pius XI, *Christus Pastorum Princeps*, 11 June 1932, *A.A.S.* 24 (1932), pp. 287-92.

The former had been consecrated by the Catholicos as Metropolitan of Niranam, with the special duty of fighting against the reunion movement. Since his reunion, Mar Severios has been Administrator Apostolic of Tiruvalla (1938) owing to the continued illness of Mar Theophilos, and in 1950 he became bishop of the same diocese. Mar Dioscoros, who was leading a retired life after his reunion passed away in 1943.

After 1950, Mar Ivanios suffered bad health, and since the middle of 1952, his illness had given cause for alarm. He asked the Holy See for an auxiliary-bishop, and Fr. Benedict-George of the Bethany Congregation was appointed by the end of the same year. The old metropolitan still had the joy of consecrating the new prelate in January 1953, under the name of Benedict Mar Gregorios. On 15 July 1953, surrounded by prelates of his rite and many other friends, Mar Ivanios went to his reward.

Since the death of Mar Ivanios, just mentioned, and the unexpected demise of Mar Severios, Bishop of Tiruvalla (18 January 1955), Mar Gregorios became Archbishop of Trivandrum, and Zacharias Mar Athanasios, who had been given to Mar Severios as auxiliary, normally succeeded to him as Bishop of Tiruvalla. The reunion movement is keeping the same pace as before, if it is not on the increase. Since 1947 the Bethany Congregation of men was raised to the interdiocesan status, and in 1956 it was given new constitutions, more in keeping with the Eastern ideal. At the end of August 1956 the Bethany Sisters, who were still of diocesan right, became a congregation of pontifical right.

In twenty-five years the reunion movement has made tremendous progress. Not only have Jacobites, Mar Thomites and Protestants been reconciled, but low-caste people have also been converted in large numbers.[1] At present (1956), the

[1] Some of those who reunite, prefer to join the Syro-Chaldaic rite as practised by the Syro-Malabar Catholics, and thus they are received into that rite and jurisdiction. There are also those who, retaining the Syro-Malankara

Syro-Malankara Church has more than 90,000 faithful and over 170 priests. Mar Ivanios founded a first grade University College a few years after World War II.

It will be noticed that the situation of the Catholic communities of the Eastern rite in Malabar is similar to that existing in Lebanon. Both countries possess a more recent community of the pure Antiochian rite, the Syrian Catholics in Lebanon and the Syro-Malankaras in Malabar, and older community long dependent on Rome, the Maronites in Lebanon and the Syro-Malabars in Malabar.

rite, remain under the jurisdiction of the Syro-Malabar Bishop of Kottayam. To meet the wishes of such as belong to this category (Suddists), the S. Oriental Congregation has granted to that prelate the privilege of using the Antiochian rite, when needed, cf. Placid of St. Joseph, op. cit. p. 98.

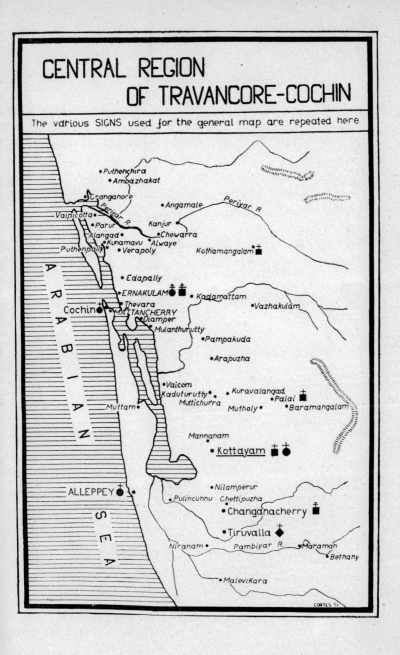

CENTRAL REGION
OF TRAVANCORE-COCHIN

The various SIGNS used for the general map are repeated here.

ARABIAN

SEA

- Puthenchira
- Ambazhakat
- Cranganore
- Periyar R.
- Angamale
- Periyar R.
- Vaipicotta
- Parur
- Kanjur
- Alangad
- Chewarra
- Kunamavu
- Alwaye
- Puthenpally
- Verapoly
- Kothamangalam

- Edapally
- ERNAKULAM
- Kadamattam
- Vazhakulam
- Cochin
- Thevara
- MATTANCHERRY
- Diamper
- Mulanthurutty
- Pampakuda
- Arapuzha

- Vaicom
- Kaduturutty
- Kuravalangad
- Muttichurra
- Palai
- Muttam
- Mutholy
- Baramangalam

- Mannanam
- Kottayam

- ALLEPPEY
- Nilamperur
- Pulincunnu
- Chettipuzha
- Changanacherry
- Tiruvalla
- Niranam
- Pambiyar R.
- Maraman
- Bethany
- Malevikara

CORTES 51

APPENDIX I

CANON LAW AND CUSTOMS OF THE SYRIAN CATHOLICS OF MALABAR

THE official ecclesiastical discipline in India before the coming of the Portuguese was fixed by prelates, who came from Mesopotamia. Therefore it could have been derived only from the discipline prevailing among the Eastern Syrians or Chaldeans. The list of Syriac works condemned at Diamper bears out this assertion. The description of the volume, the title of which reads *De Synodis* (session III, decree 14), allows us to identify it with the treatise of Abdisho of Nisibis, or *Collectio Canonum Synodicorum*. In the course of history it had replaced the previous collection of synods, or *Synodicon Orientale*, and constituted the best juridical collection of the Eastern Syrians.[1] That this work was in use in Malabar is confirmed by the fact that there is a copy extant written by Mar Jacob, when he was detained at Bassein (*Vatic. Syr. 128*), and which he completed on 17 December 1536.

But the Malabar Christians, who were living in a land of ancient civilization with strongly rooted customs, obviously did not follow the same pattern of life as their co-religionists of Mesopotamia. Moreover, since social and religious life in the East are closely interdependent, it was not surprising that popular customs, religious practices, prescriptions of Canon Law, and local, private laws were all interrelated with one another. A fairly large number of half-pagan superstitions had their place in the life of the St. Thomas Christians. Until recently a similar situation existed in some parts of Germany and the Balkans. Some of the condemnations enacted at Diamper give an indication of these Malabar customs. In the ninth session, *De Reformatione Morum*, we find but a few prescriptions of strictly juridical character. The 20th decree stated that a daughter was to receive an equal share of the heritage with the son, while, up to that time according to local custom, only males

[1] J. B. Chabot, 'L'autodafé des livres syriaques du Malabar in *Florilegium...
Melchior de Vogüé*, Paris, 1909, p. 616.

inherited. The 21st and the 22nd decrees restricted the right of adoption, though so far the Christians had been able, like the other Indians, to adopt anybody they wished, even to the prejudice of their own children.

The Christians of Malabar had accepted the caste system, probably right from the beginning, as the tradition of the country tends to prove. This acceptance was all the more strong as the Christians were reckoned among the high castes, on a par with the Nairs. In the eyes of the Brahmins, the Christians were not regarded as 'unclean', on the contrary their presence was sometimes required to purify defiled objects and even temples. The European theologians of the synod would have liked them to do away with customs which, to their unprepared minds, seemed so opposed to the genuine Christian spirit. However they were obliged to appear to be tolerant and to be satisfied with advising them to omit caste distinctions in the Portuguese territories, for no grave consequences could be feared there (decree 2). The purification of vessels, touched by members of low castes, was forbidden (decree 3). They were also forbidden to pierce their ears like the Nairs did (decree 17), and to accept of their own free will the ordeal of the fire, or the crossing of a river swarming with crocodiles (decree 16.) The synod recommended that everyone should adopt the custom of giving away to the church a tenth of the dowry which a young married woman hands over to her husband, (this custom was proper only to some parts of the diocese of Angamale—decree 14.) Was it just a pagan custom that Indians washed frequently? We would doubtless think this an excellent idea in a warm country where water was plentiful. The synod, unaware of the conditions of the land, once more concluded that in India ablutions often had a religious character, and hence such baths were condemned twice (session VIII, decree 13; session IX, decree 1). This last decree also forbade certain other practices of less importance as being superstitious. Nevertheless the practices had no clear connection with any idolatrous cult, for instance, drawing a circle with rice around the young betrothed or around a baby eating rice for the first time.

Yet, up to the present, a good number of these customs are still followed by the Catholics and other Christians of Malabar. Many of them owe their origin to social requirements. They are akin to customs in use among the Namputhiri Brahmins, and are mostly connected with the great events of life. Such customs are to be regarded as part of the discipline of the Malabar Church. It is almost certain that they are very old customs traceable to a time when Christianity was introduced in Malabar and accepted spontaneously without changing the indigenous character of the inhabitants.[1]

The theologians of Diamper, though approving the custom of churching, blamed the women for omitting to attend any service during the forty days (session IX, decree 5). Some would see in this remnants of some Jewish or Semitic customs. Namputhiri women are still now excluded from any attendance at the religious ceremonies at home for a period of equal length. It does not seem quite correct either to see a direct Jewish influence in the fact that the Christians of St. Thomas reckoned the day from evening to evening (session VIII, decree 16). This is still a custom in the Eastern Churches; and the Roman liturgy of today still regards the day as starting after vespers of the previous night.

Whatever were the local customs or the regulations made by the Catholicosate of Seleucia, the Portuguese did not lose time in trying to persuade the Christians of St. Thomas to conform to the discipline of the Latin communities. To allow Christians living in their midst to follow 'strange' usages was not acceptable to the Portuguese, especially to their clergy. Although the missionaries of those days were not wanting in zeal, they lacked the knowledge and personal appreciation of the Eastern Christians in general and of the Syro-Malabar Christians in particular. Hence their insistance on inviting the Metropolitan, Mar Abraham, to the Provincial Synod of Goa. Having refused, and rightly so, to betake himself to the second of those assemblies, in 1575, and though at the instigation of the Jesuits, he had held a diocesan synod in 1583[2] the old prelate was obliged to attend the third Provincial Synod of Goa, and what is more surprising, to sign the Acts of the third session. This

---

[1] L. K. Ananthakrishnan Ayyar, *Anthropology of the Syrian Christians*, Ernakulam, 1926. Many a custom was not discontinued after Diamper, even those connected with the purification of vessels, etc. cf. Placid of St. Joseph T.O.C.D., 'The Social and Socio-Ecclesiastical Customs of the Syrian Christians of India', in *E.C.Q.* 7 (1947), pp. 222-36.

[2] Cf. *supra* p. 44.

section was entirely devoted to his diocese. The wish was expressed that a summary of the disciplinary decrees of the Council of Trent be translated into Malayalam. Its regulations should then be applied to the archdiocese of Angamale as well as to all other suffragan dioceses of Goa. The chief points touched upon in this session were concerned with the clergy, their training and their financial support, and one of their apparently worst defects, usury.[1]

Since 1599, a fateful date and one of the darkest in the history of the relations between Latins and Orientals, the discipline of the Syro-Malabar Church has been fixed at Diamper by Alexis de Menezes and his collaborators. We have already given an account of the synod.[2] In spite of the partial failure of the Portuguese to impose their own views on every point, many decrees of Diamper passed on to posterity as the Canon Law of the Syrians of Malabar; and the Congregation of Propaganda practically acknowledged it to be the special code of the St. Thomas Christians.

The synod was specially concerned with reforming the sacramental rites. Two of the sacraments were out of use in Malabar at that time, Confirmation and Extreme-Unction, although the first of these was probably given by each priest immediately after Baptism. Here again ignorance was running counter to the old Eastern custom which does not reserve Confirmation to the bishop. The chapters of the fourth and seventh sessions dealing with these two sacraments do not as a result contain anything new. They are merely Latin disciplinary regulations. Of course missionaries living among the Eastern Christians of the Near East could have tried to find out if there was any trace of the chrismation in the baptismal rites of the Chaldeans, but it seems that, in 1599, the memory of the Holy Chrism had died out among the Christians of St. Thomas, for the *kattanars* always anointed with palm oil without any blessing at all. Therefore there could be no Confirmation where the matter of the sacrament was wanting. Declaratory or imperative formulas (session IV, *De Sacramento Baptismi*, decree 2) were forbidden during the administration of Baptism. In the eyes of the Portuguese theologians, who knew that in the question of the sacraments one must be *tutiorist*, the Latin formula was the only valid one. Moreover newly-

[1] *Bullarium Patronatus Portugalliae*, Lisbon, 1872, app. I, pp. 73-6.
[2] Cf. *supra* pp. 56-64.

born babies were to be baptized within the first week after birth (decree 5). No exception was made for the children of excommunicated persons. This measure was adopted in order to check local abuses (decree 6). Decree fourteen imposed the use of oil blessed by the bishop for the unctions. The custom of having godparents was insisted on by decree fifteen, and decree sixteen forbade the custom of giving the name of Jesus, *Isho*, at Baptism (also session VIII, decree 20). Those who bore the name, which should be pronounced with some sign of respect, were to change it when they received Confirmation. Menezes intended to administer this sacrament personally to all the Christians during his visit to Malabar. The habit of giving Old Testament names at Baptism was to be avoided; however, the names of those who were definitely regarded as saintly persons could be given. Such a detail shows how little the community of Malabar was influenced from outside, for they were obliged to look up both the Old and the New Testaments for Christian names, having no saints or martyrs of their own.

Most of the regulations of the fifth session, concerning the Holy Eucharist and the Holy Sacrifice of the Mass, will be dealt with in the second appendix. Those priests who had been ordained before they had reached the canonical age prescribed by Trent, were to abstain from celebrating, though they were under obligation to receive communion at least once a month and advised to do so every Sunday (decree 7). In order to render daily Mass easy for all priests, the synod gave permission to have the Latin Mass translated into Syriac, since the usual text of the Syriac liturgy was too long. Latin-knowing priests were allowed to celebrate Mass in Latin, in churches belonging to any diocese other than the archdiocese of Angamale (decree 4). This decision is remarkable in that it allows a sort of 'bi-ritualism', though not in the same place, and proves also that the fathers present at the synod held the view, which was unhappily traditional in the West, that the rite had a local character. The Latin bishops were asked to allow Syrian priests to say Mass in their churches, the Syriac translation of the Latin Mass being well suited for the purpose.[1]

---

[1] Decree 4 on Mass: 'Quia Missa Syriaca nimis videtur prolixa pro sacerdotibus, qui quotidie celebrare voluerint, facultatem concedit synodus, ut missa romana vertatur syriace, petitque a P. Francisco Roz s. j., ut dictam

The synod made attendance at a complete Mass on Sundays obligatory (decree 12) for all, except those who were living too far from their parish church. The latter were to attend Mass at least once a month and on the main feasts (decree 13). Decrees 5 to 11 treat of small practical points in connection with the Mass. The pious wish was expressed that the King of Portugal might provide them all with a sufficient quantity of Muscat wine, since this kind of wine was more easily preserved in India. All clerics in major orders were obliged to recite the Divine Office privately (session VII, *De Sacramento Ordinis*, decree 5). Permission was given to replace the night or the morning Office by the Pater, Ave and Gloria repeated thirty-three times. Moreover the same prayers were to be said nine times for the intentions of the dead, nine times for the Pope and nine times for the bishop.

Yearly confession was made compulsory from eight years of age onwards (session VI, *De Sacramento Paenitentiae*, decree 2). A control was to be exercised. Once the child had reached nine years of age, his Christian duties were to be noted in the *Liber Status Animarum*. All those who had not gone to confession at the required time were to be solemnly declared as excluded from church (decree 1). The canonical age for ordination was fixed (session VII, *De Sacramento Ordinis*, decree 1). Candidates to the priesthood had to be able to read and understand Syriac, just as westerners must know Latin. Young priests were to shave, older priests who grew beards were to trim their moustaches out of respect for the Precious Blood (decree 12).

The marriage discipline was the same as that fixed by the Council of Trent (session VII, *De Sacramento Matrimonii*, decrees 1-16). In the same way, the constitution of the parishes and everything

versionem adornet, quam quidem missam poterunt sacerdotes privatim cum romanis ceremoniis recitare; ceterum missae cum cantu, et solemnes, juxta syriacam, emendatam per Romum metropolitanum, recitentur; sacerdotes vero qui latine et syriace Missam legere noverint, in ecclesiis aliorum epis-copatuum possint eas latine recitare, in iis autem quae sunt hujus episcopatus, syriace tantum, ne confusio oriatur, eas recitabunt. Supplicat itaque synodus dominis episcopis harum partium, ut sacerdotibus huius episcopatus, praesulis sui legitimis demissoriis munitis, si latine legere nesciant, facultatem faciant, vel missam syriacam recitandi, vel romanam in linguam syriacam translatam inque ea romanum ritum servandi. . .' *Bullarium Patronatus*, ibid. p. 241.

connected with the priestly ministry, were regulated by Tridentine practices (session VIII, *De Reformatione Morum Ecclesiasticarum*, decrees 1-41). Noteworthy is the imposition of the Latin calendar and all the fasts of obligation, as well as the changes in fasting and abstinence. The customs of the Latin Church, which prevailed in Portugal, became compulsory, for instance the abstinence on Saturday instead of Wednesday—an introduction absolutely contrary to the legitimate and common use of the Eastern Churches. The truly Chaldean customs became only optional: the fast of the Apostles Peter and Paul, the fast of the Assumption, the fast of Jonas, or of the Ninevites and the fast preceding Our Lady's Nativity (decree 10); abstinence on Wednesday, (decree 15).[1] It is to be noted that this distinction between fast and abstinence is also contrary to the constant tradition of the Eastern Churches.

The penalties decreed upon by the synod show us which were the defects to be most stringently eliminated: complacency towards the idolatrous practices or heresy, simony and negligence in the exercise of the holy ministry. The synod reserved the absolution of certain sins (session VI, *De Sacramento Paenitentiae*, decree 9). There was a list of reserved cases in the tenth decree. The eleventh decree recommended a milder use of excommunication. Yet there were some severe penalties imposed for the purpose of protecting the faith, especially of children. Parents who sent their children to a pagan teacher exacting idolatrous practices from his pupils, were to be excommunicated; and the children were forbidden entry into the church (session III, decree 12). In a similar manner those Catholic masters who might keep in their schools any idolatrous images, whatever they might be, in order that their pagan pupils might venerate them, were to be excommunicated (decree 13). It was prohibited under pain of excommunication to sell a young Christian to a Hindu, a Muslim or a Jew (session IV, *De Sacramento Baptismi*, decree 10). Excommunication *latae sententiae* was launched against all those who would call any soothsayer to their houses for the purpose of making offerings in an idolatrous way

---

[1] Fr. Nau published as a Syro-Latin calendar of Malabar what is actually a list of the obligatory feasts according to the Synod of Diamper, cf. 'Deux notices relatives au Malabar' *R.O.C.* 17 (1912), pp. 85-7.

(session IX, decree 7). Major excommunication was also enacted against priests who pretended to fix auspicious or inauspicious days for marriage (session VII, *De Sacramento Ordinis*, decree 10). Any layman who asked for such information, was excommunicated for one year (ibid. *De Sacramento Matrimonii*, decree 14); and anybody keeping or reading any of the books condemned by the synod or listening to any of them being read, was also subject to the penalty of excommunication (session III, decree 14). With the purpose of protecting the faith, those priests were excommunicated who made a small incision with the finger nail on the consecrated bread, in order to help the penetration of the species of wine at the moment of the intinction; for such practice revealed erroneous conceptions of the Holy Eucharist (session V, *De Sacrificio Missae*, decree 3). Suspension for one year was ordered against those priests who performed superstitious exorcisms, using formulas other than those of the Latin ritual; and there was greater punishment for those who relapsed (session VII, decree 9).

In order to pull up by the roots any abuse in the administration of the sacraments, the synod declared that any priest who accepted the smallest gift after Baptism, even any sort of foodstuff, must be considered as simoniac and punished accordingly, (session IV, *De Sacramento Baptismi*, decree 18). Any priest asking for a compensation, when administering any sacrament, was to be suspended for three years, (session VII, decree 20). There were other penalties, the threats of which ensured a perfect exercise of the sacred ministry, and lighter ones, which perhaps were no less feared, such as cuts in the distributions for those who, through negligence, had not participated in the celebration on the Divine Office (session VII, decree 8); suspension for any priest who, through his own fault, had let one of his parishioners die without confession (session VI, *De Sacramento Paenitentiae*, decree 4); yearly suspension for any priest who blessed a marriage without witnesses, or without being properly deputed by the priest concerned (session VII, *De Sacramento Matrimonii*, decree 1); suspension for six months for any priest who blessed the marriage of persons of less than fourteen and twelve years of age (decree 10); and suspension for the same period for the priest who neglected to renew the Holy Oils within the month following Easter Sunday (session VIII, decree 8).

Other penalties tended to safeguard the honour of the clergy. First — an irregularity important in India — all priests suffering from leprosy must abstain from saying Mass (session VII, *De Sacramento Ordinis*, decree 3); major excommunication for all clerics who married after receiving Holy Orders (ibid. decree 16); excommunication *ferendae sententiae* for any bigamous priest, i.e. who had married a widow or a prostitute before ordination, if they refused to leave their wife (ibid); suspension for four months for those living with a Jew, a Muslim or a Hindu (decree 11); anathema to any priest who enrolled himself as a Nair, since he was liable to be called up for military service (decree 15), anathema to any cleric who did not wear the tonsure (decree 14).

The punishments directly intended to reform the morals of the laity were few: excommunication for those who participated in any game with weapons (*onam*), since they exposed themselves to death without sufficient reason (session IX, decree 4); for those who lent money at an interest higher than ten per cent (decree 9); for those who kept a concubine (decree 11); for those who denied a share of their heritage to their daughters (decree 20); anathema to married people who would separate without the intervention of the ecclesiastical authority (session VII, *De Sacramento Matrimonii*, decree 11).

There was a penalty peculiar to India. The faithful were deprived of the kissing of the hand (*caturte*), a form of greeting by which a priest let his hand be touched, either at the end of a liturgical service, when he went and stood at the entrance of the sanctuary (session VII, *De Sacramento Ordinis*, decree 4), or while visiting the houses. This penalty must be imposed for at least a full year on anyone who would purify a vessel touched by a person of low caste, (session IX, decree 3), or who would take advice from soothsayers (decree 6); for six months on anyone using charms; for two years on anyone who had received absolution from excommunication for having participated in idolatrous offerings (decree 7).

After Diamper the Syrians had a discipline so similar to that of the Latins, that little care seemed to have been taken to draw up special laws for them.

In their statutes published by Mgr. Mellano on 15 March 1879, they were barely mentioned when reference was made to their traditional feast of St. Thomas, on 3 July. In order to renew the

Holy Oils, they were allowed a delay till Pentecost, while the Latins were to use the new Oils from Easter Sunday itself. The latter probably did not have parishes far off in the hilly districts.

At the first Synod of Verapoly the Syrians were just mentioned, when the formation of the clergy was discussed: Syriac and the Syro-Malabar liturgy were to be studied; professors of Syriac were to be chosen and paid by the vicars apostolic of Trichur and Kottayam; they were to reside with the parish-priest of Puthen-pally, and should in no way interfere with the administration of the seminary.[1]

From the time the Syrians received their own prelates, their discipline was given more attention and made a little more precise in some respects. Such were the episcopal regulations published in 1891 by Mgr. Lavigne for the apostolic vicariate of Kottayam. For Changanacherry Mar Matthew Makil did the same in 1903. The regulations of Mar Louis Pareparambil and of the late Archbishop of Ernakulam, Mar Augustine Kandathil, have been promulgated in the official paper of the eparchy, *Ernakulam Missam*.

It is quite clear to any canonist that the promulgation of the Oriental Canon Law by the Pope will speed up a reform of the canonical situation of the Syro-Malabar Church. Already, religious congregations such as the Syrian Carmelites have been obliged to conform to the new law. The diocesan clergy will follow suit, and this reform will greatly help the Syro-Malabar Catholics to recover the true aspect of an Eastern Christianity.

CANON LAW OF THE SYRO-MALANKARA CHURCH

The Jacobite bishops have of course introduced in Malabar the law of the patiarchate of Antioch. It is mainly based on the *Nomocanon* of Bar-Hebraeus. This law was not in force in Malabar before the nineteenth century. Even to-day, certain local characteristics have been preserved, having their origin either in

---

[1] *Acta et decreta concilii provinciae Verapolitanae primi* . . . . . , Ernakulam, 1900, pp. 61, 65, 71.

the old law of the Chaldeans, or in local customs, or even in the legislation imposed by the Portuguese before 1653. Within the last hundred years the courts of Travancore and Cochin have had to interfere several times in the life of the Jacobite community, and their decisions possess, it seems, the force of law.

Since the reunion of Mar Ivanios and the formation of a new Catholic community in Malabar, certain regulations have settled important details. All these sources were utilized in the methodical survey prepared for the commission of the codification of Oriental Canon Law.[1] Recently Rome sent to the Malankara Church some important decisions concerning liturgical matters, for a certain number of practices were introduced which did not in any way fit with the Antiochian rite and its spirit. In this respect, as in many others, such as fasting days of obligations, the Malankara Catholics have been influenced, not always rightly, by their surrounding brethren. Needless to say many of these untimely changes are of Latin origin, and are of the worst type.

Concerning the Jacobites, it is interesting to note that parties—successively the orthodox and the Mar Thomites since 1879, the patriarch's and the metropolitan's since 1910—have brought before the courts of Travancore two different copies of the *Nomocanon*, termed respectively in the juridical texts, 'Exhibit XVIII' and 'Exhibit A'. The latter, belonging now to the metropolitan's party, conforms to the manuscripts word for word. The followers of the patriarch, however, in order to strengthen their position, presented to the courts texts of the *Nomocanan* — those from the so-called 'Exhibit XVIII' — which did not agree on many points with the manuscripts, especially as regards the powers of the patriarch. In consequence of these texts, the patriarch's party declared invalid all the episcopal consecrations performed by Patriarch Abd-ul-Massih after his deposition by the Sultan. Therefore all ordinations made by the bishops of the metropolitan party would be invalid. This shows once more with what liberty and even licence the most solid traditions regarding the power of the bishops to ordain and the

---

[1] Placid of St. Joseph T.O.C.D., *Fontes Juris Canonici Syro-Malankarensium, Fonti*, II, 8-9, Città del Vaticano, 2 vol. 1937-40.

validity of the sacraments were treated.[1] The bishops of the metropolitan's party published in 1934 in Malayalam their 'Constitution of the Orthodox Syrian Church of Malankara'.[2]

[1] Ibid. pp. 67, ff.
[2] Ibid. pp. 321-39, with the full Latin translation.

APPENDIX II

THE LITURGY OF THE SYRIAN CATHOLICS
OF MALABAR

PRACTICE BEFORE THE PORTUGUESE

Up to the arrival of the Portuguese and for some time after, the Syrians of Malabar had followed the liturgy of the Eastern Syrians of Mesopotamia. Unhappily no manuscripts dating before the sixteenth century have been preserved. Only a few belonging to that century, brought to Rome by Mar Joseph, are still extant. They comprise in all: one pontifical, copied in 1556; a collection of hymns for feast days; a ritual; a book with the ordinary office of the week; the *Kaskul*, a prayer book for monks.[1]

EARLY LATINIZATION

The Portuguese did not tolerate for very long the fact that the Christians of their empire of the Indies followed usages different from their own. Several points shocked them: the use of leavened bread, the shape of the liturgical vestments, the calendar of the feasts and fast-days, the ceremonies of the sacraments. Even before the middle of the sixteenth century, they had launched a wholesale campaign for Latinization. Mar Jacob, one of the bishops sent in 1503, had been already compelled in 1523, to protest against the priests grouped around Alvaro Penteado, who pretended to rebaptize the Christians of St. Thomas, under the pretext that the method used by the bishop was not the right one. Poor Mar Jacob! He ought to have been spared so many ordeals, because of the very efficacious help he had given the Portuguese by advising his flock to bring their pepper straight to the 'Firanguis', without passing through Muslim middlemen.[2] The general tendency, voiced by

---

[1] *B.V. Vatic. Syr. 45, 46, 62, 65, 85, 88.*

[2] G. Schurhammer, *The Malabar Church and Rome*, Trichinopoly, 1934, pp. 15-20. As early as 1518, Penteado wrote that the St. Thomas Christians were to be forced into Roman ways, ibid. p. 20. The documents quoted by

Penteado, soon swept away the opposition of Mar Jacob. When St. Francis Xavier got to know him in 1549, he was able to write of him that 'he was very obedient to the customs of our Holy Mother the Church of Rome'.[1] Does it mean that the old bishop had entirely gone over to the Latin liturgy? This does not look probable, but externals may have been imposed on the Syrians, such as vestments, a few ceremonies and perhaps the ritual.

A typical case is that of Mar Joseph, the brother of the saintly martyr Sulaqa. He was kept with Mar Elias for nearly two years at the Franciscan monastery of Bassein and forced to celebrate Mass in Latin.[2] Later, on his return from Rome, he submitted to the use of unleavened bread and Latin liturgical vestments.[3] The faithful, often more attached than the ecclesiastical leaders to their traditional ways, resisted such a compromise. Writing in 1604, Bishop Francis Roz gave an account of how a part of the population of Cranganore had fled to the hills, the Ghats, in order to escape the Latin missionaries who compelled them to eat fish on fast-days contrary to their discipline, forbade them to begin Lent before Ash-Wednesday, and prevented the *kattanars* from using leavened bread at Mass.[4] Those good missionaries would have spent their time more usefully extending the Kingdom of God!

It appeared that Mar Abraham was not very much in favour of these Latinizing measures. As far as lay within his power he tried to get away from the control of the Portuguese hierarchy. Perhaps he was encouraged secretly by some of the Jesuits of Vaipicotta, who resented interference, and who followed a more liberal policy in the question of rite. Was this broad-mindedness due to a better training, and to their contact and acquaintance with the various Eastern communities of the Near East? They had in India, at the time, one Maronite confrère, the Venerable Abraham George.[5]

Fr. Schurhammer were again published by A. da Silva Rego, *Documentaçâo para a Historia das Missôes do Padroado Portugu**ês** do Oriente, India*, Lisbon, 1947, ff. vol. II, pp. 352-6, 357-60; vol. III, pp. 543-53; vol. IV, pp. 477-81.

[1] St. Francis Xavier to King John III, Cochin, 26 January 1549, in *Epistolae S. Francisci Xaverii...*, Rome, 1945, vol. II, p. 62.

[2] Cf. *supra* p. 37.

[3] Cf. *supra* p. 40.

[4] G. Schurhammer, op. cit. p. 22.

[5] Cf. *supra* p. 46.

However, the Archbishop of Angamale could not resist going to Goa in order to be present at the third provincial synod held there in 1585. Mar Abraham was obliged to subscribe to the decisions taken during the third session which concerned the Christians of St. Thomas only. There, without having any power to do so and contrary to all prudence, the synod decided that the Latin liturgical books, breviary, missal, pontifical and ritual, be translated into Syriac (session III, decree 7).[1] It is probable that the Jesuits of Vaipicotta worked at these translations and that Abraham George was the man entrusted with this work. At any rate they started with the ritual, as they were anxious about the validity of the sacraments administered by the *kattanars*. At the time of the Synod of Diamper, the liturgical customs of the Syrians were still almost entirely the same as those of the Church of Mesopotamia. Yet a Syriac translation of the Roman ritual according to the use of Braga in Portugal must have existed at that time, since Alexis de Menezes was able during the final ceremony of the synod to hand a copy of that book to each priest appointed to a parish church. The seminarists of Vaipicotta had prepared the required copies.[2]

DIAMPER'S WORK

The liturgical prescriptions of the synod are numerous, but all of them bear witness to a tendency towards Latinization. The opposition to the Latinizing influence was rather strong, and the *kattanars* succeeded in saving the greater part of their traditional prayers, despite the endeavours of the European members of the synod to achieve complete uniformity, even in language. The regulations bearing on the sacraments have been mentioned above.

The prayers of the sacred liturgy were sifted in the course of the fifth session. This work had no other purpose than doing away with Nestorian expressions. The corrections comprised some twenty passages. For instance, the names of Nestorius, Diodorus and Theodore were removed, *Mater Dei* was substitued for *Mater Christi*. The Pope's name was to be commemorated. Several expressions were to be altered, viz. at the end of the consecration of the chalice,

---

[1] *Bullarium Patronatus Portugalliae*, Lisbon, 1873, app. I, p. 75.
[2] Cf. *supra* p. 64.

the words 'and this is a pledge *in saecula saeculorum*' were replaced by 'and this a pledge *usque ad consummationem saeculorum*', since there will be no further reason for the Eucharist after the end of the world. A rather scrupulous correction! The synod was desirous of making the Syro-Malabar liturgy as similar as possible to the Roman Mass—for instance, genuflections with one knee, a purely western practice of feudal origin, and absolutely unknown to the rite of Chaldea, were imposed. The sprinkling of Holy Water before Mass on Sunday was introduced during the eighth session (decree 17), the Latin formula for the blessing of the water being translated into Syriac. The twenty-first decree brought in a novel custom, that had its origin in local usages of the Roman rite, viz. the three Masses on Christmas. Certain ceremonies, also new in the Syro-Malabar Church, were added, those of Ash-Wednesday (decree 14), of Candlemas and the Rogation days (decree 23). The whole of the liturgical calendar was made to conform to the Latin one. Yet the principal feast of St. Thomas was kept on 3 July and the feast of the perspiration of the blood on the cross of Mylapore on 18 December (decree 9).[1]

When the account of the visitation of Archbishop Alexis de Menezes was published in Europe, a Latin translation of the corrected liturgy was printed, without pagination, as appendix to the text of the synod.[2] This translation was used by Pierre Le Brun

[1] The phrase 'hoc erit nobis pignus in saecula saeculorum' is no more used in the Syro-Malabar liturgy. The correction 'usque ad consummationem saeculorum', which is found in the official versions of the synod, is not mentioned in a Portuguese text preserved in the Roman Jesuit Archives, *Fondo Gesuitico, Missioni di Malabar*. This manuscript of the acts of the synod contains occasional omissions and additions, but as far as the decree 1 of *Actio V* relating to the Mass is concerned, there are many omissions and quite a few changes. Perhaps such divergences might be attributed to the hand of Bishop Roz himself. Decree 1 was published as *Documentum XVI* by Fr. G. M. Antão, *De Synodi Diamperitanae Natura atque Decretis*, Goa, 1952, pp. 166-70. As regards the calendar of the Syro-Malabar Church, cf. N. Nilles, 'Das syrochaldaische Kirchenjahr der Thomaschristen', in *Z.K.T.* 20 (1896), pp. 726-39; *Kalendarium manuale utriusque Ecclesiae orientalis et occidentalis*, Innsbruck, 1897, 2nd. ed., vol. II, pp. 647-76.

[2] Under the title, *Missa de que usamos antigos christianos di São Thome... purgada dos erros, et blasphemias nestorianas ... trasladade de siriaco, ou suriano de verbo ad verbum em lingua latina*, Coïmbra, 1606, 9 folios.

when comparing the liturgy of the Christians of St. Thomas with that of the Chaldeans of Mesopotamia which he knew from the Latin edition of E. Renaudot.[1] The two texts are less dissimilar than appears at first sight from their juxtaposition, because Renaudot did not reproduce several parts in full, and practically omitted the parts reserved to the deacon.[2]

VICISSITUDES OF THE SYRO-MALABAR MISSAL

For a long time only manuscript missals were available in Malabar. This evidently caused several inconveniences. The Vicar Apostolic of Verapoly, Mgr. Nicholas Szostak o.c.d., made Propaganda

---

[1] E. Renaudot, *Liturgiarum orientalium collectio*, Paris, 1716, vol. II, pp. 587-97; P. Le Brun, *Explication de la Messe*, Paris, 1726, vol. III, pp. 468-538. The latter's text was reproduced with additional notes in *Subsidium ad Bullarium patronatus Portugalliae*, Allepey, 1903, pp. 17-50.

[2] R. H. Connolly o.s.b., 'The Work of Menezes on the Malabar Liturgy', in *J.T.S.* 15 (1914), pp. 396-425, 569-89 (with an additional note of Edmund Bishop, pp. 589-93), compares very minutely the text of the Syro-Malabar liturgy, found in the translation published by Gouvea, with the so-called Liturgy of Addai & Mari, known through the text printed at Urmiah and the translations of Renaudot, Badger and Brightmann, *Liturgies Eastern and Western*, Oxford, 1896, vol. I, pp. 252-305. After having proved the substantial identity of both texts, Fr. Connolly goes on to analyze the nature of each correction, particularly the corrections made in the narration of the institution; the only passages, in which the influence of the Latin liturgy is felt are the creed, the words of the consecration, and a formula recited by the congregation, wherein some words, borrowed from the *Te igitur*, are inserted. It seems that the writer ignores the work of Le Brun, which he does not mention. J. M. Hanssens s. J., *Institutiones Liturgicae de Ritibus Orientalium*, Rome, 1930, vol. II, pp. 389-93, 502-6, compares also the Chaldean and Syro-Malabar liturgies, and gives some details concerning the history of the Syro-Malabar liturgy and the preparation of the Roman edition of 1775. Connolly and Hanssens mention, without having seen it, the work published at Brussels in 1609 by the Augustinian Friar, J. B. de Glen, *La messe des anciens chrétiens de Saint-Thomas, en l'évêché d'Angamalé, ès Indes orientales, repurgée des erreurs et blasphèmes du nestorianisme, par... Don Alexis de Meneses... y prémise une remonstrance catholique aux peuples du Pays-Bas, des fruits et utilités de la précédente histoire et de la messe subséquente,* 6 folios and 123 pages. Gouvea's Latin translation is reproduced pp. 81-123. The rest of the volume consists of an anti-Protestant controversy, in which the testimony of the St. Thomas Christians is occasionally adduced, viz. the existence among them of the Sacrifice of the Mass, of the cult of the Saints, of the use of bells, of the sign of the cross, etc.

aware of the difficulties through Fr. Ignatius of St. Hippolytus, who left for Rome during the year 1754. After a report (*votum*) made by the renowned Joseph Simon Assemani on 2 July 1757, it was decided on 17 July, in a plenary session of the *Congregatio super correctione librorum ecclestiasticorum Ecclesiae Orientalis*, that the required publication would be started. The vicar apostolic was notified of the resolution in an instruction of 3 September, in which he was asked to forward a text that corresponded to the one agreed upon at Diamper, together with a Latin translation.[1] The question was again taken up in the plenary session of 1 June 1766. Most of the cardinals were in favour of giving the Christians of St. Thomas the same missal as that of the Chaldeans of Mesopotamia. However, as it was remarked in the session, the calendars, as well as the system of scriptural pericopes, were both different. So they decided to send to Malabar a copy of the big volume which was, at that time, just being issued from the press.[2] But the Syro-Malabar Christians would not be satisfied with such a missal, for it included at the bottom of the pages an Arabic translation in Syriac characters, for which they had no use. Hence they insisted on having the manuscript which Fr. Charles of St. Conrard had brought to Rome. After some hesitation, arising from the fact that this manuscript was not identical with the one presented by Fr. Ignatius of St. Hippolytus,[3] a definite conclusion was finally arrived at during the plenary session of the Congregation on 11 May 1774. The edition of the Liturgy of the Apostles appeared in the same year, a volume in quarto of sixty pages; the lessons borrowed from the Roman missal, together with some ceremonies peculiar to certain feasts, translated from the Latin, were published the following year in the shape of a book of 862 pages of the same size. A reprint was brought out in 1844 by Propaganda under the title *Ordo Chaldaicus rituum et lectionum juxta morem Ecclesiae Malabaricae*. The Liturgy of the Apostles, or *Ordo Missae*, some sixty pages in its first edition, is usually inserted after page 440 of the *proprium*, and before the index and the corrections; it runs from page 441 to 462. Other editions came out in India, one at

[1] 'Hierarchia Carmelitana...', in *A.O.C.D.* 13 (1938), p. 37.

[2] *Missale Chaldaicum ex decreto S. C. de Propaganda Fide editum*, Rome, 1767, pp. 614 quarto.

[3] *Subsidium ad Bullarium...*, pp. 56, ff.

Mannanam in 1928, and four at Puthenpally between the years 1904 and 1931.[1]

PRESENT SITUATION

The liturgy of the Mass, or Qurbana, is celebrated in Malabar with more or less solemnity; even at Low Mass incense is used. Nowadays various degrees of solemnity can be distinguished: Low Mass, Sung Mass, Solemn Mass, very Solemn Mass. The latter is called *Raza*, more accurately *Raze*, which is merely the Syriac name for the (Holy) 'Mysteries'; together with the Sung Mass (one priest singing), this is the traditional form which is still preserved. It is the one the people were accustomed to see on important feasts, with deacons and sub-deacons and one or two assisting priests in copes (originally there were probably two deacons and two co-celebrants). The cope of the assistant priests looks Latin. It is more likely a survival of ancient times, for the cope of the Latin rite is the vestment that resembles most the Eastern chasuble or phelonion, cut as it was by the Chaldeans. The *Raza* — and this is an important point — is most commonly celebrated for the dead, but it exists under the form of a very Solemn Mass for the living. Both forms closely follow the rubrics and the order of prayers of the Chaldeans Mass as used nowadays in Mesopotamia. The pontifical Mass of the Syro-Malabar rite is a strange and altogether hybrid adaptation of the Latin rubrics to the Syrian Anaphora. On rare occasions the bishops use the pontifical *Raza* which is clearly the only form of pontifical Eucharist adapted to the rite.

The rubrics of the celebration of the 'Mysteries' (*Raza*) with a few special prayers is to be found in the missal of Puthenpally, 1929, after the Liturgy of the Apostles, pages 52-3. The full rite

[1] In the edition of Puthenpally, the Liturgy of the Apostles is inserted with a special pagination between the *Proprium Temporis* and the *Proprium Sanctorum*, pp. 1-62, and between pages 242 and 243 of the general pagination of the edition of 1929, and in the edition of Mannanam, pp. 1-64, between pages 304 and 305 of the general pagination. After the *Ordo Missae* itself, special hymns, the additions for the *Raza*, and the part of the deacon are generally given.

was printed at Mannanam in 1925 in the form of a booklet of 106 pages, in 16mo.[1]

Mar Louis Pareparambil published at Puthenpally in 1912, a book entitled *Sacrum Apostolorum Ordo Missae Syro-Chaldaeo-Malabaricae cum Translatione Latina*. The translation, though not independent of the one of 1606, is yet more literal and complete. To make them more intelligible, the rubrics are more fully described in the translation, and care is taken to indicate the differences between the Low and the Sung Mass. Since the traditional rubrics, as canonized by their insertion in the missal of 1774, were inadequate, Propaganda, duly warned in 1859, authorized Fr. Cyriac-Elias Chavara to publish at Kunamavu in 1868 a book entitled *Tukasa*. This book was reprinted at Mannanam in 1926, and in the year following its prescriptions were made compulsory for the four Syro-Malabar eparchies.

The special ceremonies of Candlemass, Ash-Wednesday and Palm Sunday were translated from the Latin. The morning service on Good Friday with the Mass of the Presanctified Gifts is a mixed composition with Eastern elements and others translated from the Latin. Holy Saturday possessed until recently no special liturgy, though in some churches the Latin ceremony is gone through with the help of a translation that was made by Fr. Cyriac-Elias Chavara with the permission of Propaganda. This translation is not to be found in the missal of Puthenpally, 1929, though this missal includes the pericopes for such Latin feasts as St. Teresa of the Child Jesus and Christ the King. The translation of the Latin service of Holy Saturday was printed separately at Mannanam in 1933.

Since the Holy Week has been recently fully restored in the Latin Church, one wonders how the Syro-Malabar liturgy could still adhere to bygone practices. It would be best of course to adopt the ceremonies of the Holy Week as performed by the Chaldeans.

---

[1] English translation by A. Kalapura, *An English Version of Rasa, or the Syriac Pontifical High Mass*, Verapoly, 1924, pp. 148, 16mo, with pages 131-48 containing devotional prayers. Fr. Fabian T.O.C.D., published a better translation of the *Raza* with liturgical and historical notes under the title *The Liturgy of the St. Thomas Christians or the Raza of the Syro-Malabar Rite*, Mannanam, 1954, pp. 205, 18mo.

PONTIFICAL, RITUAL AND OFFICE

The Roman pontifical was never translated. Since 1896, the bishops have been using the Latin text, either for the blessing of the Holy Oils or for the ordinations. When administering the Sacrament of Confirmation, they pronounce the formula in Syriac.

The ritual, as mentioned above, was translated from the Latin into Syriac before the end of the sixteenth century. Yet it was not the pure Roman ritual that was borrowed, as it was not published before 1594, but the ritual as used in Portugal, in the archdiocese of Braga. The first edition in quarto and consisting of 91 pages was printed in Rome in 1775. A second edition, a small one in octavo and numbering 196 pages, was published in Rome in 1845, under the title *Ordo Chaldaicus Ministerii Sacramentorum Sanctorum quae perficiuntur a sacerdotibus juxta morem Ecclesiae Malabaricae*. In these editions the several Baptisms are distinguished between in order to suit the convenience of the priest: Baptism of a boy, that of a girl, and of many children together. Next there follow the ceremonies of marriage, the formula of absolution, the prayers of Extreme-Unction and helping the dying, the psalms of penance and the litany of All Saints. The volume contains also some blessings—water, places, candles, Easter eggs, new fruits, bread, any food, image or statue, and new cross. It concludes with the rites for the reconciliation of a desecrated church. Since this ritual does not contain the ceremonies for the Baptism of adults, Propaganda had them translated and printed separately: *Ordo Baptismi Adultorum juxta Ritum Ecclesiae Malabaricae Chaldaeorum*, Rome, 1869, 44 pages of small print, in octavo. But this rite is not in use, and it was not reprinted in the edition of Puthenpally, 1928. The Syro-Malabar ritual has a peculiar characteristic in the administration of the Sacrament of Marriage: the priest blesses a small golden cross in place of a ring, which the bridegroom passes round the neck of his wife. The manuscript *Borgianus Latinus 155* in the Vatican Library, which belonged to the personal library of Cardinal Stephen Borgia, has the Latin translation of the Syro-Malabar ritual, made very likely when the Propaganda issued the edition of the ritual. Till very recently the blessing of the couple, which is given after the *Pater Noster*, was given by the Syro-Malabar priest immediately at the end of the sacramental rite, and not during Mass. There is no rubric to indicate when this formula is to be pronounced.

The rite for funerals and the various offices for the dead are all found in a special book printed at Mannanam in 1882, and again in 1921 and 1929. In general the old Chaldean form has been kept, but they still have traces of the Latin influence. For instance the prayers for the burial of children are translated from the Latin.

The breviary of the Syrians is incomplete. It consists of a ferial office following the tradition of the Eastern Syrians, and of the offices of some feasts, of which some parts are borrowed from the Latin. Fr. Cyriac-Elias Chavara worked to bring out an abridged edition of the office to facilitate its use. However, there is no agreement between the breviary and the sacred liturgy. The calendar of the missal is entirely at odds with that of the breviary which follows more or less the Chaldean liturgical year. In the missal the liturgy has been adjusted to the Latin calendar by a crude adoption of the pericopes of the Roman system. There are five editions of the ferial office, those of Kunamavu in 1871 and 1886, those of Mannanam in 1913 and 1932, and that of Puthenpally in 1917.

The Syro-Malabar clergy are also allowed the use of other different manuals, viz. the *Tulmada or Schola Discipulorum Ecclesiasticorum*, published at Puthenpally in 1904 by Andrew Kalapura. In them can be found prayers for some special ceremonies (Ash-Wednesday, Palm Sunday, the services of Maundy Thursday and Good Friday) the ordinary of the liturgy, the thanksgiving after the Mass, the Epistles and Gospels of the Mass.

THE SYRO-MALANKARA LITURGY

Generally speaking, the Jacobites of Malabar follow rather faithfully the pure Syrian rite of Antioch.[1] As it has been suggested

---

[1] Under a rather misleading title, the work of G. B. Howard actually deals with the Jacobite liturgy as practised in Malabar, *The Christians of St. Thomas and their Liturgies comprising the Anaphoras of St. James, St. Peter, the Twelve Apostles, Mar Dionysius, Mar Xystus, and Mar Evannis, together with the Ordo Communis, translated from Syriac Manuscripts obtained in Travancore*, Oxford and London, 1864.

previously, the Jacobite liturgical practices were introduced in their entirety not very long ago, during the first decades of the nineteenth century. Before that time the dissidents, followers of the Mar Thomases, were satisfied with the old and highly Latinized Chaldean liturgy, but they used leavened bread, hand-cross and other Jacobite externals. In the Jacobite manuscripts of the eighteenth century there can be found occasionally texts of the Antiochian rite, viz. the Anaphora of St. James, the baptismal service attributed to Bar-Hebraeus, etc.

Under Protestant influence a great deal of the liturgy is now celebrated in the vernacular, Malayalam. The Mar Thomites have altogether forsaken the use of Syriac.

In the liturgical editions of the Jacobites and later on of the Malankara Catholics, the Western Syriac text is used together with a translation into Malayalam. Till recently, most of these translations were left to the goodwill and the skill of the celebrating priest. Hence many inaccuracies crept in; but nowadays both Jacobites and Malankara Catholics, above all the latter, have books which possess a standard translation.

Since the foundation of a printing-press at the Jacobite centre of Pampakuda, many editions of various liturgical books have been printed, starting with the Book of Anaphoras. Five of these were published in 1886 and sixteen in 1931.[1] Besides this they have published many editions of various services, such as the three fast-days of the Ninivites (1933, 50 pages), the first five days of Lent (1932, 106 pages), the Holy Week (1931, 292 pages), and the various ceremonies of the year such as the blessing of the water on Epiphany day (1952). All the books listed on the next page are published by the Jacobites through the same press:

---

[1] The edition of 1886 has: Anaphoras of Mar James, Mar Dionysios Bar Slibi, Mar Matthew, Mar Eustathios, Mar Julios. The edition of 1931 contains the Anaphoras of Mar James, Mar Dionysios Bar Slibi, Mar John (of Harran, under the name of Chrysostomos, Iwannis), Mar John the Divine (Yuhannan), Mar Matthew, Mar Eustathios, Mar Julios, Mar Xystos, Mar Peter, the Twelve Apostles, Mar Abraham, Mar Lazaros, Mar Peter (Kallinikos), Patriarch of Antioch, Mar Ignatios of Antioch, Mar Marcos the Evangelist, Mar Thomas of Harkel, cf. *Anaphorae Syriacae quotquot in codicibus adhuc repertae sunt, cura Pontificii Instituti Studiorum Orientalium editae et latine versae*, Rome, 1939, vol. I, p. 46 of introduction.

1. Ritual of the Sacraments, without the Extreme-Unction, 1936.

2. Ritual of Extreme-Unction (the Service of the Lamps), 1907 and 1932.

3. Ritual of the Funeral of a Priest, 1905 and 1938.

4. Ritual of the Funeral of Lay People, 1880.

5. *Shim*, or the Ordinary Office for the week, last edition 1951.

So far the Syro-Malankara Catholics have published the following books:

1. A missal printed at Pampakuda in 1934, containing two Anaphoras, the very short one of Mar Xystos and the one of Mar James, and other common ceremonies connected with the Mass or Qurbono.

2. A missal printed at Tiruvalla in 1949, which has only the Anaphora of Mar Xystos, with the ordinary of the Mass, five common Gospels and eight supplementary *Prumion-Sedre*. This edition also possesses a standard translation in Malayalam.

3. A prayer book in Malayalam for the deacon and Mass server, in 1937 at Tiruvalla, where there exists now a printing press sufficiently equipped to print liturgical texts in Syriac and in Malayalam.

4. The *Shim*, or the Ordinary Office, 1943.

5. Three books of rubrics in Malayalam, 1941-3 and the Divine Office for the laity in the same language, 1947.

6. A translation in Malayalam of the consecration of the bishops made to agree with the newly published pontifical of the Antiochian rite, 1953.

APPENDIX III

LISTS OF BISHOPS IN MALABAR AND OF EASTERN PATRIARCHS

(a) CHALDEAN METROPOLITANS AND BISHOPS TILL 1597

The list is based on eastern sources and on local ones. The names in italics can be considered as historically reliable.

Mar Joseph of Edessa, *c.* 345?

Mar Thomas, c. 795-824

Mar Sabrisho,
Mar Peroz, } *c.* 880

Mar John, *c.* 1000

Mar Thomas, *c.* 1056

Mar John, *c.* 1110?

Mar John, *c.* 1122-9

Mar Joseph, 1231

Mar David, *c.* 1285

Mar Paulos, *c.* 1295

Mar Jacob, c. 1328

Mar Yahballaha, *c.* 1407

Mar Thomas,
Mar John, } 1490

Mar Yahballaha,
Mar Denha, } 1503

Mar Jacob, 1503-49?

Mar Joseph, 1556-69

Mar Abraham, 1568-97

(b) ARCHBISHOPS OF CRANGANORE

The list is based on Paulinus a S. Bartholomeo, *India Orientalis Christiana*, Rome, 1794, C. C. de Nazareth, *Mitras Lusitanas no Oriente*, Nova Goa, 1924, v. II, pp. 36-67, D. Ferroli s. J., *The Jesuits in Malabar*, Bangalore, 1939 & 1951 2 vol., and other authorities.

Francis Roz s. J., 1600-24

Stephen de Brito s. J., 1624-41

Francis Garzia Mendez s.J., 1641-59

After Archbishop Garzia's death, the see remained vacant, and was administered by 'governors' without episcopal character till:

James de Annunciaçiâo Justiniano, 1694-1701, who never reached India.

John Ribeiro s. J., 1701-16

Manuel Carvalho Pimentel s.J., 1721-52

John Louis Vasconcellos s.j., 1753-8

Salvador dos Reis s. j., 1753-8

Joseph Cariati, a Syro-Malabar, 1782-6, who did not occupy the see.

Joseph Caetano da Silva Coutino, 1800, who did not reach India.

Paul da S. Thomé d'Aquina e Almeida o. p., 1819-23

Joseph Joachim da Immaculada Conceiçâo Amarante o.p., 1825, who did not occupy the see.

Manuel de S. Joaquim Neves o.p., 1845-8

(By the concordat of 1886, the Cranganore jurisdiction, as a Padroado dependency, was definitely suppressed, but the title *ad honorem* was successively attributed to the Bishop of Damao, and finally to the Archbishop of Goa.)

(c) VICARS APOSTOLIC OF MALABAR AND OF VERAPOLY, AND ARCHBISHOPS OF VERAPOLY

The list is based on 'Hierarchia Carmelitana', IV, *A.O.C.D.* 11 (1936), pp. 188-98, and the works, already mentioned. We have also consulted the series of *The Madras Catholic Directory*, 1883-1911, and *The Catholic Directory of India*, 1912-54

Joseph of St. Mary Sebastiani o.c.d., 1656-63

Mar Alexander Parambil, 1663-87

Raphael de Figueredo Salgado, 1677-94, d. 1695

Custodio da Pinho, 1694-96

Angelus Francis of St. Teresa, o.c.d., 1700-12

John Baptist of St. Teresa, o.c.d., 1714-50

(Innocent of St. Leopold o.c.d., coadjutor, 1734-5)

Florentius of Jesus Nazareth o.c.d., 1750-73

Francis of Sales of Our Lady of Dolours o.c.d., 1774-80, d. 1787

John Mary of St. Thomas o.c.d., 1780-1, who died before reaching Malabar.

Aloysius Mary of Jesus o.c.d., 1784-1802

Raymond of St. Joseph o.c.d., 1803-16

Miles Prendergast o.c., 1819-31, d. 1844

Francis Xavier of St. Anne Pescetto o.c.d., 1831-44

Louis of St. Teresa Martini o.c.d., 1844-53, d. 1859

Bernardino of St. Teresa Baccinelli o.c.d., 1853-68

Leonard of St. Luis Mellano O.C.D., 1868-97, who became Archbishop of Verapoly in 1886.

Bernard of Jesus O.C.D., 1897-1919

Angel Mary Perez Cecilia O.C.D., 1919-35

Joseph Attipetty, first Indian Prelate, 1934-

(d) INDIAN PRELATES OF THE CATHOLIC SYRIANS

1. *Syro-Malabar Rite*

ERNAKULAM ARCHDIOCESE

Mar Aloysius Pareparambil, Vicar Apostolic, 1896-1919

Mar Augustine Kandathil, coadjutor, 1911-19, who became Archbishop of Ernakulam in 1923 until 1956.

Mar Joseph Parecattil, 1956-

CHANGANACHERRY

Charles Lavigne S. J., 1891-6

Mar Mathew Makil, 1896-1911

Mar Thomas Kurialacherry, 1911-27, who became residential Bishop in 1923.

Mar James Kalacherry, 1927-49

Mar Mathew Kavukatt, 1950-

TRICHUR

Adolphe E. Medlycott, 1887-96

Mar John Menacherry, 1896-1919

Mar Francis Vazhapilly, 1921-44, who became residential Bishop in 1923

Mar George Alapatt, 1944-

KOTTAYAM

Charles Lavigne S. J., 1887-96

Mar Mathew Makil, 1896-1911, then transferred to the newly erected see of Kottayam, 1911-4

Mar Alexander Chulaparambil, 1914-51, who became residential Bishop in 1923.

Mar Thomas Tharayil, coadjutor, 1945-51, residential Bishop in 1951.

14

PALAI

Mar Sebastian Vayalil, 1950-

TELLICHERRY

Sebastian Vallopilly, Administrator Apostolic, 1954-5, Bishop 1955-

2. *Syro-Malankara Rite*

TRIVANDRUM ARCHDIOCESE

George Mar Ivanios, 1932-53

Benedict Mar Gregorios, Administrator Apostolic, 1953-5, Archbishop, 1955-

TIRUVALLA

James Mar Theophilos, 1932-50, who ceased administering the diocese from 1938 onwards.

Joseph Mar Severios, who became Administrator Apostolic in 1938, residential Bishop in 1950, and Archbishop *ad personam* in 1954. Died in 1955.

Zacharias Mar Athanasios, 1955-

(e) BISHOPS OF COCHIN

List based on the works of Nazareth, Ferroli, etc.

George Themudo O.P., 1558-67
Henry de S. Jeronymo de Tavora e Brito O.P., 1567-9
Mathew de Medina, of the Order of Christ, 1578-88
Andrew de S. Maria O.S.F., 1588-1610
Sebastian de S. Pedro, O.P., 1614-24
Louis de Brito e Menezes O.P, 1628-9
Michael da Cruz Rangel O.P., 1633(34)-46

During the following vacancy, the diocese was administered by 'governors'.

Anthony de S. Dionisio O.P., 1676-83
Peter da Silva, 1688-93
Peter Pacheco O.P., 1693-1714
Francis de Vasconcellos S. J., 1721-42
Clement Joseph Colaço Leitâo S. J., 1745-75

Manuel de S. Catharina O.C.D., 1779-84
Joseph de Soledade O.C.D., 1784-99
Thomas de Noronha e Brito O.P., 1816-22
Paul de S. Thomé d'Aquino e Almeida, 1822-3, as Archbishop
of Cranganore, and governor of the diocese.
Until 1886, the diocese was administered by 'governors'
John Gomes Fereira, 1886-96
Mathew d'Oliveira Xavier, 1897-1908
Joseph Bento Martin Ribeiro, 1909-33
Abilio August Vaz das Neves, 1934-9
Joseph Vieira Alvernaz, 1942-50, who was the last prelate of the
Padroado
Alexander Edezath, 1952- , who is the first Indian prelate.

(f) DISSIDENT PRELATES OF MALABAR

The following lists are based on Placid of St. Joseph T.O.C.D., *De Fontibus Iuris Ecclesiastici Syro-Malankarensium*, Città del Vaticano, 1937-40, G. T. Mackenzie, *Christianity in Travancore*, Trivandrum, 1901, pp. 77-8, and other authorities mentioned in chapter VII.

1. *Jacobite Prelates*

Mar Thomas I (a priest), 1652-73
Mar Gregorios (a Syrian Bishop), 1665-72
Mar Thomas, (a priest), 1674
Mar Thomas II (a layman), 1676-86
Mar Basilios (a Syrian Bishop), 1685
Mar John (id.), 1685-93
Mar Thomas III (a layman), 1686-8
Mar Thomas IV (id.), 1686-1725
Mar Thomas V (id.), 1725-65
Mar Basilios (a Syrian Bishop), 1751-63
Mar Gregorios (id.), 1751-72
Mar Ivanios (id.), 1751-94
Mar Thomas VI, 1765-1808, who was consecrated bishop in 1772,
and took the title of Mar Dionyisos I
Mar Thomas VII, 1796-1809
Mar Thomas VIII, 1809-15

Mar Dionysios II, 1815-6

Mar Dionysios III, 1818-25

Mar Dionysios IV, 1825-46 (d.1853)

Matthew Mar Athanasios, 1843-75

Mar Dionysios V, 1865-1909, who assumed the title of Metropolitan of Malankara in 1876.

Mar Dionysios VI, 1908-34

PATRIACH'S PARTY	CATHOLICS' PARTY
Mar Kurillos, 1909-19	Mar Basilios I, 1912-3
Paulos Mar Athanasios, 1919-53	Mar Basilios II, 1925-9
Michael Mar Dionysios, 1954-	Mar Basilios III, 1929-

2. *Prelates of Tozhiur Church*

Mar Kurillos I, 1771

Mar Kurillos II

Mar Philoxenos I

Mar Philoxenos II

Joseph Mar Kurillos III

Joseph Mar Athanasios I

George Mar Kurillos IV

Mar Kurillos V

3. *Mar Thomite Metropolitans*

Mathew Mar Athanasios I, 1842-77

Thomas Mar Athanasios II, 1842-77

Titus Mar Thomas I, 1894-1910

Titus Mar Thomas II, 1910-44

Abraham Mar Thomas III, 1944-7

John Mar Timotheos I, 1947-

(g) CATHOLICOS PATRIARCHS OF THE CHALDEAN CHURCH

List borrowed from E. Tisserant's article on the Nestorian Church in *D.T.C.* vol. XI, 261-3.

1. *Patriarchs of the main line*

RESIDING AT SELEUCIA-CTESIPHON, WITH SOME EXCEPTIONS:

Papa, end 3rd c. to begining of 4th c.

Simon I bar Sabbae, d. 341

Shahdost, d. 342

Barbasemin, d. 348

(Vacancy 348-388)

Tomarsa

Qayyuma, retired 399

Isaac I, 399-410

Ahai, 411-14

Yahballaha I, 415-20

Mana, 420

Faraboht, 420

Dadisho I, 421 (2)-456

Babowai, 457-84

Acacios, 485-95 (6)

Babai, 497-502 (3)

Shila, 505-21 (2)

Narses & Elisha, 524-36 (7)
 or 538 (9)

Paul I, 537, or 539

Aba I, 540-52

Joseph, 551-66 (7), d. 576

Ezechiel, 567-70-81

Ishoyahb I, 582-95

Sabrisho I, 596-604

Gregory I, 605-9

(Vacancy 609-28)

Ishoyahb II, 628-44, or 646

Maremmeh, 647-50, or 644-7

Ishoyahb III, 647, or 650-7 (8)

George I, 661-80 (1)

(Nestorianism was introduced as the official creed of the Chaldean Church under the pontificate of Babai.)

John I bar Marta, 680 (1)-3

Henanisho I the Lame, 685
 (6)-699 (700)

John the Leper, intruder,
 691-2 (3)

(vacancy 700-14)

Sliba-zka, 714-28

(vacancy 728-31)

Pethion, 731-40

Aba II, 741-51

Surin, 754

James II, 754-73

Henanisho II, 773-80

RESIDING AT BAGHDAD

Timothy I, 780-9-823

Isho bar Nun, 823-28

George II, 828-30 (1)

Sabrisho II, 831-5

Abraham II, 837-50

Theodosius I, 853-8

Sergius I, 860-72

Israel of Kashkar, elected, not
 consecrated, murdered in 877

Enos I, 877-884

John II bar Narsai, 884-91

John III, 893-9

John IV bar Agbar, 900-5

Abraham III Abraza, 905-36

Emmanuel I, 937-60

Israel I, 961

Abdisho I, 963-86

Mari II bar Tobi, 987-99

John V ibn Isa, 1000-11

John VI Nasuk, 1012-16

Ishoyahb bar Ezechiel, 1020-5

Elias I, 1028-49

John VII bar Targabi, 1049-57

Sabrisho III Zanbur, 1064-72

Abdisho II ibn al-Arid, 1075-1090

Makika I, 1092-1110

Elias II bar Molki, 1111-32

Barsauma I, 1134-6

Abdisho III bar Molki, 1139-48

Ishoyahb V Baladi, 1149-75

Elias II abu Halim, 1176-90

Yahballaha II, 1190-1222

Sabrisho IV bar Qayyuma, 1222-24

Sabrisho V ibn al-Masihi, 1226-56

Makika II, 1257-65

Denha I, 1265-81

RESIDING AT MARAGHA

Yahballaha III, 1283-1318

RESIDING AT ARBELA

Timothy II, 1318-32

RESIDING AT KARAMLES

Denha II 1332–after 1364

RESIDING AT MOSUL

Simon II

Simon III

Elias IV, d. 1437

Simon IV Basidi, already Patriarch in June 1437-97

RESIDING AT GAZIRAH

Simon V, 1497-1501 (2)

Elias V, 1502-3

RESIDING AT RABBAN HORMIZD

Simon VI, 1504-38

Simon VII bar Mama, 1538-51

Simon VIII Denha, 1551-58 who remained a Nestorian

Elias VI, 1558-76

Elias VII, 1576-91

Elias VIII, 1591-1617

Elias IX Simon, 1617-60

Elias X John Maroghin, 1660-1700

Elias XI Maroghin, 1700-22

Elias XII Denha, 1722-78

Elias XIII Ishoyahb, 1778-1804, who was the last Nestorian Patriarch of this line.

RESIDING AT MOSUL

John VIII Hormez, acknowledged by Rome in 1830 as the first Catholic Patriarch of this line, and then as the only head of the Catholic Chaldeans, d. 1838

Nicolas I Isaias, 1840-47 retired, d. 1855

Joseph VI Audo, 1848-78

Elias XIV Abulyonan, 1879-94

Abdisho V Khayyatt, 1895-99

Joseph Emmanuel II Thomas, 1900-47

Joseph VII Ghanima, 1947-

2. *Patriarchs of the second line*

RESIDING AT DIARBEKIR

Simon VIII Sulaqa, 1551-5, who reunited with Rome and died as a martyr of the faith.

RESIDING AT SEERT

Abdisho IV Maron, 1555-71

Yahballaha V, 1578-80

RESIDING AT SALMAS

Simon IX Denha, acknowledged by Rome in 1581, d. 1600

Simon X, 1600-38

RESIDING AT URMIAH

Simon XI, 1638-56

Simon XII John, 1656-62

RESIDING AT KOTCHANNES

Simon XIII Denha, 1662-1700, who reverted to Nestorianism, and broke the Catholic succession of this line.

Simon XIV Solomon, 1700-40

Simon XV Michael Muktes, 1740-80

Simon XVI John, 1780-1820

Simon XVII Abraham, 1820-61

Simon XVIII Ruben, 1861-1903

Simon XIX Benjamin, 1903-18, murdered in Persia.

Simon XX Paul, 1918-20

Simon XXI Isaias, 1920- , who went into exile in 1932, and finally took refuge in the U.S.A. in 1941.

It is important to note that the present Catholic patriarchate of Babylon of the Chaldeans owes its origin to the reunion with Rome of the principal line of patriarchs, whereas the Nestorian patriarchate of to-day descends from the patriarchs, who were Catholic for more than a century (1551-1662).

(h) Syrian Patriarchs of Antioch since 1653

List based on *AA.SS.* July, vol. IV, p. 145 'De Patriarchis Antiochenis', H. Mousset, *Histoire du Christianisme spécialement en Orient*, Jerusalem-Harissa, 1948-49, vol. II, pp. 218-26 and vol. III pp. 240-9, and on data provided by the Right Reverend Mgr. Zacharias Malke, Chorepiscopus, President of the Syrian Catholic Patriarchal Seminary of Sharfe, Lebanon.

1. *Jacobite Patriarchs*

Residing at Deir as-Zafran near Mardin

Shukr-Allah I, 1640-62(?)

Simon of Tur-Abdin, 1640-62, an anti-Patriarch, cf. next list.

Joshua II Qamceh, 1655-61, an anti-Patriarch

Andrew I Akhidjian, 1662-77, who became a Catholic, cf. next list.

Abd-ul-Massih I er-Rahaui, 1662-86

Habib el-Mezziati, 1674-86, d. ?, anti-Patriarch at Tur-Abdin.

Peter VI Shahbadin, 1678-1702, who became Catholic, cf. next list.

George II, 1686-1708 or 1709

Basilios Isaac II, 1709-24

George III, 1746-68

George IV, 1768-81

Michael III Djarweh, 1782-1801, who became Catholic in 1783, cf. next list.

Matthew Ben Abdel, 1782-1817

George V Sayyar, 1819-36, who twice became Catholic, but reverted to Jacobitism before his patriarchal election.

Elias II Ankaz, 1838-47

Jacob II, 1847-72

Peter VII, 1872-95, who visited Malabar in 1875-6.

Abd-ul-Massih II, 1895-1906, who was deposed and died in 1914. He visited Malabar in 1912-13, and became Catholic in 1913.

Abdallah II Sattuf, 1906-16, who was a Catholic between 1895-1906, reverted to Jacobitism to become Patriarch, and visited Malabar in 1909.

Elias III Shakar, 1917-33, who died in Malabar when trying to settle the dispute between the two Jacobite parties.

Ephrem Barsom, 1933, who transfered his residence to Homs in Syria.

2. *Catholic Patriarchs*

RESIDING AT ALEPPO, WITH SOME EXCEPTIONS, AND BEARING THE TITLE OF THIS CITY

Simon of Tur-Abdin, 1640-62, whose union with Rome is not certain.

Andrew I Akhidjian, 1662-77, who had become Catholic before his episcopal consecration in 1656.

Peter VI Shahbadin, 1677-1702 or 1703, who became Catholic at the time of his election, was exiled and imprisoned in 1701.

(Vacancy 1703-1783)

RESIDING AT SHARFE, LEBANON

Michael III Djarweh, 1783-1801, who had become Catholic as Archbishop of Aleppo.

Michael IV Daher, 1802-10 retired, d. 1822

Simon II Hindi, 1814-18 retired, d. 1838

Peter VII Djarweh, 1820-51, acknowledged by Rome in 1828, and who transferred his residence to Aleppo.

RESIDING AT MARDIN

Anthony I Samheri, 1853-64

Philip I Arkus, 1866-74

George V Shelhot, 1874-91

Cyril Behnam II Benni, 1893-7

RESIDING AT BEIRUT

Ephrem II Rahmani, 1898-1929, who transferred his residence to Beirut in 1899.

Gabriel I Tappuni, 1929, who was created Cardinal in 1935.

Since 878 the Syrian patriarchs have the custom of prefixing the name of Ignatius to their own patriarchal name. Nowadays such a custom is followed by both the Catholic and Jacobite patriarchs.

APPENDIX IV

CHRONOLOGICAL EVENTS

St. Thomas the Apostle lands at Cranganore	? 52
Bishop David leaves Basrah for India	c. 295
Syrian emigrants arrive at Cranganore	c. 345
Bishop Theophilos visits India	c. 354-356
Synod of Seleucia, archbishopric of Seleucia-Ctesiphon	410
Archbishop of Seleucia-Ctesiphon assumes the title of catholicos	c. 421
Synod of Markabta. The Church of Mesopotamia becomes independent from Antioch	424
The Indian Church is firmly connected with Seleucia-Ctesiphon	c. 450
Cosmas Indicopleustes visits India	c. 535
Theodore, a Frankish monk, visits Mylapore	590
Dispute between India and Seleucia	650-60
The metropolitan see of India is created	714/728
Bishop Thomas Cana arrives in Malabar	? 825
The Syrian Church of India is granted full status	852/858
Mar Sabrisho and Mar Peroz arrive in Malabar	c. 880
King Alfred's embassy to Mylapore	883
Mar John, Archbishop (?) of India, visits Rome	1122
Marco Polo visits India	1293
Fra John of Monte-Corvino visits India	1293
Haythonus, a Norbertine canon, visits Malabar ?	? 1300
Mar Jacob, Metropolitan of India	1315
Fra Jordan Catalani visits Thana, near Bombay	1321
Fra Oderico de Pordenone visits Thana and Malabar	1321
Fra Jordan Catalani visits Quilon	1322
Fra Jordan Catalani becomes the first Latin Bishop of Quilon	1329
Fra John Marignola visits Quilon	1348-9
Nicolas de Conti visits Mylapore and Malabar	1415-38
The Syro-Malabar priest, Joseph, goes to Mesopotamia	1490

He comes back from Mesopotamia with two bishops,
    Mar Thomas and Mar John   c. 1496
Vasco de Gama's first landing in India near Calicut   25 May 1498
Mar Yahballaha, Mar Denha, and Mar Jacob arrive in
    Malabar   1501
Vasco de Gama's first meeting with the Syrian Christians
    of Malabar   1503
Cochin falls under Portuguese rule   1503
Cranganore is captured by the Portuguese   1504
The bishopric of Funchal is created with jurisdiction
    over Portuguese India   1514
The tomb of St. Thomas is discovered at Mylapore   1523
Goa is made suffragan bishopric of Funchal   1539
St. Francis Xavier's first visit to Malabar   1544
A seminary is opened at Cranganore   1546
A Persian cross is discovered at Mylapore   1547
St. Francis Xavier's second visit to Malabar   1549
The Chaldean Church is reunited with Rome   1552
A Jesuit college opens at Cochin   1552
Mar Joseph and Mar Elias reach Goa   1556
Goa becomes an archbishopric, and Cochin its suffra-
    gan bishopric   1557
First Jesuit mission among the Syrian Christians   1557-60
Mar Joseph and Mar Elias arrive in Malabar   1558
The King of Cochin publishes an edict of tolerance in
    favour of Christian converts   1560
Mar Joseph is obliged to go to Europe   1561
Mar Joseph returns to Malabar   1564
Mar Joseph is sent back to Europe   1565
Mar Abraham arrives in Malabar   1563
Mar Abraham escapes to Mesopotamia   1564
Mar Abraham comes back to Malabar   1565
First Council of Goa   1567
Mar Joseph dies in Rome   1569
Second Council of Goa   1575
A seminary is founded at Vaipicotta   1577
A Nestorian bishop, Mar Simon, comes to Malabar   1577
First Synod of Angamale   1583

Third Council of Goa 1585
Fourth Council of Goa 1592
Alexis de Menezes becomes Archbishop of Goa 1595
Mar Abraham's death 1597
Alexis de Menezes begins his visit in Malabar, 27 December 1598
Synod of Diamper 1599
Fr. Francis Roz s. j., becomes Bishop of the Syrians 1599
Second Synod of Angamale 1606
Angamale again becomes an archbishopric 1608
Bishop Roz' death 1624
Fr. Francis Donati o.p. in Malabar 1628
Thomas de Campo becomes archdeacon 1637
A monk, called Athallah, reaches Mylapore 1652
Coonan Cross Oath 1653
Athallah is burnt in Goa 1654
First Carmelite mission to Malabar 1657
The first Latin Vicar-Apostolic of Malabar is conse-
crated. His is called Bishop Sebastiani 1659
Bishop Sebastiani lands at Cochin. Second Carmelite
mission in Malabar 1661
Quilon is captured by the Dutch 1661
Cranganore is captured by the Dutch 1662
Cochin is captured by the Dutch 6 January 1663
Bishop Sebastiani consecrates Bishop Mar Alexander de
Campo, and leaves Malabar 1 February 1663
Mar Gregorios, the first Jacobite Bishop, comes to
Malabar 1665
A seminary is founded at Verapoly 1682
Second Jacobite mission to Malabar 1685
Angelus Francis of St. Mary o.c.d. is nominated Vicar
Apostolic of the Syrians 1700
Mar Simon of Adana, a Catholic Chaldean bishop,
arrives in Malabar 1700
Mar Thomas IV tries to reunite with Rome 1704
Death of a Nestorian bishop, Mar Gabriel 1730 or 1731
A certain Mar John, Nestorian Bishop, comes to Malabar 1747
Mar Thomas V tries to reunite with Rome 1748
Third Jacobite mission to Malabar 1751

The Seminary of Verapoly is revived   1764

Joseph Cariati, a Syro-Malabar priest, is nominated
Archbishop of Cranganore   1782

Joseph Cariati dies at Goa   1786

Cochin is captured by the British   1795

Mar Dionysios I becomes Catholic for six months   1799

Mar Dioscoros, a Jacobite bishop, comes to Malabar   1807

The first Anglican missionaries arrive in Travancore   1816

Mar Jacob is sent to Malabar by the Jacobite patriarch   1825

A congregation of Syro-Malabar and Latin Carmelite
Tertiaries is founded   1829-31

The first synod of the Malabar Jacobites   1836

A breach occurs between the Jacobites and the Protestant missionaries   1837

The apostolic vicariate of Verapoly is created   1838

Mar Kurillos, a Jacobite bishop, comes to Malabar   1846

The Carmelite Tertiaries become a congregation of
diocesan character   1855

Mar Kurillos enforces the Syrian rite of Antioch on the
Jacobites of India   c. 1857

The Carmelite Tertiaries become a canonical Third
Order Regular   1860

Mar Rokos, a Chaldean bishop from Mesopotamia,
arrives at Cochin   1861

He returns to Mesopotamia   1862

Mar Mellus, a Chaldean bishop from Mesopotamia,
arrives in Malabar   1874

The Jacobite Patriarch, Peter VII, reaches Malabar   1875

The Second Jacobite synod   1876

Mar Mellus, excommunicated by Rome, leaves India   1882

The Seminary of Puthenpally becomes the central
seminary for the Syrians and the Latins   1886

The Catholic hierarchy is established in India   1886

The apostolic vicariates of Kottayam and Trichur are
created for the Syro-Malabar Catholics   1887

Two new apostolic vicariates are created at Ernakulam
and Changanacherry for the same, the vicariate of
Changanacherry replacing that of Kottayam   1896

The 'Mellusians' of Trichur become Nestorian — 1907

A delegate of the Jacobite patriarch resides in Malabar — 1908

The Jacobite Patriarch, Abdallah, visits Malabar — 1909

The Jacobites of India split into two parties — 1910

The apostolic vicariate of Kottayam is created for the Catholic Syrians of the Suddist community — 1911

The deposed Jacobite Patriarch, Abd-ul-Massih, comes to Malabar and erects a catholicosate — 1912

The two Bethany congregations are founded by Fr. P. T. Givargheese, the future Mar Ivanios — 1919

The Syro-Malabar hierarchy is erected — 1923

Fr. P. T. Givargheese becomes a Jacobite bishop and assumes the name of Mar Ivanios — 1925

Mar Ivanios becomes Metropolitan of Bethany, and one of his Bethany monks becomes his suffragan Bishop of Tiruvalla, under the name of Mar Theophilos — 1929

Mar Ivanios and Mar Theophilos become Catholic — 1930

The Jacobite Patriarch, Elias III, comes to Malabar — 1931

The Syro-Malankara hierarchy and ecclesiastical province are erected. Mar Ivanios becomes Archbishop of Trivandrum, and Mar Theophilos Bishop of Tiruvalla — 1932

The Seminary of Puthenpally is transferred to Alwaye — 1933

Elias III dies in Malabar — 1933

Mar Severios, Jacobite Bishop of Niranam, becomes Catholic — 1937

Mar Dioscoros, Jacobite Bishop of the Suddists, becomes Catholic — 1939

The new Syro-Malabar diocese of Palai is erected — 1950

Jubilee celebrations of St. Thomas and St. Francis Xavier — December 1952

Mar Ivanios dies — 1953

Cardinal Eugene Tisserant, secretary of the S. Oriental Congregation, visits the Syrian Catholics of Malabar — 1953

The new Syro-Malabar diocese of Tellicherry is erected — 1954

Mar Severios dies — 1955

Mar Gregorios becomes Archbishop of Trivandrum and Mar Athanasios suffragan Bishop of Tiruvalla — 1955

Mar Augustine Kandathil, first Syro-Malabar Archbishop of Ernakulam, dies — 1956

The jurisdiction of the Syro-Malabar hierarchy is considerably extended inside Travancore-Cochin, in Madras State and in Mysore State — 1956

The new Syro Malabar diocese of Kothamangalam is erected — 1956

Official contacts between the Catholicos' party of the Indian Jacobites and the Greek patriarchate at Constantinople take place — 1956

TRAVANCORE-COCHIN STATE

MALABAR DISTRICT
MADRAS STATE

MALABAR DT.

MADRAS STATE

ARABIAN

Cannanore
Tellicherry

CALICUT

Ponnani R.

Anjur
Palayur · Arthad
TRICHUR
· Elthuruth

Cranganore

Kothamangalam
ERNAKULAM   Periyar R.
Cochin
MATTANCHERRY

N

Palai ·
Kottayam

ALLEPPEY
· Changanacherry
· Tiruvalla   Pambiyar R.

S E A

Nevalacara
QUILON

TRIVANDRUM: capital of State
QUILON: district head-quarters.
TRIVANDRUM: above 100.000 inh.
QUILON: above 50.000 inh.
Kottayam: above 20.000 inh.
Parur: other places of interest
Latin archdiocese, dioceses
Syro-Malabar archdiocese, dioceses
Syro-Malankarese
    archdiocese, dioceses

TRIVANDRUM

English Miles
Kilometers

KOTTAR
Cape Comorin

BIBLIOGRAPHY

(a) GENERAL WORKS OF REFERENCE

Achan P. A., *Annual Report of the Archaeological Department of the Cochin State for the year 1103 M.E. (A.D. 1927-8)*, Ernakulam, 1929

—— *Annual Report of Archaeological Department of the Cochin State for the year 1110 M. E. (A.D. 1934-5)* Ernakulam, 1936.

—— *Annual Report of the Archaeological Department of the Cochin State for the year 1120 M.E. (A.D. 1944-5), 1121 M. E. (A.D. 1945-6)*, Ernakulam, 1947, 2 vols.

—— *Annual Report of the Archaeological Department of the Cochin State for the year 1122 M.E. (A.D. 1947-8, A.D. 1949)*, Ernakulam, 1949-50, 2 vols.

Aiya V. N., *The Travancore State Manual*, Trivandrum, 1906, 3 vols.

Annual Bibliography of Indian Archaeology, Leyden, 1926-47, 15 vols.

Annuario Pontificio, Rome-Vatican City, 1912-54, 43 vols.

Assemani J. S. & E. E., *Bibliothecae Apostolicae Vaticanae Codicum Mss Catalogus*, Rome, 1758, vol. II.

Ayyar A. S. R., *Annual Report of the Archaeological Department of the Travancore State for the year 1099 M. E. (A.D. 1923-4.)* Trivandrum, 1924.

Ayyar A. S. R., *Travancore Archaeological Series*, Trivandrum, 1927, vol. V, part III and vol. VI, part I.

Ballini A., 'India (1915-24), Bolletino Bibliografico', *Aevum*, I (1927), pp. 71-281, 413-16.

Bardenhewer O., *Geschichte der altkirchlichen Literatur*, Freiburg i. B., 1913, vol. I.

Battandier A. (contd. by Chardavoine E.), *Annuaire Pontifical Catholique*, Paris, 1898-1947, 42 vols.

Baumstark A., *Geschichte der syrischen Literatur*, Bonn, 1922.

Coussa A, *Epitome Praelectionum de Jure Ecclesiastico Orientali*, Rome-Venice, 1941-50, 3 vols.

Dey N. L., *The Geographical Dictionary of Ancient and Medieval India*, London, 1927

15

Encyclopaedia of Islam, Leyden, 1913–36, 4 vols. and supplement.

Gierarchia Cattolica, Rome, 1871–11, 40 vols.

Golubovich G, *Biblioteca bio-bibliografica della Terra Santa e dell' Oriente francescano*, Karachi, 1906–23, 4 vols.

Hanssens J. M. s.j., *Institutiones Liturgicae de Ritibus Orientalium*, vol. II and III, appendix of vol. III, Rome, 1930–2.

Hatch E. G., *Travancore. A Guide Book for the Visitor*, London 1933.

Hosten H. s.j., List of Books and Articles for a Study of the St. Thomas Question, *in Antiquities from S. Thomé and Mylapore*, Mylapore (Madras), 1936, pp. 196–228.

—— 'The Marsden Mss. and Indian Missions Bibliography', *B.S.O.S.* 3 (1923–5), pp. 129–50.

The Imperial Gazeteer of India, Oxford, 1907–09, vols. X, XVII, XXIV.

Innes C.A., *Malabar and Anjengo*, Ed., F. B. Evans, Madras, 1915 (Madras District Gazeteers)

Iyer L. K. Anantha Krishna, *The Cochin Tribes and Castes*, Madras, 1912, vol. II.

Jugie M. A.A., *Theologia dogmatica christianorum orientalium ab Ecclesia catholica dissidentium*, Paris, 1935, vol. V, *De Theologia Dogmatica Nestorianorum et Monophysitarum*.

Lenain de Tillemont M., *Mémoires pour servir à l'histoire ecclésiastique des six premiers siècles*, Venice, 1732, vol. I.

Lequien M. o. p., *Oriens Christianus in quatuor patriarchatus digestus, quo exhibentur ecclesiae, patriarchae, caeterique praesules totius Orientis*, Paris, 1740, 3 vols.

Logan W., *Manual of the Malabar District*, Madras, 1887 and 1906, 2 vols.

The Madras Catholic Directory, Madras, 1883–1911, 29 vols, followed by *The Catholic Directory of India*, Madras, 1912–5, 4 vols. *The Catholic Directory of India, Burma and Ceylon*, 1916–50, 35 vols., and *The Catholic Directory of India*, New Delhi, 1954–56, 2 vols.

Menon C. A., *The Cochin State Manual*, Ernakulam, 1911.

Moares G., *Bibliography of Indological Studies, 1942 and 1943*, Bombay, 1946 and 1952, 2 vols.

Placidus of St. Joseph t.o.c.d., 'Statistica Christianorum S. Thomae', *O.C.P.* 3 (1937), pp. 292–5.

Poduval R.V., *Administration Report of the Archaeological Department, Government of Travancore, 1113-19 M.E. (A.D. 1937-43)*, Trivandrum, 1939-5, 6 vols.

—— *Archaeology in Travancore*, Trivandrum, 1941.

—— *Topographical List of Travancore Inscriptions*, Trivandrum, 1941.

Quasten J., *Patrology*, Utrecht and Westminster (U.S.A.), 1950, vol I.

Rangacharya V., *A Topographical List of the Inscriptions in the Madras Presidency (collected till 1915)*, Madras, 1919, 3 vol.

Rao T. A. G. & Aiyer K. V. S., *Travancore Archaeological Series*, Trivandrum, 1920, vol. I-II.

Ritzler R. & Seferin P., *Hierarchia Catholica Medii et Recentioris Aevi. 1503-1730*, Münster i. W.-Padua, 1923-52. 3 vols.

Rommerskirchen G. & Dindinger G. o. m. i., *Bibliografia Missionaria, 1934-53*, Rome, 1936-54, 17 vol.

Sewel R., *List of the Antiquarian Remains in the Presidency of Madras*, Madras, 1882, vol. I.

Sewel R., 'List of Inscriptions, and Sketch of the Dynasties of Southern India', *Archaeological Survey of Southern India*, Madras, 1884, vol. II.

Statistica con cenni storici della gierarchia dei fideli di rito orientale, Rome, 1932.

Streit R. & Dindinger G. o. m. i., *Bibliotheca Missionum*, Aachen, 1916-34, vol. I, IV, V, VI, & VIII.

Thurston E., *Castes and Tribes of Southern India*, Madras, 1909 vol. VI.

Ward & Conner, *Geographical and Statistical Memoir of the Survey of the Travancore and Cochin States from July 1816 to the end of the year 1820*, Trivandrum, 1863.

Zotenberg H., *Catalogues des manuscrits syriaques et sabéens (mandaïtes) de la Bibliothèque Nationale*, Paris, 1874.

(b) MANUSCRIPT SOURCES

Some modern writers have concerned themselves with unpublished sources, but nearly always in a very limited way. The Jesuits have naturally emphasized the work of their Order, as is illustrated by D. Ferroli s. j., *The Jesuits in Malabar*. He relied mainly on Jesuit sources. K. Werth had made a valuable contribution by going through many documents of the Propaganda

Archives. His volume *Das Schisma des Thomas-Christen unter Erzbischof Franz Garzia* has largely renewed the knowledge and the usual interpretation of the breach of 1652. Another fundamental work was completed in 1939 by Fr. Ambrose of St. Teresa O. C. D., who published the series IV of his *Hierarchia Carmelitana*, under the title *De praesulibus missionis Malabaricae*. He is entirely concerned with Carmelite documentation. Perhaps there is only one writer who tried to synthetize the local traditions of Malabar, and who gathered fairly abundant material, the late Fr. Bernard of St. Thomas T. O. C. D., in his *History of the St. Thomas Christians*. Unfortunately for the public at large, he wrote in Malayalam, and his English résumé, *A Brief Sketch of the History of the St. Thomas Christians*, does not give full credit to his vast knowledge of the subject.

The present work was mainly built on printed documentation. Yet we have occasionally quoted some of the available manuscripts. We enter them here below together with the chief unpublished sources, which were consulted in order to check the veracity of some published ones. No attempt is made here to list all the manuscripts that lie in the many archives of Europe (Brussels, Evora, Lisbon, London, Paris, Rome, etc.) and India (Cochin, Goa, Verapoly, etc.).

ARCHIVUM VATICANUM (ROME)

The *Acta Consistorialia*, *Acta Camerae*, 13, and *Acta Miscellanea*, 53, were consulted for the nomination of Fr. Roz S. J. as Bishop of Angamale.

BIBLIOTHECA APOSTOLICA VATICANA (ROME)

Mar Joseph, one of the last Chaldean Bishops of Malabar, brought to Rome, where he died, several Syriac manuscripts, some of which were copied in Malabar. They are entered as *Vatic. Syr.* no. 2, 3, 4, 17, 22, 45, 46, 62, 65, 85 and 88.

ARCHIVUM S. CONGREGATIONIS DE PROPAGANDA FIDE (ROME)

We have examined a part of the pertinent material between 1622 and 1662, which were found in the two sections called *Scritture Originali* (*Lettere Antiche*) no. 98, 105, 109, 128, 135, 138, 142, and *Scritture Referite Antiche*, no. 191, 192, 194, 232, 233, 234, 252.

ARCHIVUM ROMANUM SOCIETATIS JESU (ROME)

In the Indian sections called *Goani Catalogi* (*1552-1608*) and

Catalogi Triennales Coccinenses et Malabarenses (1604-1752), all the lists of Jesuits working for the benefit of the Syrians of Malabar were examined. In other sections, such as *Epistolae Goanae et Malabaricae*, no. 8-21, id. (1603-80), no. 47-56, and *Goana Historia (1539-1753)*, no. 31-5, all the letters, annual and private, were consulted. We have duly quoted some of them when speaking of the preparation and aftermath of the Diamper synod. The *Summario de las cosas que perteneçen a la Provincia de la India Oriental y al governo della*, written by Fr. A. Valignano s. J., was also checked as far as the Syrians of Malabar were concerned. We also carefully read the copy of the acts of the Diamper synod, found under n. 62. It is to be noted that the archives of Madura Province of the Society of Jesus (Shembaganur, Madurai District, India) preserve many accurate copies and English translations of the Roman material just mentioned. They are entered there as *Letters and Documents on the Syrian Christians*, vol. I (1581-1644), vol. II, (1648-1738) and vol. III (letters of Bishop Roz and of Fr. J. M. Campori s. J.). In the same collection one can find two very useful but unpublished, histories of Jesuit activities in South India, L. Besse s. J., *History of the Malabar Province* 2 vols, and J. Castets s. J., *Histoire de l'ancienne Mission du Madura*.

BRITISH MUSEUM (LONDON)

Add. 9853, *Reports of the Jesuit Missions in India 1601-59*, which contains among others the following documents: *Relação da Christandade de S. Thomé scryta pello Sor Bispo Dom Francisco Roz*, ff. 32-5; *Relação da Christiandade da Serra, 1604*, ff. 85-99; Sloane Mss., no. 2748 A., *Traité de l'Antiquité du Christianisme aux Indes en portugais*; Sloane Mss., 2749 A., *Breve Relação da antiquissima Christandade da Serra do Mallavar*.

BIBLIOTECA NACIONAL (LISBON)

N. 536, *Noticias do Reyno de Malabar*, a well written account of the various communities existing among the Christians of Malabar at the end of the eighteenth century.

(c) PRINTED SOURCES
I. Collection of Sources

Acta Apostolicae Sedis, Rome-Vatican City, 1909-54, 46 vols.

Acta et Decreta S. Conciliorum Recentiorum (Collectio Lacencis), Freiburg i. B., 1876, vol. II.

Acta Sanctae Sedis Ephemeridia, Rome, 1865-1908, 39 vols.

Bullarium Patronatus Portugalliae Regum, Lisbon, 1868-79, 3 vols. and 2 appendices, completed by *Subsidium ad Bullarium Patronatus Portugalliae Regum*, Alappey, 1903.

Bullarium Pontificium S. Congregationis de Propaganda Fide, Rome, 1839-41, 5 vols. with *Index Analyticus Bullarii Pontificii S. Congregatione de Propaganda Fide*, Rome, 1858. Completed by *Appendix ad Bullarium Pontificium....*, Rome, s.d., 2 vols.

Collectanea S. Congregationis de Propaganda Fide, Rome, 1907, 2 vols.

Concilium Tridentinum, Diariorum, Actorum,.. Nova Collectio, Ed., S. Ehses, Freiburg i. B., 1919, vol. VIII.

Corpo Diplomatico Portuguêz, Lisbon, 1902, vol. XI & XII.

De Martinis, R., *Jus Pontificium de Propaganda Fide*, Rome, 1888-97, 7 vols.

'Ecclesiastical Councils of Goa and the Synod of Diamper', *Archivo Portuguêz Oriental*, 1862.

Giamil S., 'Documenta relationum inder S. Sedem Apostolicam et Assyriorum Orientalium vel Chaldeorum Ecclesiam.... (XVII-XVIII ss.), *Bessarion*, 7 (1900), pp. 92-136, 318-54. Republished in the form of a book, Rome, 1902.

Hefelé & LeClercq, *Histoire des Conciles*, Paris, 1913, vol. V.

LeClercq, C., 'Conciles des Orientaux Catholiques', *Histoire des Conciles*, Paris, 1949-52, vol. II, 2 parts.

Leo XIII, *Leonis Pontificis Maximi Acta*, Rome, 1887-8, vol. VI & VII; also Bruges, 1898, vol. V-VII.

Mai A., *Scriptorum Veterum Nova Collectio*, Rome, 1838, vol. Xa,

Placid of St. Joseph T. O. C. D., 'De Fontibus Juris Ecclesiastici Syro-Malankarensium Commentarius Historico-Canonicus', *C.C.O. Fonti, series II, fasc. VIII-IX*, Rome, 1937-40, 2 vols.

Prévost, Abbé, *Histoire générale des voyages*, The Hague, 1755, 2nd ed., vol. XIII.

Rabbath, A., *Documents inédits pour servir à l'histoire du christianisme en Orient*, Paris-Leipzig, 1910, vol. II.

Sastri, K. A. Nilakanta, *Foreign Notices of South India, from Megasthenes to Mahuan*, Madras, 1940.

Schurhammer, G. s.J., *Die zeitgenössischen Quellen zur Geschichte*

Portugiesisch Asiens und seiner Nachbarländer zur Zeit des Hl. Franz Xaver (1538-52), Leipzig, 1932.

Silva Rêgo A. da, *Documentaçâo para a Historia das Missôes do Padroado Português do Oriente, India*, Lisbon, 1947-53, 10 vols.

2. Greek and Latin Writers and Authorities

Acta Apostolorum Apocrypha, Ed., Lipsius & Bonnet, Leipzig, 1893-1903, 2 vols.

—— Scherman, T., *Propheten und Apostellegenden*, Leipzig, 1907.

—— James, M.R., *The Apocryphal New Testament*, Oxford, 1924, 2nd ed., 1950.

—— *Supplementum Codicis Apocryphi. I. Acta Thomae Graece partim cum novis codicibus contulit partim primum edidit recensit, praefatus est, indices adiecit* M. Bonnet, Leipzig, 1883.

Ambrosius, *Enarrationes in Psalmum XLV*, P.L. 14, 1198.

Cosmas Indicopleustes, *Topographia Christiana*, P.G. 88, 51-576.

—— McCrindle, J. W., *The Christian Topography of Cosmas*, London, 1897.

—— Windstedt, E. O., *The Christian Topography of Cosmas Indicopleustes*, Cambridge, 1909.

(Pseudo-) Dorotheus Tyrensis, *De LXX Domini Discipulis*, 7, P.G. 92, 1072.

Eusebius Caesarensis, *Historia Ecclesiastica*, Bk 5, 10, P.G. 20, 456.

Gaudentius Bzesciensis, *Sermo XVII, De Diversis Capitulis Septimus*, P.L. 20, 961-5.

Gelazius Cyzicensis, *Concilium Nicaenum*, P.G. 85, 1314.

Gregorius Nazianzenus, *Oratio XXXIII ad Arianos*, II, P.G. 36, 228.

Gregorius Turonensis, *In Gloria Martyrum*, c. 31, 32, *Monumenta Germaniae Historica, Scriptores Rerum Merov.*, vol. 1 b.

Hieronymus, *De Viribus Illustribus*, 36, P.L. 23, 683.

—— *Epistola LIX ad Marcellam*, P. L. 22, 288 ff.

Origen, *In Genesim*, Bk III, P.G. 12, 92.

Paulinus Nolensis, *Poema XIX. Carmen XI in S. Felicem*, P.L. 61, 514.

The Periplus of the Erythraean Sea, Ed., W. H. Schoff New York, 1912.

Philostorgos, *Ecclesiastica Historia*, Bk III, ch. IV & VI, P.G. 45, 482-90, and G.C.S. 21 (1913), pp. 33-5.

Recognitiones Clementinae, Bk. IX, c. 29, P.G. 1, 1415.

Boschius, P. s. j., 'Tractatus Historico-Chronologicus de Patriarchis Antiochenis', *AA. SS.* July, vol. IV, Antwerp, 1725, pp. 1-145.

Gelzer, H., *Patrum Nicaenorum Nomina*, Leipzig, 1898.

Honigmann, E., 'La liste originale des Pères de Nicée', *Byzantion* 14 (1939), pp. 17-76.

McCrindle J. W., *Ancient India as described by Ktesias the Knidian*, Calcutta, 1882.

—— *Ancient India, as described by Megasthenes and Arrian*, Calcutta, 1926.

—— *Ancient India as described by Ptolemy*, Ed., S. Majumdar Calcutta, 1927.

Mercati A., *Monumenta Vaticana veterem diocoesim Columbensem (Quilon) et eiusdem primum episcopum Iordanum Catalani O.P. respicientia....*, Rome, 1923.

N. B. A detailed list of Greek and Latin authorities on the St. Thomas question is given by A. C. Perumalil s. j., *The Apostles in India*, pp. 135-8.

3. *Oriental Writers and Authorities*

Acta Thomae, M. A. Bevan, *Hymn of the Soul contained in the Syriac Acts of St. Thomas*, London, 1897.

Anaphorae Syriacae quotquot in codicibus adhuc repertae sunt, cura Pontificii Instituti Studiorum Orientalium editae et latine versae, Rome, 1939, ff. vol. I.

Chronica Ecclesiae Arbelensis, 'La Chronique d'Arbèles', Ed., A. Mingana in *Sources Syriaques*, Mosul, 1907, vol. I, pp. 1-75, 76-108.

—— Ed., F. Zorell *O.C.* 8 (1927), n. 31, pp. 141-204.

—— Ortiz de Urbina, I. s. j., 'Intorno al valore storico della Cronica di Arbela', *O.C.P.* 2 (1936), pp. 5-33.

—— P. Peeters s. j., 'Le passionnaire d'Adiabène', *A.B.* 43, (1925), pp. 261-304.

—— Sachau E., 'Die chronik von Arbela Ein. Beitrag zur Kenntnis des ältesten Christentums in Orient', *Abhandlungen der kgl. preuss. Akademie der Wissenschaften*, No. 6, Berlin, 1915.

Chronique de Seert, *Histoire nestorienne inédite*, Ed., A. Scher *P.O.* 4, fasc. 3, 5, fasc. 2, 7, fasc. 2, 13, fasc. 4.

Doctrine d'Addai, Ed., Cureton *Ancient Syriac Documents*, London, 1864.

Ephrem Syrus, *Carmina Nisibena*, Ed., Bickell, Leipzig, 1866.

Ephrem Syrus, *Hymni et Sermones*, Ed., J. T. Lamy, Mechlin, 1902, vol. IV

Gregorius Barhebraeus, *Chronicon Ecclesiasticum*, Ed., J. B. Abbeloos & T. J. Lamy, Paris-Louvain, 1877, vol. III.

—— *Nomocanone*, Ed., G. Riccioti, Rome, 1931, *C.C.O. Fonti, fasc. III, Disciplina Antiochena (Siri)*, I

Ishoyabh III, *Liber Epistolarum*, Ed., R. Duval, *C.S.C.O. Scriptores Syri*, ser 2, 64, Paris, 1905.

Jacob of Sarug, 'Gedicht des Jacob von Sarug über den Palast, de der Apostel Thomas in Indien baute', Ed., R. Schroeter, *Zeitschrift der deutschen morgenland. Gesellschaft*, 25 (1871), pp. 321-77.

—— Schroeter R., 'Nachträge zu dem in dieser Zeitschrift Bd. 25, s. 321 ff. veröffentlichen Gedicht der Jakob von Sarug..', ibid. 28 (1874), pp. 584-626.

Liber Patrum, Ed., J. M. Vosté, Vatican City, 1940, *C. C. O. Fonti*, ser II, *fasc. XVI, Caldei, Diritto Antico*, III.

Liber Rasae, Mannanam, 1905, 1925.

Missale Chaldaicum ex decreto S. Congregationis de Propaganda Fide Editum, Rome, 1767.

Missale Syro-Malabaricum, Rome, 1774, 1844; Puthenpally, 1904, 1931; Mannanam, 1928.

Officium Defunctorum, Mannanam, 1882, 1921.

Officium Divinum Feriale, Kunamavu, 1876, 1886; Mannanam, 1913 1932; Puthenpally, 1932.

—— *East Syrian Daily Office*, Ed., A. J. Maclean, London, 1894.

Officium Divinum Festivum, Mannanam, 1894.

Ordo Chaldaicus Ministerii Sacramentorum Sanctorum quae perficiuntur a Sacerdotibus iuxta morem Ecclesiae Malabaricae, Rome, 1845, Puthenpally, 1914.

Ordo Judiciorum Ecclesiasticorum, collectus, dispositus, ordinatus et compositus a Mar Abdisho Metropolita Nisibis et Armeniae, Ed., J. M. Vosét O.P., Vatican City, 1940, *C.C.O. Fonti*; ser. II, fasc. XV, *Caldei-Dirotto Antico*, II.

Severus of Antioch, *Conversão de un rei da India ao christianismo. Homilia do archanjo S. Michael* pro Severo, arcebispo de Antiochia, Ed., J. M. Esteves Pareira, Lisbon, 1900.

Solomon of Basrah, *The Book of the Bee*, Ed., E. A. Wallis Budge, Oxford, 1886, *Anecdota Oxoniensia, Semitica*, ser. I.

Synodicon Orientale, Ed., J. B. Chabot, Paris, 1902, *Notices et Extraits des manuscrits de la Bibliothèque Nationale et d'autres bibliothèques*, vol. XXXVII.

Vosté, J. M. O.P., *Droit ancien: Synodes (Synodicon Orientale), Collectio Canonum Synodicarum d'Ebedjésus de Nisibe*, Rome, 1931, *C.C.O. Fonti, fasc. 4, Discipline Chaldéenne (Chaldéens)*, I.

Assemani, J. S., *Bibliotheca Orientalis Clemento-Vaticana*, Rome 1725-8, vol. III, parts 1 & 2.

—— *Catalogus Patriarcharum Syro-Jacobitarum*, ibid. vol. II. pp. 479-1721.

—— *De Catholicis seu Patriarchis Chaldaeorum et Nestorianorum. Commentarium Historico-Chronologicum*, Rome, 1775.

Bihlmeyer, D. P., 'Un texte non interpolé de l'Apocalypse de Thomas', *Revue Bénédictine*, 28 (1911), pp. 270-82.

Breve Ragguaglio sulla questione del Malabar, Rome, 1920.

Brightmann, F. T., *Liturgies Eastern and Western*, Oxford, 1896.

Budge, E. A. Wallis, *The Contendings of the Apostles, being the Histories of the Lives and Martyrdoms and Deaths of the Twelve Apostles and Evangelists, translated from the Ethiopic Manuscripts of the British Museum*, Oxford, 1935.

—— *The Monks of Kublai Khan, Emperor of China*, London, 1928.

Fabian T.O.C.D., *The Liturgy of the St. Thomas Christians or the Raza of the Syro-Malabar Rite*, Mannanam, 1954.

Ferrand, G., *Relations de voyages et textes géographiques arabes, persans et turques relatifs à l'Extrême Orient du VIIIe au XVIIIe siècles*, Paris, 1913, vol. I.

Gismondi, H. S. J., *Maris, Amri et Slibae de Patriarchis Nestorianorum Commentaria*, Rome, 1896-9.

Hindo, P., *Lieux et Temps Sacrés-Culte Divin-Magistère Ecclésiastique-Bénéfices et Biens Temporels Ecclésiastiques*, Vatican City, 1943, *C.C.O. Fonti*, ser. II, fasc. 28, *Disciplina Antiochena Anticha, Siri*, IV.

Hindo, P., *Les Personnes*, Vatican City, 1951, ibid. fasc. 26, ibid. II.

—— *Textes concernant les Sacrements*, Vatican City, 1941, ibid. fasc. 27, ibid. III.

Hosten H., 'The St. Thomas Christians of Malabar (A.D. 1490-1504)', *K.S.P.* ser. 5, (1930) pp. 225-59.

Kalapura A., *An English Version of Rasa, or the Syriac Pontifical High Mass*, Verapoly, 1924.

Letters of Mar Abdisho, Patriarch of Babylon, and of Leo XIII, Mosul, s.d.

Libellus Memorialis circa questionem et petitionem Malabaricorum Syro-Chaldaeorum, Mosul-Rome, 1896.

Libellus supplex SSmo D.N. Pio X, Summo Pontifici, . . . oblatus a Sacerdotibus Ritus Syro-Chaldaici Trium Vicariatuum Apostolicorum Malabariae, s.l., 1908.

Nainar S.M.H., *The Knowledge of India possessed by Arab Geographers down to the 14th century A.D., with special reference to South India*, Madras, 1943.

Neale J. M. & Littledale R.F., *The Liturgies of SS. Mark, James, Clement, Chrysostom, and Basil, and the Church of Malabar* London, s.d.

Nilles N. s.j., *Kalendarium manuale utriusque Ecclesiae Orientalis et Occidentalis*, Innsbruck, 1896.

Renaudot E., *Liturgiarum Orientalium Collectio*, Paris, 1716. 2 vols.

Studi Storici sulle Fonti del Diritto Canonico Orientale, Vatican City, 1932, C.C.O. Fonti, fasc. 8.

Tisserant E., *Specimina Codicum Orientalium*, Rome-Bonn, 1914.

4 Portuguese Sources

Albuquerque A., *Commentarios do Grande Afonso de Albuquerque*, Ed., A. Baião, Coïmbra, 1923, 2 vols. English translation by W. De Gray Birch, London, 1880, Hakluyt Society, III.

Barbosa D., *Livro em que dá relação do que viu e conviu no Oriente*, Ed., A. R. Machado, Lisbon, 1946. Portuguese text and English translation by M. L. Danves, London, 1918-21, 2 vols. Hakluyt Society, 2nd ser. n. 49.

Barros J. de & Couto D. de, *Da Asia: dos Feitos que os Portuguezes fizeram na terra e mares do Oriente*, Lisbon 1778-83, 24 vols.

Barros J. de, *Da Asia*, Lisbon 1777, 8 vols. and 6th ed. by H. Cidade & M. Murias, Lisbon 1944-7, 4 vols.

Castanheda F. Lopes de, *Historia do descrobimento & Conquista da India pelos Portuguezes*, Ed., P. de Azevedo, Coïmbra, 1923-4, 3rd ed. 4 vols.

Correa G., *Lendas da India*, Ed., R.J. de Lima Felner, Lisbon 1860-1922, 4 vols.

Couto D. de, cf. Barros J, de

Denvers F.C., *Report to the Secretary of State for India in Council on the Portuguese Records relating to the East Indies contained in the Archivo da Torre do Tombo and the Public Libraries at Lisbon and Evora*, London, 1892.

Faria y Souza M. de, *Asia Portuguesa*, Lisbon, 1666, 1674-1703, 3 vols. 1945, 2 vols.

Gouvea A. de, *Iornada do Arcebispo de Goa, Dom Frey de Menezes . . . quando foy as Serras de Malabar*, Coïmbra, 1606; French translation under the title *Histoire Orientale des grands progrès de l'Eglise Catholique et Romaine en la réduction des anciens Chrétiens dits de S. Thomas*, etc., translated into French by F. Jean-Baptiste de Glen O.E.S.A., Brussels, 1609.

Historia des Descobimentos e Conquistas dos Portuguezes no novo mundo, Lisbon, 1786, 4 vols.

Historia dos Portuguezes no Malabar. Ms arabe do seculo XVI, publicado por David Lopes, Lisbon, 1898.

Lopes F.F. O.F.M., 'Para a Historia da Ordem Franciscana em Portugal. Fontes Narrativas e Textos Legais, Provincia de S. Tomé na India Oriental, Provincia de Madre de Deus da India Oriental', *Archivo Ibero-Americano*, 7 (1937), pp. 39-68; 8 (1948), pp. 112-19.

Nazareth C.C., *Mitras Lusitanas no Oriente*, Nova Goa, 1924, 2nd ed. vol. II.

Vasco de Gama, *Diário da Viagem de Vasco da Gama. Facsimile do Codice Original transcriçao e versao em grafia actualizada* (with special studies), Ed., D. Peres, etc. Porto, 1945, 2 vols.

5 Jesuit Sources

Bartoli D., *Dell'Istoria della Compagnia di Gesù. L'Asia. Parte Prima*, Rome, 1673; Piacenza, 1819; Venice, 1833.

Catalogus Operiarorum Societatis Jesu qui inter Sancti Thomae Christianos Malabarenses aliquando laboraverunt, Ed., L. Besse s.j. Trichinopoly, 1917.

Collegii Coccinensis Socii juxta Catalogos Provinciae Malabaricae ab anno 1707 ad annum 1655, Ed., L. Besse s.j. Trichinopoly, 1919.

Compendium Indicum Societatis Jesu, Rome, 1737.

De Souza F., *Oriente conquistado a Jesu Christo pelos Padres da Compañhia de Jesus da Provincia de Goa*, Lisbon, 1710; Bombay, 1881, 2 vols.

Documenta Indica, Ed., J. Wicki s. j., Rome, 1945-56. 4 vols.

Fenicio J. s.j., *Livro da Seita dos Indios Orientais e principalmente dos Malavares*, Ed., J. Charpentier, Uppsala, 1933.

Francis Xavier St., *Epistolae S. Francisci Xaverii aliaque eius scripta*. Nova Editio, Ed., G. Schurhammer & J. Wicki s. j., Rome, 1944-5, 2 vols. *M.H.S.J.* vol. 67-8. *M.M.S.I.* vol. I-II.

Franco A., *Synopsis Annalium Societatis Jesu in Lusitania, 1540-1725*, Augsburg & Graz, 1726.

Gonçalves D. s. j., *Historia do Malavar*, Ed., J. Wicki, s. j., Münster i.w., 1955.

Guerreiro F., *Relacam annual das cousas que fizeram os Padres da Compañhia de Jesus na India e Japao nos annos 1600-1/ 1602-3/ 1604-5/ 1606-7/ 1607-8*, successively published at Evora, 1603, and at Lisbon, 1605, 1607, 1609, 1611. New edition of all the 'relations' by A. Viegas, Coïmbra & Lisbon, 1930-42, 3 vols.

Guzman L. de, *Historia de la Missiones de la Compañia de Jesus en la India Oriental, en la China y Japon desde 1540 hasta 1600*, Alcala, 1601, 2 vols. Bilbao, 1891, 1 vol.

Hay J., *De rebus japonicis, indicis, et peruanis, epistolae recentiores*, Antwerp, 1605.

Hazart C., *Kerkelijcke Historie van de gheheele wereld*, Antwerp 1682, vol. I.

Hosten H., 'Jesuit Annual Letters from Goa and Cochin, 1618-24', *The Examiner*, 1912, pp. 47-8, 57-8, 67-8, 97-9, 107-9, 111-19, 127-8, 137-9.

—— 'Jesuit Statistics for Goa and Cochin, 1600-8', ibid. 1911, pp. 437-8.

Jarric P. du, *Histoire des choses les plus mémorables adventures tant ez*

Indes Orientales, que autres pais de la Descôuverte des Portugais, en l'établissement et progrez de la foy chrestienne et catholique; et principalement de ce que les religieux de la Compagnie de Jesus y ont fait et enduré pour la mesme fin, Paris, 1608-14, 3 vols. Latin translation, Thesaurus Rerum Indicarum, Ed., M. Martinez Cologne, 1615-16, 3 vols.

Kreningh J., Conquistas na India em apostolicos missôes da Companhia de Jesus ... ate o anno 1744, Lisbon, 1750.

Lettres des pays estrangers, ou il y a plusieurs choses curleuses d'édfication. Envoyées des Missions de ces pays là, Chaignon, Paris, 1668.

Lettres de Jersey, St. Helier, 12-15 (1893-6)

Lettres d'Uclès, Uclès, 1888-94.

Lettere annue d'Etiopia, Malabar, Brasil e Goa, 1620-4, Rome, 1627

Maffei J.P., Historiarum Indicarum Libri XVI, Selectarum item ex India Epistolarum Libri IV. Accessit liber recentiorum Epistolarum, a Joanne Hayo Dalgattiensi Scoto ex eadem Societate nunc primum excusus, cum Indice accurato, Cologne, 1590, Antwerp, 1605. Preceded by the same author's Latin translation of E. Acosta, Rerum a Societate Jesu in Oriente gestarum ... commentarius ... Dillingen, 1571, Paris, 1572, Naples, 1573, Cologne, 1574, 1583.

Nouveaux advis de l'estat du christianisme ès pays et royaulmes des Indes Orientales et Jappon, Paris, 1582.

Orlandini N, continued by Sacchini F., Poussives P., Jouvancy J. de, & Cordara J., Historia Societatis Jesu, Rome, 1615-1750 & 1859, 6 vols.

Pimenta N., Nova relatio historica de rebus in India Orientali a Patribus Societatis Jesu anno 1598-9 gestis ... Mayence, 1601.

——— Exemplar epistolae P. Nicholai Pimentae Provinciae Indiae Orientalis Visitatoris, ad Adm.Rev.P.Cl. Aquavivam Praepositum Generalem S.J., de statu Rei Christianae in India Oct. Kal. Dec. anno 1600 datae, Rome, 1602, Mayence, 1602.

Raguagli d'alcune Missioni fatte dalli Padri della Compagnia di Gesù nelle Indie Orientali, Rome, 1615.

Relation de ce qui s'est passé dans les Indes Orientales ... par les Pères de la Compagnie de Jésus, Paris, 1657.

Relation des missions des Pères de la Compagnie de Jésus dans les Indes Orientales, ..., Paris, 1659.

Relatione delle Missioni e Christianità che appartengono alla Provincia di Malabar della Compagnie di Gesù, Rome, 1645.

Roz F., *De Erroribus Nestorianorum*, Ed., J. Hausherr s.j., O.C. 11 (1928), n. 1.

Saulière A. & Hosten H., 'Extracts from some Jesuit Annual Letters, Malabar and the Fishery Coast', *The Indian Athenaeum*, 1 (1923), pp. 49-58.

—— 'Annual Letter of 1582,' ibid. pp. 11-16.

Schurhammer G., 'The History of Malabar of Fr. Diogo Gonsalvez s.j. (1615)', *K.S.P.* 1 (1930), pp. 307-8.

—— 'Das "Livro da seita dos indios orientais" der P. J. Fenicio s.j. (1609)', *A.H.S.I.* 3 (1934), pp. 142-7.

Valignano A., *Historia del principio y progresso dela Compañia de Jesu en las Indias Orientales (1542-1564)*, Ed., J. Wicki s.j., Rome, 1944. On this work, cf. also J. Wicki s.j., 'Der zweite Teile der Historia Indica Valignano's', *A.H.S.I.* 7 (1938), pp. 275-85

Wicki J., s.j., 'Auszüge aus den Briefen der Jesuitengeneräle an die Obern in Indien (1549-1613)', *A.H.S.I.* 22 (1953), pp. 114-69.

—— 'Die, "Historia do Malavar" des P. Diago Gonçalves s. j.,' *A.H.S.I.* 14 (1946), pp. 73-101.

6 *Carmelite Sources*

Ambrose of St. Teresa, *Bio-Bibliographia Missionaria O.C.D. (1584-1940)*, Rome, 1941.

—— 'Hierarchia Carmelitana, IV, De Praesulibus Missionis Malabaricae, a Ecclesiae Verapolitanae', *A.O.C.D.* 11 (1936), pp. 188-205, 12 (1937), pp. 12-32, 13 (1938), pp. 17-37, 142-68, 209-47, 285-303, 14 (1939), pp. 27-56.

—— 'Initium Missionis Carmelitarum Discalceorum in Serra Malabarica', ibid. 11 (1936).

Eustache of St. Mary, *Istoria della Vita, Virtù, Doni e Fatti del Ven. Monsignor Fr. Giuseppe di S. Maria de Sebastiani*, 1719.

Joseph of St. Mary, *Prima Spedizione all' Indie Orientali del Padre Giuseppe di S. Maria C.D., delegato apostolico ne regni de Malavari, ordinata da Nostro Signore Alessandro Settimo*, Rome, 1666.

—— *Seconda spedizione all' Indie Orientali di Monsignor Sebastiani, Fr. Giuseppe di S. Maria C.D., prima vescovo di Hierapoli, hoggi di Bisignano e barone di S. Sofia, ordinata da Alessandro VII di gloriosa memoria*, Rome, 1672.

Paulinus of St. Bartholomew, *Examen Historico-Criticum Codicum Indicorum Bibliothecae Sacrae Congregationis de Propaganda Fide*, Rome, 1792.

——   *India Orientalis Christiana*, Rome, 1794.

——   *Musei Borgiani Velitris Codices Manuscripti Avenses Peguani Siamici Malabarici Indostani*, Rome, 1793.

——   *Notitia topographica, civilis, politica, religiosa missionis malabaricae ad finem saeculi XVIII*, Ed., Ambrose of S. Teresa o.c.d., Rome, 1938, *Monumenta Missionum Carmelitarum*, II.

——   *Viaggio all' Indie Orientali*, Rome, 1796. English translation by W. Johnston, *A Voyage to the East Indies*, London, 1800.

Valerius of St. Joseph, 'Relatio de statu atque de fructibus spiritualibus missionum nostrarum Orientis saeculo XVII. Nunc primum edita ac notis illustrata a P. Fr. Ambrosio a S. Theresa o.c.d., a.o.c.d., 13 (1938), pp. 68–97, 179–90.

Vincent Mary of St. Catherine, II *Viaggio all Indie Orientali*, Rome, 1672.

(d) INDIAN AND LOCAL SOURCES

1. *Literary and other Documents*

Acta et Decreta Concilii Provincia Verapolitanae Primi . . . , Ernakulam, 1900.

Burkitt F.C., 'The Buchanan Mss. at Cambridge' *K.S.P.* 1928 pp.1–29.

The Carmelite Congregation of Malabar, Mannanam, 1904–56.

Fabian t.o.c.d., cf. Oriental Writers and Authorities.

Itturiotz C., 'Three St. Thomas Documents', *K.S.P.* 2 (1932), pp. 205–24.

Land, *Anecdota Syriaca*, Leyden, 1862, vol. I. The sections concerning Malabar were translated by H. Hosten s.j., 'Land's Anecdota Syriaca on the Syrians of Malabar translated from the Latin', *The Indian Athenaeum*, 56 (1927), pp. 41–6, 81–88.

Le Brun P., *Explication de la Messe*, Paris, 1726, vol. III.

Luke P.W., *The Ancient Songs of the Syrian Christians of Malabar*, Kottayam, 1910.

Missa de que usamos antigos christianos di Sâo Thome ... purgada dos erros, et blasphemias nestorianas ... trasladade de siriaco, ou siriano, de verbo ad verbum em lingua latina, Coïmbra, 1608. A French translation with notes was published at Brussels in 1609 by J. B. de Glen o.e.s.a., *La messe des anciens chrétiens de Saint Thomas, en l'évêché d'Angamalé, ès Indes orientales, repurgées des erreurs et blasphèmes du nestorianisme, par ... Don Alexis de Meneses*.

Nau F., 'Deux Notices relatives au Malabar', *R.O.C.* 17 (1922), pp. 74-82.

Pareparambil A., *The Syrians in Malabar, Mar Roccos and Mar Mellos*, s.l., s.d.

——— *An account of a very important period of the history of the Catholic Syrians of Malabar*, Ernakulam, 1920.

Placid of St. Joseph T.O. C.D., *De Fontibus ...* cf. Collection of Sources.

Rocca F.X. s.j., 'La Leggenda di S. Tomaso Apostolo (Canto popolare del Malabar)', *O.C.P.* 22 (1933), pp. 168-79.

Saldanha A., *The Syriac-Malayalam Hymnal*, Cannanore, 1937.

Schurhammer G. s.j., 'Letters of Joâo da Cruz, a Nair Ambassador, c. A.D. 1515-37' *K.S.P.* 6 (1930), pp. 304-7.

Synodo diocesano da Igrega e bispado de Angamale dos antigos christâos de San Thome des Serras do Malavar das partes de India Oriental, celebrado pello Revmo Senhor Dom Frey Aleixo de Menezes ..., Coïmbra, 1606.

Taylor W., 'Brief Notice and Translation of a Tamil Manuscript, containing a legendary Account of the Apostle St. Thomas, with his miracles in Kereladesam, and at Mylapore, or St. Thomé,' *South India Christian Repository*, 1 (1837), pp. 263-6, republished by H. Hosten s.j., in *The Indian Athenaeum*, 1 (1923), pp. 8-17.

Wrede F., 'Account of S. Thomé Christians on the Coast of Malabar', *Asiatick Researches*, 7 (1805), pp. 364, ff.

2. *Archaeological and Epigraphical Documents*

Abraham C. & Joseph T.K., 'The Old Church at Kotamangalam and a Chattannur Inscription of A.D. 1273', *K.S.P.* 2 (1932), pp. 277-8.

Achan P. A., 'A Hebrew Inscription from Chennamangalam', *I.A.* 59 (1930), pp. 134-5.

Arayathinal T., 'St. Georges' Church, Irapoly, Malabar', *E.C.Q.* 3 (1938-9), p. 34.

Ayyar A.S.R., 'A new Persian Cross from Travancore', *The Ceylon Antiquary and Literary Register*, 9 (1924), pp. 188-96.

Burnell A.C., 'The oldest known South Indian Alphabet', *I.A.* 1 (1872), pp. 229-30.

—— 'The Original Settlement Deed of the Jewish Colony at Cochin', ibid. 3 (1874), pp. 333-4.

—— 'Pahlavi Inscriptions', ibid. 2 (1873), pp. 183 and 273.

—— 'On some Pahlavi Inscriptions in South India', ibid. 3 (1874), pp. 308-16. Printed at Mangalore, 1873, as a separate booklet.

—— *South Indian Palaeography*, London, 1878.

Cotton J.J., *List of Inscriptions on tombs or monuments in Madras, possessing historical or archaeological interest*, Madras, 1905.

Daniel K.N., 'The Archuvannam and the Manigramam of the Kottayam plates of Tarur Iravi or the Jews and Christians of Malabar', *I.A.* 53 (1924), pp. 257-61.

—— 'An Inscription of Iraya Chirika (Raja Simha) Perumal', *I.A.* 58 (1929), pp. 158-60.

—— 'Kottayam plate of Vira-Raghava Chakravarti', ibid. 53 (1924), pp. 185-96, 219-29, 244-51.

Ellis F.W., 'Analysis of the Copper-Grant in the possession of the Jews', *Madras Journal of Literature and Science*, 12 (1844), pp. 1-17.

Figueiredo N. de, 'Epigrafia Indica. O Tumúlo de S. Tomé em Meliapôr', *Boletim do Instituto Vasco da Gama*, n. 18 (1933), pp. 82-93.

—— *St. Thomas the Apostle in Mylapore. Three documents: his Tomb (1543); his Relics (1601); Stone Cross (1601)*, Madras, 1935.

'Grant to the Early Christian Church of India', *J.R.A.S.* 7 (1843), pp. 343-4, with six lithographs.

Gundert H., 'Translation and Analysis of the Ancient Documents engraved on copper in possession of the Syrian Christians and Jews of Malabar', *Madras Journal of Literature and Science*, 13 (1845), I, pp. 115-46; II, pp. 11-14.

Hallegue E.I. & Joseph T.K., 'A Hebrew Inscription of A.D. 1269 from Chennamangalam in Cochin', *K.S.P.* 2, ser. 10, (1932), p. 234.

Harlez M. de, 'L'inscription Pahlévie de la Croix de S. Tomé' *Actes du IIe Congrès International des Orientalistes*, Paris, 1899, vol. I, section 1 pp. 249-52.

Hosten H. s.j., 'Saint Thomas and San Thomé, Mylapore. 1. Altar Crosses in Malabar and at San Thomé', *The Indian Athenaeum*, 1 (1923), pp. 67-85.

——— 'Thomas Cana and his Copper-Plate Grant', *I.A.* 56 (1927), pp. 121-8, 147-55, 177-86.

Hultzsch E., 'Cochin Plates of Bhaskara Ravivarman', *Epigraphia Indica*, Calcutta, 1894-5, vol. III, pp. 66-9.

Joseph T.K., 'Another enigmatic Inscription from Travancore', *I.A.* 56 (1927), p. 129.

——— 'Christian and Non-Christian Crosses in Ancient India', *J.I.H.* 28 (1950), pp. 111-22.

——— 'A Hebrew Inscription from Parur', *K.S.P.* ser 3 (1930), pp. 166-7.

——— 'The *Magna Carta* of the Malabar Christians', *Asiatic Review*, (1925), pp. 299-304.

——— 'The Malabar Christians Copper-Plates', *K.S.P.* ser. 4 (1930), pp. 201-4.

——— '*Malabar Christians and Their Ancient Documents*' Trivandrum, 1929.

——— 'Malabar Miscellany. I. Another Persian Cross in Travancore. II. A Greek Inscription at Chayal', *I.A.* 52 (1923), pp. 355-7.

——— 'Malabar Miscellany. V. A. Rajasimha Inscription at Talehkad in Cochin. VI. Inscription in the reverse of the Talehkad Rajasimha Stone', *I.A.* 57 (1928), pp. 24-31.

——— 'A Pahlavi Inscription round a Persian Cross at Katamaram, Travancore', ibid. 53 (1924), p. 123.

——— 'A Travancore Inscription in Greek Script', *J.I.H.* 27 (1949), pp. 179-84.

Jouvreau-Dubreuil G., 'Les ruines romaines de Pondichéry', *Bulletin de l'Ecole Française de l'Extrême-Orient*, 40 (1940), pp. 448-50.

——— 'The Temple of Augustus in the South of India', *The Q. J. M. S.* 19 (1929), pp. 180-1.

Kielhorn F., 'The Date of the Kottayam Plate of Vira-Raghava', *Epigraphia Indica*, Calcutta, 1900-1, vol. VI pp. 83-4.

Kukkil K.N., 'Memorandum on the Syrian and Jewish Copper-Plate of Malabar', *Madras Journal of Literature and Science*, 21 (old ser. 1859-60), nos. 9-10, pp. 30-55.

Loewe H., 'Hebrew inscription from Parur', *K.S.P.* ser. 5 (1930), p. 286.

Love H.D., *Vestiges of Old Madras, 1640-1800*, London, 1913, vol. I.

Manhali V., *A Brief History of the Palayur Church*, Trichur, 1926.

Marshall J., *A. Guide to Taxila*, Delhi, 1936, 3rd ed.

—— *Taxila*, Cambridge, 1951, 3 vols.

Modi J.J., 'A Christian Cross with a Pahlavi Inscription recently discovered in the Travancore State', *J.B.B.R.A.S.* 2 (new series, 1926), pp. 1-18.

Monteiro d'Aguiar J., Hosten H. s.j., Joseph T.K., 'The Magna Carta of the St. Thomas Christians', *K.S.P.* ser. 4 (1930), pp. 169-200.

Pisharoti K.R., 'Cranganore', *I.H.Q.* 2 (1926), pp. 617-22.

Quadros J., 'Epigrafia Indica. Uma Inscriçâo em Pahlavi', *Boletim do Instituto Vasco da Gama*, 14 (1932), pp. 1-31.

Schurhammer G. s.j., 'Some Malayalam words and their identification', *K.S.P.* ser. 4 (1930), pp. 221-3 (ibid. pp. 223-4, notes by T.K. Joseph).

Venkayya V., 'Kottayam Plate of Vira-Raghava', *Epigraphia Indica*, Calcutta, 1896-7, vol. IV pp. 290-7.

Wariar A.G., 'Some Historical Sites and Monuments of Kerala', *I.H.Q.* 4 (1929), pp. 534-44.

West E.W., 'Inscriptions around Crosses in South India', *Epigraphia Indica*, Calcutta, 1896-7, vol. IV pp. 174-6.

—— 'Some Remarks on the Malabar Copper-Plates', *J.R.A.S.* 1870, pp. 388-90.

Winckworth C.P.T., 'A new Interpretation of the Pahlavi Cross-Inscriptions of Southern India', *J.T.S.* 30 (1929), pp. 237-44. Reprinted in *K.S.P.* ser. 3 (1930), pp. 159-68.

—— 'Revised Interpretation of the Pahlavi Cross Inscriptions of South India', *K.S.P.* ser 5. (1930) pp. 267-9.

—— & Burkitt F.C., 'Notes on the Pahlavi, Kufic and Hebrew Signatures to the Quilon Plates', ibid. ser. 6 (1930), pp. 320-3.

(e) VARIOUS SOURCES AND DOCUMENTS

Anquetil du Perron, *Zend-Avesta*, Paris, 1771, vol. Ia, pp. CLVI-CXCI.

Baldaeus P., *A True and Exact Description of the Most Celebrated East-India Coasts of Malabar and Coromandel, and also of the Isle of Ceylon*, London, 1703, 3 vols.

Biermann B. o.p., 'Documenta quaedam initia Missionum Ordinis Praedicatorum in India Orientali illustrantia (1503-48)' *A.F.P.* 10 (1940), pp. 132-57.

Bihl M. and Moule A.C., 'De duabus Epistolis Fratrum Minorum Tartariae Aquilonaris an. 1323', *A.F.H.* 15 (1923), pp. 89-112.

—— 'Tria nova documenta de Missionibus Fratrum Minorum Tartariae Aquilonaris annorum 1314-22' ibid. 17 (1924), pp. 55-71.

Bracciolini P., *Historia de Varietate Fortunae*, Paris, 1723.

Cerri U., *An Account of the State of the Roman Catholic Religion throughout the World*, London, 1715.

Domenichelli T., *Sopra la Vita e i Viaggi del Beato Odorico da Pordenone dell' Ordine de' Minori. Studi con documenti rari ed inediti del Chierico Franscecano T. Domenichelli sotto la direzione del P. Marcellino da Civizza M.O.*, Prato, 1881.

Dubois J.P.J., *Vie des gouverneurs-généraux de la Compagnie des Indes, avec l'abrégé de l'histoire des établissements hollandais aux Indes Orientales*, The Hague, 1703.

Cunes F., *Memoir of Commander Frederick Cunes ... on 31st December 1750*, Madras, 1908, *Selections from the Records of the Madras Government, Dutch Records*, no. III.

Galletti, Van der Borg & Groot P. s.s.j., *The Dutch in Malabar being a translation of selections nos. 1 and 2 with introduction and notes*, Madras, 1911, ibid. no. XIII.

Geddes M., *The History of the Church of Malabar from 1501 till 1599, giving an account of the persecution and violent methods of the Roman prelates to reduce them to the Church of Rome, together with the Synod of Diamper*, London, 1694.

India in the Fifteenth Century, edited with an introduction by H.R. Major, London, 1857. *Hakluyt Society.*

Jordanus Catalani, *Mirabilia Descripta. Les Merveilles de l'Asie. Texte Latin, fac-similé et traduction française avec introduction et notes par H. Cordier.* Paris, 1925. An English translation of the same was published by Yule in London, 1863, *Hakluyt Society*.

La Croze M. Veyssière de, *Histoire du Christianisme des Indes*, The Hague, 1724.

Longhena M., *Viaggi in Persia, India e Giava di Nicolo de Conti* Milan, 1929.

Marignola J., *Chronicle*, Ed., J. Emler, Praga, 1882, *Fontes Rerum Bohemicarum*, vol. III, pp. 496-507.

Fracanzono da Montalboddo M., *Paesi novamente retrovati, et novo mondo da Alberico Vesputio Florentino*, Vicenze, 1507.

Norbert O.M. CAP., *Mémoires Historiques*, Lucques, 1745, 3 vols.

Polo Marco, *The Book of Ser Marco Polo the Venetian*, Ed., H. Yule London, 1875, 2 vols. *Hakluyt Society*.

—— *Il Millione*. Prima edizione integrale a cura di Professore Luigi Foscolo Benedetto sotto il patronato della città di Venezia, Florence, 1928.

—— *The most noble and famous travels of Marco Polo together with the travels of Nicolo de' Conti*. Edited from the Elizabethan translation of John Frampton with introduction, notes and appendices by N. M. Penzer, London, 1929.

—— *The Travels of Marco Polo* translated into English from the text of L. F. Benedetto by Prof. Aldo Ricci, London, 1931.

—— *The Description of the World*, Ed., A. C. Moule & P. Pelliot London, 1938-9, 2 vols.

Poujade J., *La route des Indes et ses navires. Documents d'Ethnographie navale*, Paris, 1948.

Raulin I.F. O.E.S.A., *Historia Ecclesiae Malabaricae cum Diamperitana Synodo apud Indos Nestorianos, S. Thomae Chritianos nuncupatos, coacta ab Alexio de Menezes Augustinensi Anno Domni MDXCIX, nunc primum e Lusitano in Latinum versa cui accedunt, cum Liturgia Malabarica tum Dissertationes variae: omnia perpetuis animadversionibus illustrata*, Rome, 1755.

Sassetti F., *Lettere sopra i suoi viaggi nelle India Orientali dal 1578 al 1588*, Reggio, 1844.

Sebastiani Joseph of St. Mary, *Breve racconto della vita, missioni, e morte gloriosa del Ven. P. M. F. Donati O.P.*, Rome, 1669.

Swanston C., 'A Memoir of the Primitive Church of Malay-Ala, or of the Syrian Christians of the Apostle Thomas, from its first rise to the present time', *J.R.A.S.* 1834, pp. 171-92, 1835, pp. 51-62, 234-47.

Valentyn, *Oud- en Nieuw Ost-Indië*, Amsterdam-Dordrecht, 1711-13, 4 vols.

Van Angelbeek J.G., *Memoir of Johan Gerard Van Angelbeek . . . in the year 1793*, Ed., P. Groots s.j., Madras, 1908, *Selections . . . , Dutch Records*, no. IV.

Van Gollenesse Stein, *Memoir on the Malabar Coast 1743 A.D.*, Madras, 1908, ibid. no. I

Van Rheede H.A., *Memoir written in the year A.D. 1677* Madras, 1911, ibid. no. XIV.

Van den Wijngaert A., o.f.m., *Sinica Franciscana*, Karachi, 1929, vol. I.

Varthema L. di, *The Itinerary of Ludovico di Varthema of Bologna from 1502 to 1508*, as translated from the original Italian edition of 1510, by John Winter Jones f.s.a. in 1863 for the Hakluyt Society with a Discourse on Varthema and his travels in South India, Ed., R. C. Temple, London, 1928.

Voste J. M. o.p., 'Missio duorum fratrum Melitensium o.p. in Orientem saeculo XVI, et relatio, nunc prima edita, eorum quae in istis regionibus gesserunt', *A.O.P.* 33 (1925), pp. 261-78.

Waigand J., *Missiones Indiarum Orientalium S. Congregationi de de Propaganda Fide conceditae, iuxta Visitationem Apostolicam 1859-1862*, Rome 1940. unpublished dissertation.

Weijerman G., *Memoir of Commandeur Godefridus Weijerman . . . on the 22nd February 1765*, Ed., P. Groots s.j. Madras, 1910, *Selections . . . , Dutch Records* no. XII.

Wicki J. s.j., 'Zur Orientreise des päpstlichen Nuntius Ambrosius Buttigeg o.p. (1553-1556)', *O.C.P.* 19 (1953), pp. 350-71.

Wytfliet C., Magin A., etc., *Histoire Universelle de la Conversion des Indiens*, Douai, 1605-7, 3 vols.

(f) MODERN WORKS

1. *Works dealing with the St. Thomas Christians or closely related subjects*

Abraham C.E., 'Malpan Abraham and the Reform Movement in

the Syrian Church', *National Christian Council Review*
15 (1937), pp. 33-41.

Abraham C. E., 'The Syrian Church] of Malabar. Its contribution
to the Church in India', *The Indian Journal of Theology*, 1
(1952) 2, pp. 22-9.

Adeney W.F., *The Greek and Eastern Churches*, New York, 1938.

Agur C., *The Church History of Travancore*, Madras, 1903.

Aiyar M.S.R., 'The Apostle Thomas and India', *Q. J.M.S.* 20,
(1929-30), pp. 271-83.

—— 'Apostle Thomas. Was it a Mysore Maharaja that brought
him to India?', ibid. pp. 26-31.

Alori A. o.p., 'I Domenicani nell' India dal Secolo XIII al Secolo
XIX', *Missioni Domenicane*, 11 (1937), pp. 79-81, 99-101.

—— 'II P. Francesco Donati O.P. Missionario e Martire nelle
Indie (1596-1635)', ibid. 13 (1940), pp. 30-1, 34-6.

Amann E., 'Apocryphes du Nouveau Testament', *D.B.S.* vol. I,
460-533.

—— 'La Théologie de l'Eglise Nestorienne', *D.T.C.* vol. II,
289-313.

—— 'Rites Malabares', ibid. vol. IX, 1704-45.

André de Sainte-Marie o.c.d., 'Vers la fin d'un long schisme',
Les Missions Catholiques, 1931, pp. 509-14.

Antâo G.M., *De Synodi Diamperitanae Natura atque Decretis*, Goa,
1952.

Anthony K.J., *Verapoly Archdiocese. A Short History*, Ernakulam,
1947.

Arayathinal T., 'The Missionary Enterprises of the Syrian Catholics
of Malabar', *E.C.Q.* 7 (1947), pp. 236-51.

Attwater D., *The Christian Churches of the East*, London and Mil-
waukee, 1935 and 1947, 2 vols.

—— *Eastern Catholic Worship*, New York, 1945.

Aubert R., *Pie XI*, Paris, 1952, *Histoire de l'Eglise*, vol. XX

Ayyar A.S.R., 'Cheraman-Perumal-Nayanan', *I.A.* 54 (1925),
pp. 7-15.

—— 'The Martyrdom of St. Thomas the Apostle', *J.B.B.R.A.S.*
21 (1925), pp. 508-48.

Ayyar K.V.K., *The Zamorins of Calicut from the earliest times down to
A.D. 1806*, Calicut, 1938.

Ayyar R.B.L.K.A., *Anthropology of the Syrian Christians*, Ernakulam, 1926.

Badger G.P., *The Nestorians and their Rituals*, London, 1852, 2 vols.

Baiâo A., Cidade H., Murias M., (Editors) *Historia da Expansao Portuguesa no Mundo*, Lisbon, 1937-40, 3 vols.

Balme F. O.P., 'Un Missionnaire Dominicain en Orient au quatorzième siècle. Le B. Jourdain de Sévérac, Evêque de Coulam, sur la côte de Malabar, aux Indes Orientales, 1318-36', *L'Année Dominicaine*, 1886, pp. 4-10, 58-70, 217-25, 255-60, 297-305.

Bamboat Z., *Les voyageurs français aux Indes aux XVIIe et XVIIIe siècles*, Paris, 1933.

Barone G., *Vita, precursori ed opere del P. Paolino da S. Bartolomeo (Filippo Werdin)*, Naples, 1888.

Barthold W., *La découverte de l'Asie*, Paris, 1947.

—— *Zur Geschichte des Christentums in Mittel-Asien bis zur mongolischen Eroberung*, Tübingen, 1901, and Leipzig, 1929.

Bartholomew of Jesus T.O.C.D., *The Syrian Christians in Malabar*, Mangalore, 1917.

Bateman J., *The Life of the Right Reverend Daniel Wilson*, London, 1860, 2 vols.

Battandier A., 'Les Eglises Syriennes du Malabar', *An. P. Cat.*, 22 (1929), pp. 497-513.

Beach H.P., *The Cross in the Land of the Trident*, London, 1896

Beauvoir Priaulx O. de, *The Indian Travels of Apollonius of Tyana and the Indian Embassies to Rome from the reign of Augustus to the death of Justinian*, London, 1873.

Bello S., *La Congrégation de S. Hormisdas et l'Eglise Chaldéenne dans la première moitié du XIXe siècle*, Rome, 1939, O.C.A. no. 122.

Beltrami G., 'La Chiesa Caldea nel Secolo dell 'Unione', *O.C.* 29 (1933), fasc. 83.

Benedict O.I.C., 'The Malankara Rite', *C.M.* 16 (1952), pp. 403-6

Bernard of St. Thomas T.O.C.D., *A Brief Sketch of the History of the St. Thomas Christians*, Trichinopoly, 1924.

—— *The History of the St. Thomas Christians* (in Malayalam), Palai-Mannanam, 1916-21, 2 vols.

Besse L. S.J., *La Mission du Maduré*, Trichinopoly, 1914.

Bertrand J. S.J., *Mémoires historiques sur les Missions des ordres religieux et spécialement sur la question du Clergé Indigène et des Rites Malabars*, Paris, 1862.

Biermann B.M., 'Der erste Bischof in Ost-Indien. Fray Duarte Nunez O.P.', *N.Z.M.W.* 9 (1953), pp. 81-90.

Bonin C.E., 'Notes sur les anciennes chrétientés nestoriennes de l'Asie Centrale (XIIIe-XIVe siècles)', *J.A.* 15 (1900), pp. 584-92.

Bornkamm G., *Mythos und Legende in den apokryphen Thomas-Akten*, Göttingen, 1933.

Brière M., 'Histoire du couvent de Rabban Hormizd de 1808 à 1832', *R.O.C.* 15 (1910), pp. 410-24; 16 (1911), pp. 113-27, 349-54, 346-55.

Bragança Pereira A.B. de, *Historia Administrativa de Goa*, Bastora, 1937, 2 vols.

—— *Historia Politica, Diplomatica e Militar de Goa*, Bastora, 1936, vol. I.

—— 'Historia Religiosa de Goa', *Oriente Portuguêz*, 1932, fasc. 213, pp. 34, ff.

Brodrick J. s.j., *Saint Francis Xavier*, London, 1952.

Brou A. s.j., 'La disparition des Jésuites de l'Inde après les décrets de Pombal', *R.H.M.* 10 (1933), pp. 69-78.

—— 'L'Evangélisation de l'Inde au Moyen-Age', *Etudes*, 87 (1901), pp. 577-605.

—— 'Les origines du clergé indigène l'Inde', *R.H.M.* 7 (1930), pp. 46-73.

—— *Saint François Xavier, 1506-1548*, Paris, 1912, 2 vols.

Brown L.W., *The Indian Christians of St. Thomas*, Cambridge, 1956

Browne E.F., 'The Syrian Church of Malabar', *The Christian East*, 5 (1924), pp. 45-7.

Browne L.E., *The Eclipse of Christianity in Asia from the time of Muhammad till the fourteenth century*, Cambridge, 1933.

Buchanan C., *Christian Researches in India*, London, 1812 and 1858.

Burkitt F.C., *Early Christianity outside the Roman Empire*, Cambridge, 1899.

—— *Early Eastern Christianity. St. Margaret's Lectures 1904 on the Syriac-speaking Church*, London, 1904.

—— 'The Original Language of the Acts of Judas-Thomas', *J.T.S.* 1 (1900), pp. 280-90, 3 (1902), pp. 94, ff.

Burkitt F. C., 'Saint Thomas', *Encyclopaedia Brittanica*, 11th ed. vol. XXVI.

Burnell A., 'Earliest Christian Missions in South India. A Reply to Rev. A. Collins', *I.A.* 4 (1875), pp. 181-3.

—— 'Malabar Christians', ibid. 5 (1875), pp. 25-6.

The Carmelite Congregation of Malabar, 1831-1931, Trichinopoly, 1932.

Castets J. s.j., 'The Portuguese Missions of Goa, Cochin and Ceylon', *The Examiner*, 1922, pp. 193-5, 203-4, 213-15, 223-5.

Chabot J.B., 'L'autodafé des livres syriaques au Malabar', *Florilegium . . . Melchior de Vogüé*, Paris, 1909, pp. 613-23.

Charles P. s.j., 'Europe and the Far East', *European Civilization*, Ed., E. Eyre, London, 1939, vol. VII, pp. 595-811.

Charlesworth M.P., *Trade Routes and Commerce of the Roman Empire*, Cambridge, 1924.

Charpentier J., 'Cesare de Federici and Gasparo Balbi', *I.A.* 53 (1924), pp. 49-61.

—— 'St. Thomas the Apostle and India', *Kyrkohistorisk Arsskrift*, 27 (1927), pp. 21-47.

Chatfield R., *A Historical Review of the Commercial, Political and Moral State of Hindoostan, from the earliest period to the present time: The Rise and the Progress of Christianity in the East, its present condition, and the means and probability of its future Advancement*, London, 1808.

Chatterjee K.R., 'Side-Lights on the Racial Origin of Nambudri Brahmans of South India', *Annals of the Bhandarkar Institute*, 21 (1941), pp. 266-9.

Chatterton E., *A History of the Church of England in India,* London, 1924.

Cheriyan P., *The Malabar Christians and the Church Missionary Society: 1816-1840*, Kottayam, 1935.

Clemen C., *Der Einfluss des Christentums auf anderen Religionen*, Leipzig, 1933.

Codrington K. de B., *Ancient India from the earliest times to the Guptas*, London, 1926.

Collins R., 'Malabar Christians', *I.A.* 4 (1875), pp. 311-14.

—— 'Manicheans on the Malabar Coast', ibid. pp. 153-5.

—— *Missionary Enterprise in the East with especial Reference to the Syrian Christians of Malabar and the Results of Modern Missions*, London, 1873.

Conner, 'Christians (in Memoir of the Survey of Travancore)', *The Madras Journal of Literature and Science*, 1, (1834), pp. 78-82.

Connolly R.H., O.S.B., 'A Negative Golden Rule in the Syriac Acts of Thomas', *J.T.S.* 36 (1935), pp. 353-7.

Costa, A. de Jesus da, *Acçâo missionaria e patriotica de Dom Frei Aleixo de Meneses, Arcebispo de Goa e Primaz de Oriente*, Lisbon 1940, *Congreso do mundo Português, Publicaçoes, vol. IV*.

Crivelli C. s.J., 'Una "Chiesa" Protestante di Rito Orientale', *La Civiltà Cattolica*, 93 (1942), pp. 354-66.

Cros L.J.M. s.J., *Saint François Xavier. Sa Vie et ses Lettres*, Toulouse, 1900, 2 vols.

Cruz F.M. d', Ed., *Goa and St. Francis Xavier and St. Thomas Apostle in India*, Arsikere, 1952.

Cunha Riviera J. H. da, *A Conjuraçâo de 1787 em Goa e Varias Cousas disse Tempo. Memoria Historica*, Nova Goa, 1875.

Cunningham A., *Ancient Geography of India*, Calcutta, 1924.

Dahlmann J. s.J., *Indische Fahrten*, Freiburg i. B., 1908, 2 vols.

—— *Die Thomas-Legende und die ältesten historischen Beziehungen des Christentums zum fernen Osten in Lichte der indischen Altertumskunde*, Freiburg i. B., 1912.

Daniel K.N., *A Brief Sketch of the Church of St. Thomas in Malabar*, Kottayam, 1933.

—— 'The Burial Place of St. Thomas', *J.I.H.* 30 (1952), pp. 205-11.

—— *The Date of Parkara Iravi Varma, Emperor of Kerala*, Tiruvalla, 1945.

—— 'Roman Catholicism and the Church of Malabar before the 16th century', *Y.M.I.* April 1923, pp. 26, ff.

—— 'Rome and the Malabar Church', *K.S.P.* 2 ser. 11 (1933) pp. 307-40.

—— *The South Indian Apostolate of St. Thomas*, Serampore, 1950.

—— 'Vira Ravi Varma of Travancore, 1594-1604, and the Portuguese', *J.I.H.* 26 (1948), pp. 169-87.

Daniel I., *The Syrian Church in Malabar*, Madras, 1949.

Danvers F. C., *The Portuguese in India, being a History of the rise and decline of their Eastern Empire*, London, 1894, 2 vols.

Dauviller J., 'Droit Chaldéen', *D.D.C.* vol. III, 292-388.

—— 'Les Provinces Chaldéennes "de l'Extérieur" au Moyen -

Age', *Mélanges offerts au R. P. F. Cavallera* s.j., Toulouse, 1948, pp. 260-316.

Day F., *The Land of the Permauls of Cochin, its Past and its Present*, Madras, 1863.

D'Cruz F.A., *St. Thomas the Apostle in India. An Investigation based on the last researches in connection with the time-honoured tradition regarding St. Thomas in Southern India*, Madras, 1929, 2nd ed.

Deb H. K., 'St. Thomas and a Kushan King' *J.B.B.R.A.S.* 29 (1933), pp. 311, ff.

—— 'Vikramaditya and his era', *Zeitschrift für Indologie u. Iranistik*, 1 (1922), pp. 250-302.

De Backer L., *L'Extrême Orient au Moyen-Age*, Paris, 1877.

Delduque Da Costa A., 'Os Portugueses e os Reis da India', *Boletim do Instituto Vasco da Gama* 1932, no. 13, pp. 1-45, no. 15, pp. 1-38; 1933, no. 18, pp. 1-28, no. 20, pp. 1-40.

Devos P. s.j., 'Le miracle posthume de S. Thomas l'Apôtre' *A.B.* 66 (1948), pp. 231-75.

De Witte C. M. o.s.b., 'Les bulles pontificales et l'expansion portugaise au XVe siècle', *R.H.E.* 48 (1953), pp. 683-718, 49 (1954), pp. 438-61. 51 (1956), pp. 413-53.

Donauer F., *Auf Apostelwegen in Indien. Der Schweizer Bischof Aloisius Benziger vom Ordern der unbeschuhten Karmeliter, 1864-1942*, Einsiedeln, 1944.

Donovan D., 'The Death of Mar Ivanios', *Unitas*, 5 (1953), pp. 149-52.

D'Orsey A. J. D., *Portuguese Discoveries, Dependencies, and Missions in Asia and Africa*, London, 1893.

Doyle J., 'St.Thomas of Mylapur', *Catholic Encyclopaedia*, vol. XIII, p. 382.

D'Sa M., *The Martyrs of Thana*, Bombay, 1915.

Duchesne L., *Eglises Séparées*, Paris, 1905.

Dupont P., 'Voyageurs Européens aux Indes du XIIe au XIVe siècle', *Bulletin des Amis de l'Orient*, no. 13, pp. 27-42.

Edelby N., 'Note sur le catholicosat de Romagyris', *P.O.C.* 2 (1952), pp. 39-46.

Etheridge J. W., *The Syrian Churches, their early History, Liturgies and Literature*, London, 1846.

Ettumanukaram J., 'St. Thomas. The Witness of Greek and Latin Fathers', *St. Thomas the Apostle. . .* , pp. 81-8.

Farquhar J. N., 'The Apostle Thomas in North India', *B.J.R.L.* 10 (1926), pp. 80-111. Reprint, Manchester, 1926.

——— , 'The Apostle Thomas in South India', ibid. 11 (1927), pp. 20-50.

Felix O. M. CAP., *Historical and Traditional Records on Early Christianity in Northern India*, Agra, 1908.

Ferreira Martins J. F., *Cronica dos Vice-Reis e Governadores da India*, Nova Goa, 1919.

Ferroli D. S.J., *The Jesuits in Malabar*, Bangalore, 1939-51, 2 vols.

Filliozat J., 'Intercourse of India with the Roman Empire during the opening centuries of the Christian Era' *J.I.H.* 28 (1950), pp. 23-44.

Fleet J. F., 'Salivahana and the Saka Era', *J.R.A.S.* 1916, pp. 809-20.

Fleet J.F., 'St. Thomas and Gondaphernes', ibid. 1905, pp. 223-36, 1906, pp. 706-11.

Fortescue A., *The Lesser Eastern Churches*, London, 1913.

Garbriel O.I.C., 'Bethany', *E.C.Q.* 11 (1955), pp. 136-40.

Garbe R., *Indien und das Christentum*, Tübingen, 1914.

Garsten W. A., 'The Syrian Christians in the Indian States of Travancore and Cochin', *The Christian East*, 18 (1938), pp. 40-8.

George V. C., 'St. Francis Xavier and St. Thomas Christians', *St. Francis Xavier. Souvenir of the Fourth Centenary of the Death of St. Francis Xavier*, Ernakulam, 1952, pp. 85-108.

——— 'Thomas, Emperor of India', *The New Review*, 14 (1941), pp. 113-21.

Germann W., *Die Kirche des Thomaschristens. Ein Beitrag zur Geschichte den orientalischen Kirchen*, Gütersloh, 1877.

Gracias J. B. A., 'Portuguese na India', *O Oriente Português*, 1934-5, pp. 393-434.

Graf G., 'Garweh', *L.F.T.K.* vol. IV, 290-91.

Grierson G., 'Bhakti-Marga. 5. Influence of Christianity', *E.R.E.* vol. II, pp. 548-50.

——— 'Modern Hinduism and its debt to the Nestorians' *J.R.A.S.* 1907, pp. 311-35, 477-503.

Grousset R., Auboyer J., Buhor J., *L'Asie Orientale des origines au XVe siècle*, Paris, 1941, *Histoire du Moyen-Age*, X.

Gubernatis A. de, *Storia dei Viaggiatori Italiani nelle Indie Orientali*, Livorno, 1875.

Hambye. E. R. s.j., 'St. Thomas and India'. *C.M.* 16 (1952), pp. 363-75.

—— The Syrian Church in India till the Advent of the Portuguese', ibid. 16 (1952), pp. 376-89.

—— 'The Syrian Jacobites in India', *E.C.Q.* 11 (1955), pp. 115-29.

—— 'The Syrians and the Jesuits', *Deepika Special Number*, Kottayam, 1952, pp. 243-48.

Harnack A., *Die Mission und Ausbreitung des Christentums* Leipzig, 1924, 4th ed., 2 vols.

Hasan Khan M., *History of Tipu Sultan*, Calcutta-Dacca, 1954.

Heazell-Margoliouth, *Kurds and Christians*, London, 1913.

Heck K., *Hat der heilige Apostel Thomas in Indien das Evangelium gepredigt? Ein historisches Untersuchung*, Radolfzell, 1911.

Heras H. s.j., *The Conversion Policy of the Jesuits in India*, Bombay, 1933.

—— 'The Syrian Christians of Malabar', *The Examiner*, 89 (1938), pp. 81-2, 91-3, 104-5, 120-21, 135-6, 151-2, 170-1, 181-8, 207, 225-6, 242-3, 258, 278-9, 294, 310-11, 327, 344-5, 359, 373-5, 389-90, 422-3.

—— *The Two Apostles of India*, Trichinopoly, 1944.

Hindo P., *Primats d'Orient. . . . et Maphriens Syriens*, Rome, 1936.

History-Album of St. Joseph's Apostolic Central Seminary, Verapoly-Puthenpally-Alwaye, South India, Alwaye, 1932.

Hosten H. s.j., *Antiquities from San Thomé and Mylapore*, Calcutta-Mylapore, 1936.

—— 'Cheli, Chincheos (Chorii, Tochasi) and Chinese in India according to Manoel Godinho de Eredia (1613)', *J.B.B.R.A.S.* 26 (1930), pp. 457-66.

—— 'Christian Archaeology in Malabar', *The Catholic Herald of India*. 20 (1922), pp. 829. ff.

—— 'Is S. Thome in civitate Iothabis ?', *I.A.* 10 (1931), pp. 53-8.

—— 'Peter Louis s.j., or the first Indian Jesuit', *K.S.P.* ser. 1 (1928), pp. 1-3.

Hosten H., s.j., 'St. Thomas in India, or Tattah Fakirs and Fr. B. Burthey s.j', *The Indian Athenaeum*, 1 (1923), pp. 1-6.

—— 'St. Thomas and San Thome, Mylapore', *J.B.B.R.A.S.* 19 (1923), pp. 153-236.

—— 'The St. Thomas Christians of Malabar A.D. 1490-1564', *K.S.P.* ser. 5 (1931), pp. 225-59.

—— 'Thomas Cana by T. K. Joseph B.A. Further remarks on the same', *I.A.* 56 (1927), pp. 161-6; 57 (1928), pp. 103-6; 117-24, 160-5, 209-14.

—— 'Zadoe, or St. Thomas' Monastery in India (about A.D. 363)', *J.B.B.R.A.S.* 20 (1924).

Hough J., *History of Christianity in India*, London, 1839, 2 vols.

Howard G. B. Ed., *The Syrian Christians of Malabar, otherwise called the Christians of St. Thomas*, by Philippose Edevalikel, Oxford-London, 1869.

Hümmerich F., *Vasco da Gama und die Enstehung des Seewegs nach Ostindien*, München, 1898.

Hunt W. S., *The Anglican Church in Travancore and Cochin, 1816-1916* Kottayam, 1920, 2 vols.

—— 'The South Indian Syrian Churches', *The Christian East*, 5 (1924), pp. 132-4.

Huonder A. s.j., 'Deutsche Jesuitenmissionäre des 17 und 18 Jahrhunderts', *Stimmen aus Maria-Laach*, (*Erzählungshefte zu den*), Freiburg i. B., 1899.

Inacio de Santa Tereza O.S.A., 'As Cristandades do Padroado do Oriente em 1732', *Anais da Propagação da Fé*, 9 (1939), pp. 180-4.

Ivanios Mar, 'The Malabar Re-Union', *Pax*, April 1931, no. 114, pp. 1-5.

—— 'A New Branch of the Tree of Life: the Syro-Malankara Church', *The Eastern Branches of the Catholic Church*, New York, 1938, pp. 27-35.

Iyer L. A. K., 'Marriage Customs of the Nambutiris', *The New Review*, 32 (1950), pp. 36-43.

—— 'Nambutiri', ibid. 29 (1949), pp. 169-78.

Janin R. A.A., *Les Eglises Orientales et les Rites Orientaux*, Paris, 1935, 3rd ed., 1956, 4th ed.

—— *Les Eglises séparées d'Orient*, Paris, 1930.

—— 'L'Eglise Syrienne du Malabar', *E.O.* 16 (1913), pp. 526-35.

Jann P. A. O.M. CAP., *Die katholischen Missionen in Indien, China und Japan. Ihre Organisation und das portugiesische Patronat von 15 bis in 18 Jahrhundert*, Paderborn, 1915.

Job K. E., *Christianity in Malabar*, Changanacherry, 1927.

—— 'Seven Churches of Malabar', *St. Thomas the Apostle . . .*, pp. 46-55.

—— 'St. Thomas in Parthia and Indo-Parthia', ibid. pp. 109-14.

—— *The Syrian Church of Malabar. Its cultural contribution*, Changanacherry, 1938.

Joseph T. K., 'A Christian Dynasty in Malabar', *I.A.* 52 (1923), pp. 157-59.

—— 'Citerior India and Extra-Indian Indias; a rejoinder', *J.I.H.* 26 (1947), pp. 175-87.

—— 'Citerior India of Rufinus circa 400 A.D.', ibid. 23 (1944), pp. 110-15.

—— 'Constantine and Indias', ibid. 28 (1950), pp. 1-7.

—— 'Divu of Theophilus the Indian', *I.A.* 60 (1931), p. 248.

—— '"India", a Continuation of Egypt and Ethiopia', *J.I.H.* 26 (1948), pp. 201-7.

—— 'The India of Greeks and Romans of 326 B.C. to A.D 641.', *J.B.O.R.S.* 33 (1947), pp. 19-70.

—— 'An Indian Christian Date, A.D. 317, from Hindu Documents', *J.I.H.* 26 (1948), pp. 27-44.

—— 'King Alfred and St. Thomas', *J.B.H.S.* 4 (1931) pp. 181-4.

—— 'Kings and Christians in Kerala', *K.S.P.* ser. 8 (1931), pp. 121-3.

—— 'King Pallivacnavar, 317 to ?346 A.D.', *Caritas*, Alwaye, 1948, December number.

—— 'The Malabar Christians' Date for Manikka-Vachakar and for the foundation of Quilon', *Q.J.M.S.* 22 (1931), pp. 228-31.

—— 'Malabar Miscellany III. Calamina. IV. Some Place-names in Travancore', *I.A.* 53 (1924), pp. 93-7.

—— 'The Malaya Mountain', *J.I.H.* 25 (1947), pp. 263-7.

—— 'Mar Sapor and Mar Prodh', *I.A.* 57 (1928), pp. 46-8.

—— 'Ports and Mounts of Malabar (A.D. 50-150). Some new identifications', *J.I.H.* 26 (1948), pp. 121-9.

17

Joseph T.K., *Propagation of Christianity in the Early Centuries* (in Malayalam), Tiruvalla, 1950.

—— 'A Query: St. Thomas in Parthia or India?', *I.A.* 61 (1932), p. 159.

—— 'St. Thomas and the Cross', *Q.J.M.S.* 14 (1923).

—— 'St. Thomas Crosses and St. Thomas Tradition', *I.H.Q.* 8 (1932), pp. 785-9.

—— 'St. Thomas in Iothabis, Calamina, Kantorya or Mylapore' *I.A.* 60 (1931), pp. 231-4.

—— 'St. Thomas in South India', ibid. 55 (1926), pp. 221-3.

—— 'The Saint Thomas Traditions of South India', *Bulletin du Comité International des Sciences Historiques*, July 1933, no. 20, pp. 560-9.

—— 'Thomas Cana', *I.A.* 56 (1927), pp. 161-6, 57 (1928), pp. 103-6.

—— 'Was St. Thomas in South India?', *Y.M.I.* July and Dec. 1927.

—— 'Was St. Thomas in South India?', *I.A.* 58 (1929) pp. 133, ff.

—— 'What the Apostle Thomas wrote from India', *Y.M.I.* May 1926.

Jouvreau-Dubreuil G., 'India and the Romans', *I.A.* 52 (1923), pp. 50-3.

Kaithanal P., *Christianity in Malabar*, Trichinopoly, 1938.

Karka D. J., *History of the Parsis*, London, 1884, 2 vols.

Kaye J. W., *History of Christianity in India*, London, 1859.

Keay F. E., *A History of the Syrian Church in India*, Madras, 195.

Kennedy J., 'The Child Krishna, Christianity and the Gujars' *J.R.A.S.* 1907, pp. 951-91.

—— 'The Child Krishna and his Critics', ibid. 1908, pp. 505-21.

—— 'The Gospels of the Infancy, the Lalita Vistava, and the Vishnu Purana: or the transmission of religious legends between India and the West', ibid. 1917, pp. 209-43, 469-540.

—— 'St. Thomas and his tomb at Mylapore', *East and West* 5 (1907), pp. 192-201.

Kennet, *St. Thomas Apostle of India*, Madras, 1882.

Kidd B. J., *The Churches of Eastern Christendom*, London, 1927.

Kierkels L. P., c.p., *To commemorate the sixtieth anniversary of the Catholic Hierarchy in India and Ceylon, 1886-1946*, Bangalore, 1946.

Kizhakkethayil J., 'A Sanskrit Scholar and Malayalam Poet. Ernst Hanxleden', *The New Review*, 6 (1937), pp. 127-38.

Korolevskij C., 'Antioche', *D.H.G.E.* vol. III, 563-703.

—— 'Joseph Audo', ibid. vol. V, 326-32.

Kowasky, N. O.M.I., 'Der Stand der katholischen Missionen um das Jahr 1765..III. Indian und Tibet', *N. Z.M.G* 12 (1956), pp. 20-34.

Kuruvilla K.K., *A History of the Mar Thoma Church and its Doctrines*, Madras, 1951.

—— 'The Mar Thoma Church and its doctrines', *The Guardian*, 28 (1950)pp. 308, ff

Labourt L., *Le Christianisme dans l'Empire Perse sous la dynastie Sassanide (224-632)*, Paris, 1904.

—— *De Timotheo I Nestorianorum Patriarcha (788-823) et Christianorum Orientalium Condicione sub Califis Abbasidis*, Paris, 1904.

Langlois C. V., *Jordan Catala Missionnaire, Histoire Littéraire de la France*, Paris, vol. XXXV, pp. 260-7.

Lassen C.H, *Indische Altertums-kunde*, Leipzig, 1856, vol. III, B, 1861, vol. IV, B.

Latourette K. S., *A History of the Expansion of Christianity*, London, 1937-45, 7 vols.

La Vallée-Poussin L. de, *Dynasties et Histoire de l'Inde depuis Kanishkra jusqu'aux invasions musulmanes*, Paris, 1935, *Histoire du Monde*, vol. VI, 2.

—— *L'Inde aux temps des Mauryas et des Barbaros, Grecs, Scythes, Parthes et Yue-Tchi*, Paris, 1930, ibid. vol. VI, 1.

LeClerq H., 'Inde', *D.A.C.L.* vol. VIII, 517-30.

—— 'Kosmas Indicopleustes', ibid. vol. VIII, 820-49.

—— 'Malabar', ibid. vol. X, 1260-77.

Lemmens L., *Geschichte der Franziskanesmissionen*, Münster, 1929.

—— 'Notae criticae ad initia unionis Chaldaeorum', *Antonianum*, 1 (1926), pp. 205-18.

Levi S., 'Notes sur les Indo Scythes. III. Saint Thomas, Gondophares et Mazdeo', *J.A.* 9 (1897), pp. 27-42. English translation in *I.A.* 32 (1903), pp. 381-426, 33 (1904), pp. 10-16, 110-16. Comments in 'Bulletin des publications hagiographiques', *A.B.* 18 (1899), pp. 275-9.

Levi della Vida G., *Ricerche sulla formazione del più antico fondo di manoscritti orientali della Biblioteca Vaticana*, Vatican City, 1939.

Lima Felner R. J. de, *Subsidio para a historia da India Portugueza*, Lisbon, 1878.

Lobley J. A., *The Church and the Churches in Southern India: a review of the Portuguese missions to that part of the world in the sixteenth century with special reference to the Syrian Christians and to modern missionary efforts in the same quarter*, Cambridge, 1870.

Lord J. A., *The Jews in India and the Far East*, Bombay, 1907

Lourenço A., *Utrum fuerit Schisma Goanum post Breve 'Multa Praeclare' usque ad annum 1849*, Goa, 1947.

Lubeck K., *Die christliche Kirchen des Orients*, Kempten, 1911.

Lukose K. K., 'The History of the Development of the variety of Christians in Malabar', *C.Q.R.* 138 (1944), pp. 204-33. A similar article appeared in the form of a booklet at Nagercoil, 1943.

Mackensie G. T., 'History of Christianity in Travancore', *The Travancore State Manual*, vol. II, pp. 135-223. Published previously under the title *Christianity in Travancore*, Trivandrum, 1901.

—— 'The Syrian Christians in India', *The Dublin Review*, 139 (1906), pp. 105-22.

Mac Gillivray G. J., 'The Nestorian and the Chaldean Churches', *C.R.* 1 (1931), pp. 578-85.

—— 'Nestorians and Chaldeans in Modern Times', ibid. 2 (1931), pp. 47-57.

Maclean A. J. & Browne W. H., *The Catholicos of the East and his people*, London, 1892.

Malavielle L., 'Le littoral de l'Inde par Pomponius Mela', *Revue de Philologie*, 24 (1890), pp. 19-30.

Marcellino da Civezza o.f.m., *Storia Universale delle Missioni Francescane*, Rome-Florence, 1857-95, 11 vols.

Marshall J., 'Greeks and Sakas in India', *J.R.A.S.* 1947, pp. 3-32.

Martin J.P.P., *Les origines de l'Eglise d'Edesse et des Eglises Syriennes*, Paris, 1889.

Martins M., 'Os Portugueses e a Literatura dos Cristâos Malabares', *Broteria*, 45 (1947), pp. 265-82.

Mateer S., *The Land of Charity. An account of Travancore and its Devil Worship*, London, 1871.

—— *Native Life in Travancore*, London, 1883.

Mateos F. s.J., 'El Asia Portuguesa, campo de apostolado de San Francisco Javier', *Missionalia Hispanica*, 9 (1953), pp. 417-81.

Mathew J., 'Travancore a hundred years ago: the times of the Ranis and Colonel Munro', *K.S.P.* ser. 8 (1931), pp. 123-33. App. pp. i-xxxii.

Mathew Th., *The Syrian Church of Malabar. Its present situation*, Kottayam, 1938.

Medlycott A.E., *India and the Apostle St. Thomas. An Inquiry with a critical analysis of the Acta Thomae*, London, 1905.

—— 'St. Thomas Christians', *Catholic Encyclopaedia*, vol. XIV, pp. 678-88.

Meersman A., *The Friars Minor or Franciscans in India, 1291-1940*, Karachi, 1943.

Meile P., 'Les Yavanas dans l'Inde Tamoule', *J.A. (Mélanges Asiatiques)*, 132 (1940-1), pp. 85-123.

Meinsma P. A. van der, *Geschiedenis van de Nederlandsche Oost-Indische Bezettingen*, The Hague, 1872-75, 3 vols.

Menant D., 'Les Parsis', *Annales du Musée Guimet, Bibliothèque d'Etudes*, Paris, 1898.

Menon K.P. & Menon S.T.K., *A History of Kerala, written in the form of Notes on Visscher's letters from Malabar*, Ernakulam. 1929-33, 3 vols.

Menon K.P.P., 'Notes on Malabar and its Place-names', *I.A.* 31 (1902), pp. 338-50.

Menon P. S., *A History of Travancore from the earliest times*, Madras, 1878.

Michaud M., 'Chambre Apostolique', *D.D.C.* vol. III, 405-7.

Mingana A., 'The Early Spread of Christianity in Central Asia and the Far East.' *B.J.R.L.* 9 (1925). Reprint with additions, Manchester, 1925.

—— 'The Early Spread of Christianity in India', ibid. 10 (1926), pp. 435-95. Reprint, Manchester, 1926.

Monneret de Villard U., 'La Fiera di Batnae e la Traslazione di S. Tommaso a Edessa', *Rendiconti della Academia Nazionale dei Lincei. Cl. di Scienze Morali*, 6 (1951) pp. 77-104.

Mootheden Th., 'The Apostolate of St. Thomas in India', *E.C.Q.* 9 (1952), pp. 349-58.

Mortimer K. J., 'The Monks of St. Hormisdas', Ibid. 7 (1948) pp. 477-82.

Moule A. O., 'Brother Jordan de Sévérac', *J.R.A.S.* 1928, pp. 349-76.

Mukherjee K., 'St. Thomas of India', *The Indian Review*, 44 (1943) pp. 563-64.

Müllbauer M., *Geschichte der katholischen Missionen in Ostindien*, Freiburg i. B., 1852.

Musset P., *Histoire du Christianisme spécialement en Orient*, Harissa-Jerusalem, 1948-49, 3 vols.

Nau F., 'L'expansion nestorienne en Asie', *Annales du Musée Guimet, Bibliothèque de Vulgarisation*, 40 (1913), pp. 193-388.

Nyberg H.S., (Review of T. K. Joseph's *Malabar Christians and their Ancient Documents*), *Le Monde Orientale*, 25, (1933), pp. 349-50.

Oaten E., *Early European Travels in India*, London 1909.

Ogilvie J. N., *Apostles of India*, London, s.d.

Osborne D., *India and its Missions*, Philadelphia, 1884.

Panikkar K. M., *Malabar and the Dutch, being the History of the Fall of the Nayar Power in Malabar*, Bombay-London, 1932.

—— *Malabar and the Portuguese (1500-1663)*, Bombay, 1929.

Panjikaran J. C., 'Christianity in Malabar with special reference to the St. Thomas Christians of the Syro-Malabar Rite', *O.C.* 6 (1926), no. 23, pp. 93-136.

—— 'L'entrée des évêques jacobites de l'Inde dans l'obédience du Pape', *Missions Catholiques*, 1930, pp. 534-5.

—— *The Syrian Church in Malabar*, Trichinopoly, 1914.

Panjiker T. K. G., *Malabar and its Folk*, Madras, 1943, 3rd ed.

Parry, O.H., *Six months in a Syrian monastery*, London, 1895.

Pascal L. A., *The Latin and Syrian Hierarchies of Malabar*, s. l., 1937.

Pastor L. voii, *The History of the Popes from the close of the Middle-Ages*, London, 1924-53, vol. XIII—XL.

Peeters P. s.j., (Reviews on St. Thomas question, in *Bulletins des Publications Hagiographiques*), *A.B.* 18 (1899), pp. 275-9, 25 (1906), pp. 196-200, 32 (1913), pp. 75-7, 44 (1926), pp. 402-3.

Perumalil A. C. S.J., *The Apostles in India: Fact or Fiction*, Patna, 1953.

—— 'The Apostles of Kalyana (Bombay): St. Bartholomew the Apostle and St. Pantaenus', *J.I.H.* 22 (1943), pp. 71-92.

Perumalil A. C. S.J., 'Citerior India of Rufinus, circa 400 A.D. A reply', ibid. 24 (1945), pp. 110-23.

—— 'Citerior India. Another rejoinder', ibid. 26 (1948), pp. 199-200.

—— 'The India of the early Greeks and Romans from the time of Alexander's invasion till the fall of Alexandria (326 B.C. to A.D. 641)', *J.B.O.R.S.* 28 (1942), pp. 225-65, 341-83.

Philipps W. R., 'The connection of St. Thomas the Apostle with India', *I.A.* 32 (1903), pp. 1-15, 145-60, 33 (1904), pp. 31-32.

Philippose A., 'The Apostolic Origin and the Early History of the Syrian Church of Malabar', *The Madras Christian College Magazine*, 5, pp. 547-58, 621-33, 663-74.

Pillai P. S., *Some Early Sovereigns of Travancore*, Tinnevelly and Madras, 1943, 2nd ed.

Pisharoti, K. R., *Ancient Cochin*, Ernakulam, 1942.

—— 'Cranganur. A Study', *Rama Varma Research Institute Bulletin*, 1 (1930), pp. 33-6.

—— 'Glimpses of Cochin History from literary sources (1342-1505)', *Journal of Oriental Research* 4 (1930), pp. 141-51.

Placid of St. Joseph T.O.C.D., 'Divided Christendom', *C.M.* 16 (1952), pp. 390-402.

—— 'The Dhariyaikal Christians of Thiruvancode', *Indica, the Indian Hist. Research Institute Silver Jublee Commemoration Volume*, 1953, pp. 317-19.

—— 'The Efforts for Reunion in Malankara, South India', *Unitas*, 5 (1953), pp. 7-15, 89-98

—— 'Um die Einheit der Kirche in Indien. Zum Uebertritt des jakobitischen Bischofs Mar Severios', *Katholische Missionen*, 66 (1938), pp. 94-8.

—— 'The Social and Socio-Ecclesiastical Customs of the Syrian Christians of India', *E.C.Q.* 7 (1947), pp. 222-36.

—— 'The South Indian Apostolate of St. Thomas', *O.C.P.* 18 (1952), pp. 229-45.

Placid of St. Joseph T.O.C.D., 'Die St. Thomas Christen oder die Syrischen Christen von Malabar', *Ostkirchliche Studien*, 4 (1955), pp. 261-88.

—— 'St. Thomas in South India', *Ninth All-India Oriental Conference*, Trivandrum, 1937, pp. 19.

—— 'St. Thomas in South Indian Tradition', *St. Thomas the Apostle* . ., pp. 1-14.

—— 'St. Thomas in Syriac Writings, and Liturgies', ibid. pp. 68-80.

—— *The Syrian Church of Malabar*, Changanacherry, 1938.

—— 'Les Syriens du Malabar', *L'Orient Syrien*, 1 (1956), pp. 375-424.

Poonen T. I., *A Survey of the Rise of the Dutch Power in Malabar (1603-1678)*, Trivandrum, 1948.

Pothacamury T., 'The Struggle of the Church in Travancore', *The Month*, 182 (1946), pp. 282-8.

Radaelli G., 'Un Visitatore Apostolico Indigeno nel Malabar', *Il Pensiero Missionario*, 14 (1942), pp. 122-35.

Rae G. M., *The Syrian Church in India*, London, 1892.

Rama Varma Raja K., *A Contribution to the History of Cochin*, Trichur, 1914.

Rawlinson H. G., *India, a Short Cultural History*, London, 1937.

—— *Intercourse between India and the Western World from the earliest times to the Fall of Rome*, London, 1926, 2nd ed.

Rayanna P.s.j., *The Indigenous Religious Congregations of India and Ceylon*, Madura, 1948.

Reinaud M., *Relations politiques et commerciales de l'Empire Romain avec l'Asie Orientale pendant les cinq premiers siècles de l'ère chrétienne*, Paris, 1863.

Richards W. J., *The Indian Christians of St. Thomas, otherwise called the Syrian Christians of Malabar. A Sketch of their History, and an Account of their Present Condition, as well as a Discussion of the Legend of St. Thomas*, London, 1908.

Richter J., *Indische Missionsgeschichte*, Gütersloh, 1924, 2nd ed.

Robertson W., *Historical Disquisition concerning the knowledge which the Ancients had of India; and the Progress of Trade with that country prior to the Discovery of the Passage to it by the Cape of Good Hope*, London, 1891.

Robinson T., 'Historical Account of the Christians on the Malabar

Coast', *Madras Journal of Literature and Science*, 1 (1834), pp. 7-13, 94-104, 255-69, 342-50.

Robinson T., *Last Days of Bishop Heber*, Madras, 1829.

Sankar K. G., 'The date of Manikyavacaka', *Q.J.M.S.* 22 (1931) pp. 45-55.

Santos A. s.j., 'Dos Javieres en la India', *Miscelánea Comillas*, 18 (1952), pp. 27-87.

——— 'Francisco Roz s.j., Arzobispo de Cranganor, primer Bispo Jesuita de la India (1557-1624)', *Missionalia Hispanica*, 5 (1948) pp. 325-93, 6 (1949), pp. 79-142. Madrid, reprint, 1948.

——— 'Jeronimo Javier s.j., Arzobispo Electo de Cranganor', *Studia Missionalia*, 7 (1952), pp. 125-75.

Schmidlin J., *Catholic Mission History*, Techny (Illinois), 1933.

Schurhammer G. s.j., 'Iniquitriberim and Beteperuman Chera and Pandya Kings in Southern India, 1544', *J.B.H.S.* 3 (1930), pp. 1-40.

——— 'Joâo da Cruz, a Chetti, not a Nair', *K.S.P.* ser. 10 (1932), p. 276.

——— *The Malabar Church and Rome during the Early Portuguese Period and Before*, Trichinopoly, 1934.

——— 'Some Remarks on Series 4 of K.S.P. (Thomas Cana's Plates, Mar Jacob's Orthodoxy, and Earliest Tamil Printing)', *K.S.P.* ser 5, (1930), pp. 303-4.

Shah L. T., *Ancient India. History of Ancient India for 1000 years*, Baroda, 1940, 3 vols.

Sherring M. B., *The History of the Protestant Missions in India*, London, 1884.

Silva Correia A. C. Germano da, *Historia da Colonização Portuguesa na India*, Lisbon, 1948-50, 3 vols.

Silva Rego A. da, *Historia das Missôes do Padroado Português do Oriente. I. India (1500-1542)*, Lisbon, 1949.

——— *O Padroado Português do Oriente. Esboço Historico*, Lisbon 1940.

Smit J., *Val en Opstanding van een Groot Christenvolk, de Chaldeën in Perzië, Indië en Azië*, Heemstede, 1950.

Smith G., *The Conversion of India from Pantaenus to the present time A.D. 193-1893*, London, 1893.

Smith V. A., *The Early History of India from 600 B.C. to the Mu-*

hammadan Conquest including the invasion of Alexander the Great, Oxford, 1924.

Smith V. A., 'The Indo-Parthian Dynasties', *Z.D.M.G.* 60 (1906), pp. 49-72.

Srinivasachari C. S., 'The St. Thomas Tradition and Recent Discovery in Travancore', *I.H.Q.* 7 (1931), pp. 837-9.

Sternbach L., 'Jews in Mediaeval India as mentioned by Western Travellers', *Proceedings of the Indian Historical Congress, 8th Session*, Allahabad, 1945, pp. 169-96.

Stewart J., *Nestorian Missionary Enterprise. The Story of a Church in Fire*, Edinburgh, 1928.

'Syrian Christians in Travancore', *The S. India Christian Repository*, 2 (1838), pp. 189-205.

Tarn W. W., *The Greeks in Bactria and India*, Cambridge, 1951, 2nd. ed.

Teles R. C., *Os Franciscanos no Oriente e seus conventos*, Nova Goa, 1922.

Temple R. C., 'Regarding the Christians of St. Thomas in South India', *I.A.* 52 (1923), pp. 103-7.

Tfinkdji J., 'L'Eglise Chaldéenne autrefois et aujourd'hui, *An.P.Cat.* 17 (1914), pp. 7-21, pp. 465-9.

Themotheos, Johannan Mar, The Mar Thoma Syrian Church. What it stands for', *National Christian Council Review*, 17 (1939), pp. 404-12.

Thomas P., *Christians and Christianity in India and Pakistan*, London, 1954.

Thomas P. J., 'An Ancient Monastery of St. Thomas in Mylapore' *The Catholic Register*, June 1937, pp. 5-8, reprinted in *St. Thomas the Apostle in Mylapore*, 1934, pp. 15-19.

—— 'A Hindu Tradition on St. Thomas', *Indian Historical Records Commission, Proceedings and Meetings*, Calcutta, 6 (1924), pp. 121-9.

—— 'The India of the Early Christian Fathers', *Y.M.I.* March 1928, and *The Catholic Register*, October 1937, pp. 6-9.

—— 'The India of the Early Christian Fathers', *St. Thomas the Apostle. . .*, pp. 89-107.

—— 'The Literary Activities of Catholic Missionaries in South India', Trichinopoly, *St. Joseph's College Magazine*, 4 (Sept. 1915).

Thomas P. J., 'The Literary Heritage of the Malabar Christians', *The New Review*, 1 (1934), pp. 461-7.

—— *The Marriage Customs of the Syrian Christians of Malabar*, Madras, 1936.

—— 'Palli Vana Perumal—A Royal Disciple of St. Thomas?' *St. Thomas the Apostle*... pp. 56-65.

—— 'Roman Trade Centres in Malabar', *K.S.P.* ser. 10 (1932), pp. 259-69.

—— 'St. Thomas in South India', *Y.M.I.* Nov. 1927, and Jan. 1928,

—— 'St. Thomas in South India', *I.A.* 57 (1928), pp. 7-10.

—— 'St. Thomas in Southern India', ibid. 60 (1931), pp. 105-9.

—— 'The South Indian Tradition of the Apostle Thomas', *J.R.A.S. Centenary Supplement*, 1903, pp. 213-23.

—— 'The Tradition of St. Thomas Christians', *St. Thomas the Apostle*..., pp. 15-45.

—— 'Was The Apostle Thomas in S. India? A Brief Statement of the Problem', *The Catholic Leader*, 11 (1930), pp. 21-3, and *The Catholic Register*, Feb. 1937, pp. 7-9. Also in the *Bulletin of the Catholic University of Peking*, 7 (1930), pp. 103-10.

Thurston H. s.j., 'Saint Thomas', *Catholic Encyclopaedia*, vol. XIV, pp. 658-9.

Tinling J. F. B., *Early Roman Catholic Missions in India*, London, 1871.

Tisserant E., 'Droit Canonique de l'Eglise Nestorienne. La Liturgie des Eglises Nestoriennes et Chaldéennes', *D.T.C.* vol. XI, 313-63.

—— 'L'Eglise Nestorienne', ibid. 157-288.

—— 'L'Eglise Syro-Malabare', ibid. vol. XIV, 3089-162.

—— 'Timothée I', ibid. vol. XV, 1121-39.

Tournebize F., 'Arménie', *D.H.G.E.* vol. IV, 338-42.

Tripathi R. S., 'Harsa and Christianity', *J.R.A.S.* 1928, pp. 629, ff.

Valerian t.o.c.d., *The Servant of God, Fr. Cyriac Elias Chavara, Founder and Prior General, 1805-1871*, Mannanam, 1953.

Van de Aalst P., 'Die missionering door de Nestoriannsche Kerk', *C.O.V.* 5 (1952-53), pp. 245-68.

Van Lohuizen-De Leeuw J. E., *The Scythian Period, an Approach to the History, Art, Epigraphy, and Paleography of North India from the 1st century B.C. to the 3rd century A.D.*, Leyden, 1949.

Varekat A. P., *The Latin and Syrian Hierarchies of Malabar*, Trichur, 1937.

Väth A. s.j., *Der Hl. Thomas der Apostel Indiens. Ein Untersuchung über den historischen Gehalt der Thomas-Legende*, Aachen, 1925.

—— *Die Inder*, Freiburg i. B., 1934.

Vaz F. X., 'Bispo Theophilo, o Indo', *O Oriente Português*, 5 (1908), pp. 89-97.

Vigouroux F., 'Saint Thomas', *D.B.* vol. V, 2198.

Vine, *The Nestorian Churches*, London, 1937.

Vithuvattikal L. T.O.C.D., 'Indische Ostkirche', *Katholische Missionen*, 3 (1953), pp. 70-3.

Von Gutschmid, *Die Königsnamen in den apocryphen Apostelge-schichten*, Cologne, 1864.

Warmington E. H., *The Commerce between the Roman Empire and India*, Cambridge, 1928.

Werth K.P. s.m., *Das Schisma der Thomaschristen unter Erzbischof Franciskus Garzia, dargestellt nach den Akten des Archivs der Sacra Congregatio de Propaganda Fide*, Limburg a.d.L., 1937.

Wheeler R.E.M., Ghosh A., Krishna Deva, 'Arikamedu: an Indo-Roman Trading-Station on the East Coast of India', *Ancient India*, no. 2 (1946), pp. 17-124.

Wherry E. M., *Islam and Christianity in India and the Far East*, London, 1907.

Whitehouse T., *Lingerings of Light in a Dark Land, being researches into the past history and the present conditions of the Syrian Church of Malabar*, London, 1873.

Whiteway R. S., *The Rise of Portuguese Power in India, 1497-1550* Westminster, 1899.

Wicki J. s.j., 'Pedro Luis, Brahmane und erste-indische Jesuit (ca 1532-1596)', *N.Z.M.W.* 6 (1950), pp. 115-26.

Wilford F., 'Origin and Decline of the Christian Religion in India', *Asiatick Researches*, 10 (1808), pp. 27-126.

Wilson R. S., *The Indirect Effects of Christianity in India and the Far East*, London, 1907.

Yule H., *Cathay and the Way Thither*, new edition by H. Cordier, London, 1915- 16, 4 vols. *Hakluyt Society*.

Yule H., 'Malifattan', *I.A.* 4 (1875), pp. 8-10.

Zacharias H.C.E., 'The Church of Saints Thomas and Bartholomeo in Malabar', *Pax*, 1928, pp. 2-22, 139-155.

Zaleski L. M., *The Apostle St. Thomas in India. History, Tradition and Legend*, Mangalore, 1912. The same book was published in French, Mangalore, 1912.

—— *Les Origines du Christianisme aux Indes*, Mangalore 1915.

Zaleski L. M., *The Saints of India*, Mangalore, 1915.

Ziadé I., 'L'Eglise Syrienne', *D.T.C.* vol. XIV, 3017-88.

2 *Works dealing with the Liturgy of the St. Thomas Christians or closely related subjects*

Attwater D., cf. previous section.

Badger G.P., *The Nestorians and their Rituals*, London, 1852, 2 vols.

Battandier A., 'Rite et Calendrier Syro-Malabares', *An. P. Cat.* 5 (1902), pp. 19-22, 25-8.

Benediction of the Bl. Sacrament among the Syro-Malankarese, Pax, Oct. 1932, p. 162.

Botte B. O.S.B., 'L'anaphore chaldéenne des Apôtres', *O.C.P.* 15 (1949), pp. 259-76.

—— 'L'épiclèse dans les liturgies syriennes orientales', *Sacris Erudiri*, 6 (1954), pp. 48-72.

Burkitt F. C., 'The Old Malabar Liturgy', *J.T.S.* 29 (1930), p. 155.

—— 'St. Thomas and his Feasts', *K.S.P.* 1930, pp. 287-302.

Codrington H., 'The Chaldean Liturgy', *E.C.Q.* 2 (1937), pp. 79, ff. 138, ff., 202.

—— The Syrian Liturgy', ibid. 1 (1936), pp. 10 ff., 40, ff., 87 ff., 135. These two articles were reprinted in 1954 under the title *Studies of the Syrian Liturgies*, London.

Connolly R.H. O.S.B., 'The Work of Menezes on the Malabar Liturgy', *J.T.S.* 5 (1914), pp. 396-425, 509-89, with additional note of Edmund Bishop pp. 589-93.

Daniel K. N., *A Critical Study of the Primitive Liturgies, especially that of St. Jams*, Tiruvalla, 1949, 2nd ed.

Dauvillier J., 'L'ambon ou bêma dans les textes de l'Eglise Chaldéenne et de l'Eglise Syrienne au moyen-âge', *Cahiers Archéologiques*, 6 (1952), pp. 11-30.

Etheridge J. W., cf. previous section.

Fortescue, A., id.

Hambye E.R. s.j., 'Le baptême dans les Eglises syriennes de l'Inde L'Orient Syrien, 1 (1956), pp. 255-66.

Howard G. B., The Christians of St. Thomas and their Liturgies, Oxford-London, 1864.

Janin R., cf. previous section.

King A. A., The Rites of Eastern Christendom, London, 1947-8, 2 vols.

Leclerq H., 'Malabar', cf. previous section.

Mousses C., 'Les huit éditions du Missel Chaldéen', P.O.C. 1 (1951), pp. 209-20.

—— 'La Liturgie chaldéenne des Apôtres', P.O.C. 2 (1952), pp. 125-41.

—— 'Les missels chaldéens d'après les manuscrits', P.O.C. 4 (1954), pp. 26-32.

Nilles N., 'Das syro-chaldäische Kirchenjahr des Thomaschristen', Z.K.T. 20 (1896), pp. 726-39.

Placid of St. Joseph T.O.C.D., 'De Syro-Malabaren en hun Ritus', C.O.V. (1953) pp. 110-24.

Raes A. s.j., 'Le rite de la confession chez les Malankares', O.C.P. 16 (1950), pp. 448-59.

INDEX

ABBASID Caliphs, xiv

Abdallah Sattuf, Mar Ignatios, Jacobite Patriarch, and his visit to Malabar, 153

Abdisho, a Chaldean writer, 15

Abdisho of Nisibis, Chaldean Metropolitan and writer, theological treatise and Paradise of Eden, 62; canonical treatise, 163

Abdisho IV, Catholic Chaldean Catholicos, 35, 39, 40-1, 47

Abdisho V Khayyatt, Catholic Chaldean Catholicos, 120

Abd-ul-Massih, (Jacobite Patriarch), and Malabar, 153-4, 157, 173

Abraham, Mar, Chaldean Metropolitan of India, election and arrival in India, 40; difficulties, 42-7, 165-6, 176-7; church built by, 62

Abraham, George, Maronite Jesuit, and Malabar, 46, 48, 71, 176-7

Abraham, Jacob, Catholic Chaldean monk and Bishop, *see* Uraha

Abraham, Malpan, Indian Jacobite priest, and reformer, 148, 150

Acts of Judas-Thomas, 2-6

Aden, 27

Afghanistan, 2

Africa, 27

Ajuti, Latin Archbishop, and apostolic delegate to the East Indies, 131, 155

Alangad, Syro-Malabar parish and church, Persian cross at, 16; visited by Menezes 53; fake consecration of Archdeacon Thomas at, 79-80; consecration of the Carmelite Vicar Apostolic, Angelo Francis of St. Teresa, at, 90; residence of the vicar apostolic at, 95

Alapatt, Mar George, Syro-Malabar Bishop of Trichur, 127

Alburquerque, Alfonso de, Portuguese Admiral and Viceroy, 32

Albuquerque, John de, Bishop of Goa, 69

Aleppo, 84, 87, 88

Alexander VII, Pope, 83

Alexander de Campo, first Syro-Malabar Vicar Apostolic, 86-8, 122, 141

Alexander of St. Joseph, Prior General of the Syrian Carmelite Tertiaries, 136

Alexandria, xiii, 3, 11, 25, 27, 71, 121

Alexandretta, 87

Alfred the Great, King of England, and embassy to the tomb of St. Thomas the Apostle, 19

Alkosh, Chaldean monastery near Mosul, 112, 113, 118

Alwaye, Seminary conducted by the displaced Carmelites at, 100; Jacobite synod at, 154

Amanton, Latin Archbishop, Apostolic Delegate in Mesopotamia, 108, 110

Ambazhakat, Jesuit seminary at, 88, 89-90, 99

Angamale, Syro-Malabar centre, archdiocese of, 10, 39, 41, 42-5, 48, 53, 55, 61, 64, 72-5, 83, 123, 137, 141, 164, 166-7, 177; churches at, 62; Synod of, 44, 66

Angelo Francis of St. Teresa, Carmelite Friar, reached Malabar, 88; Vicar Apostolic of Malabar, 89-92

Anglican, missionaries in Travancore, 146-7, 149, 151, 153; Book of Common Prayer, 146; churches, 155; Sisters in Bengal, 158

Anquetil du Perron, French indologist, in India, 93

Anthony the founder, Syro-Malabar priest, supporter of the Chaldean jurisdiction in Malabar, 106

Antioch, patriarchate of, xiv, 17, 140-1, 142, 147, 153, 155, 157, 172

Antiochian rite, 130, 140, 143, 148-58, 160, 162, 173, 184-5

Antonio da Porto, Portuguese Franciscan Friar, Guardian at Bassein, 36-8

Aquaviva, Claudio, Jesuit General, 46

Aqra, Chaldean diocese of, 113

Arabic language, xiii-iv, 24, 41, 121, 184

Arabs, 12, 27, 31

Arakuzha, convent of the Syro-Malabar Carmelite Tertiary Sisters at, 129

Arbela, Chronicle of, 7, 12

Arikamedu, Roman trade-centre on the Coromandel coast, 5

Armenian, schism of the 19th century, 113-4; hierarchy, 126

Arthad, Syro-Malabar and Jacobite parishes of, 4

Assemani J. S., Maronite scholar, 10, 180

Athallah, the so-called Patriarch of India, 78-80, 102

Athanasios, Mar, Syrian Jacobite Bishop, in Malabar, 147

Athanasios, Matthew Mar, Mar Thomite Metropolitan, 148-50, 152

Athanasios, Thomas Mar, Mar Thomite Metropolitan, 150, 152

Augustine, Carmelite Friar and missionary, forwarded Mar Thomas IV's petitions to Rome, 143

Augustine, Chaldean monk and Chorepiscopus, and Malabar, 118-9

Avignon, 22

Axum, in Ethiopia, xiii, 7

Ayres d'Ornellas de Vasconcellos, Archbishop of Goa, 115

Aziz, Philip, Chaldean monk, visited Malabar, 112; wrote to the Vicar

Apostolic of Verapoly, 114; his methods, 115

BABAI, Chaldean Catholicos, and Nestorianism, 18, 140

Babylon, Patriarchate of, 52, 53, 55, 60, 71, 103, 120

Baccinelli, Joseph, *see* Bernardinus of St. Teresa

Baghdad, 9, 12, 87; Latin Archbishop of, 105; British Consul at, 108, 113; Chaldean priests at, 109; Vilayet of, 114; Syrian Catholic Metropolitan of, 157

Bahrayn, 14

Balkans, 163

Bangalore, 133, 137

Baptism, 51-2, 58, 64, 156, 160, 166-7, 170, 183

Baramangalam, Syro-Malabar parish of, 129

Bardesanes, Syrian writer, 2

Bar Hebraeus, Jacobite writer, 14-5, 172-3, 185

Barreto, Francis, Portuguese Governor of Bassein, 36

Barreto, Nunez, Jesuit missionary and Provincial, 82

Bartholomew of S. Concordio, Dominican Friar, and India, 20

Bartholomew of the Holy Ghost, Carmelite Friar and missionary, 88

Basilios, Mar, Maphrian of the East, 143

Basilios, Mar, Jacobite Metropolitan, and Malabar, 143

Basilios Shukrallah, Mar, Jacobite Metropolitan, and Malabar, 144

Basilios II, Mar, Indian Jacobite Catholicos, 158

Basilios III, Mar, Indian Jacobite Catholicos, 154, 159

Basrah, 7, 62, 87, 102, 108, 119

Bassein, near Bombay, 36-8, 40, 41, 163, 176

Beith Qataraye, in the Persian Gulf, 11-2

Bengal, 158

Benziger, Aloysius, Carmelite Bishop of Quilon, 156, 159

Bethany, religious Congregations of, 155, 158-9, 161; episcopal see in Malabar, 158

Berardi, Anthony, see Marcellinus of St. Teresa

Bernard of Jesus, Carmelite Friar, missionary, and Superior of the Syro-Malabar Carmelite Tertiaries, coadjutor to Mgr. Mellano, 136

Bernardinus of St. Teresa, Carmelite Vicar Apostolic of Verapoly, 98-100, 107, 110, 123

Biondi, Fabio, Latin Archbishop and Apostolic Collector of Portugal, 70-1

Bojador, Cape, on the West African coast, 33

Book of the Bee, see Solomon of Basrah

Book of Charms, 62

Book of Chastity, see Ishodenah

Book of the Fathers, 62

Book of Ordinations, 62

Bombay, 1, 21; Vicar Apostolic of, 115-7; Mar Philipos Jacob Uraha at, 118; Jacobites at, 155

Bonnel, Charles, French Jesuit and missionary, 127-8

Braga, archbishopric of Portugal, rite of, 177, 184

Brahmins, 63, 88, 164-5

Bras of St. Mary, Portuguese Augustinian Friar, and Malabar, 49-50

Brito, Stephen de, Jesuit Archbishop of Cranganore, 75-8

Buchanan, Claudius, British Protestant missionary, and Malabar, 146

Burnell, English writer, on the Malabar copper-plates, 15

Busnaya, Joseph, Chaldean monk, 62

Buttigeg, Ambrose, Maltese Dominican Bishop, and India, 35-6, 38

Byzantine rite, 66, 107; theology, 165

Byzantium, 11, French ambassador at, 113

CABRAL, Pedro, Portuguese Admiral, 25, 27

Calcutta, 131, 133, 147; Jacobites at, 155

Calixtus III, Pope, relations with the Militia Christi, 33

Canhur, see Kanjur

Cannanore, 30

Capuchins, 78

Cariati, see Kariatil

Carmelites, Displaced, and Malabar, 80-100, 104; lack of missionaries, 106; Chaldean opposition to their jurisdiction, 107, passim, 114; complaints against the, 105, 116; asked Rome to condemn certain writings, 122-3; opposed the appointment of a Syro-Malabar vicar general, 123-4; their jurisdiction after 1886, 125-6; their mistrust of Mar Thomas VI, 145

Carmelites, Syro-Malabar Tertiaries, early history, 98; work against Mar Rokos, 109-10; monastery at Mannam, 111, 116, 127; chapel at Trichur, 115; seminaries of, 128, 130; apostolate among the low castes, 130; work against the Mellusians, 132; successive progress, 136-7; work for the reunion of the dissidents, 139; and Oriental Canon Law, 172

Carmelite, Syro-Malabar Tertiary Sisters, 129, 137

Castelli, Cardinal, Perfect of the Congregation of Propaganda, 94

Castells, Latin Archbishop and Apostolic Delegate in Mesopotamia, 113

Castets, French Jesuit in India, 46-7

Catalonia, 72

Catholicos, Indian Jacobite prelate, 154-5, 159

Cazet, Jesuit Vicar Apostolic of Northern Madagascar, 131

Ceylon, early Christianity in, 13; visited by Friar John Marignola 23; centre of trade, 85

Chaldea, *see* Mesopotamia

Chaldean, name and rite of the East Syrian Christians, 1, 10, *passim* 36, 42, 45, 52, 66, 71, 74, 103, 123, 126, 142, 150, 156, 161, 163, 166, 169, 173; liturgy, 175, *passim*

Changanacherry, Syro-Malabar centre Seminary at, 128; Tertiary Sisters of St. Francis, 129; vicariate apostolic of, 129, 134, 172; bishopric of, 135; archbishopric of, 136; work among the dissidents from, 139, 156

Charles Borromeo, St., 67

Charles of St. Conrad, Carmelite Vicar Apostolic of the Great Mogul, 96, 180

Chavara, Cyriac Elias, Syro-Malabar Carmelite Tertiary and Superior, 109, 178; Vicar General, 109-10,

Chegeree, *see* Chewarra

Chengamangalam, *see* Vaipicotta

Chettipuzha, Syro-Malabar Carmelite monastery, and catechumenate, 130

Chewarra, Syro-Malabar parish, visited by Archbishop de Menezes, 53

China, xiv, 14-5, 19-20, 21, 34

Chinese Bishops, 121

Chittagong, 131

Chulaparampil, Mar Alexander, Syro-Malabar Bishop of Kottayam, 139

Church Missionary Society, 146, 147, 148, 151, 153

Chrism, Chrismation, 51-2, 58, 64, 128, 166-7, 184

Chronicle of Seert, 7

Clement VIII, Pope, 46, 48, 53, 65

Cochin, visited by St. Francis Xavier, 32; centre of Portuguese activities, and of the Padroado, 31, 38, 43-4, 50, 54, 57, 69, 70, 71, 73-4, 75, 77, 79, 81, 85, 88, 90, 92; fell to the Dutch, 86, 89, 121; fell to the British, 97; Jacobite bishop at, 105; State of, 72, 135, 144, 154, 173

Coimbatore, Latin diocese of, 135

Collectio Canonum Synodicorum, 163

Comorin, Cape, 1

Confession, in the Syro-Malabar rite, 168, 170

Confirmation, the Sacrament of, *see* Chrism

Constantinople, *see* Byzantium

Constantius, Roman Emperor, 7

Coonan Cross, oath taken by the Syro-Malabar Christians on the, 79

Coptic, xiii-iv

Cornelius of Jesus of Nazareth, Carmelite Friar and missionary, 87

Cosmas Indicopleustes, on Socotra and India, 11-13

Cranganore, old trading centre and Christian settlement in Malabar, 6; origin of social divisions, 8-10; book written at, 17; Syro-Malabar parish priest of, 26; Franciscan school and Seminary of, 32, 69, 99, 146; visited by St. Francis Xavier, 32; school of the Jesuits at, 70; residence of Bishop Roz, 73; visited by the Carmelites, 81; archdiocese of, 83, 90, 91, 92, 95-7, 103, 105; Syro-Malabar Christians depending on, 115, 122; deserted by the Syro-Malabars, 176

Custodio de Pinho, Latin Indian Vicar Apostolic of Bijapur and Golconda, 88

Cyrene, 49

Cyril of Alexandria, St., 61

DAHLMANN, German Jesuit writer, and St. Thomas in India, 3, 5

Danish factory and mission, *see* Tranquebar

David, Chaldean Bishop of Basrah, and India, 7

Dehok, Eliseus, Chaldean monk, and Malabar, 112

Deir as-Zafaran, Jacobite monastery and see of the Jacobite patriarch, 148

Denha, Mar, Chaldean Bishop, sent to India, 25, 30-1

Denha Bar-Yona, Chaldean priest, and Malabar, 106

De Souza, Dominique, Dominican Friar and Vicar General of Cochin, 33

Diamper, Syro-Malabar parish, visited by Archbishop de Menezes, 55; Synod of, 53, 56-68; Chaldean books burnt by order of the Synod of, xiii, 24, 62, 101; decrees of the Synod of, 163-71, 177-9, 180; customs after the Synod of, 164-5

Diarbekir, Chaldean diocese of, 90

Diodorus of Tarsus, 13, 45, 55, 177

Dionysios I, Mar, Indian Jacobite Metropolitan, see Thomas VI, Mar

Dionysios III, Mar, Indian Jacobite Metropolitan, 147

Dionysios IV, Mar, Indian Jacobite Metropolitan, 148-9

Dionysios V, Joseph Mar, Indian Jacobite Metropolitan, 130, 150, 152, 155, 157

Dionysios VI, George Mar, Indian Jacobite Metropolitan, 153, 157, 159

Dioscoros, Mar, Indian Jacobite Metropolitan, 160-1

Dominicans, in India, 69, 72; at Mosul, 113

Donati, Francis, Dominican Friar and missionary, and Malabar, 75-8

Dutch, enterprises in the East, 28; navy, 81; conquests on the Malabar coast, 84-6, 121

East India Company, The British, 109, 146

Eastern Syrians, see Chaldeans

Edapally, Syro-Malabar parish, 81, 88; congregation of priests at, 77

Edessa, xiii, 2-3, 9-10

Egypt, 31, 39

Elias, Mar, Chaldean Bishop, and Malabar, 35-8, 40, 176

Elias II, Ignatius Mar, Jacobite Patriarch, 148

Elias V, Chaldean Catholicos, 25

Elias VII, Nestorian Catholicos, 43

Elias XI, Nestorian Catholicos, 92

Elias Abu'l-Yonan, Catholic Chaldean Patriarch, 119

Elthuruth, Syro-Malabar Seminary of, 99; Syro-Malabar Carmelite monastery, 132

Ephesus, Oecumenical Council of, 60

Ephrem II, Ignatius Mar, Rahmani, Syrian Catholic Patriarch, 157

Ernakulam, Syro-Malabar centre, printing press at, 100; vicariate apostolic of, 134; archbishopric of, 135-9, 172; Syro-Malabar Carmelite house at, and College at Thevara near, 137; Christian newspapers published at, 137; Syro-Malabar Congregation at, 156

Ethiopia, xiii-iv, 25, 27-30, 121

Eucharist, Holy, 36-7, 54, 58, 146, 148, 167-8, 170-1, 176-82

Eugene, Mar, monastery of, 24

Eusebius of Caesarea, 6-7

Extreme-Unction, Sacrament of, 166, 183

Fanam, Indian coin, 54

Farquhar J.N., on St. Thomas the Apostle, 3, 5

Fars, province of South-West Persia, 14-5

Federl, Eustachius, see Francis of Sales of the Mother of Dolours

Figueredo Salgado, Raphael, Vicar Apostolic of Malabar, 88

Florentius of Jesus Nazareth, Carmelite Vicar Apostolic of Malabar, 93, 179

Flos Sanctorum, see Ishodenah

France, French, 21, 29, 68, 126-7

Francis of Sales of the Mother of

Dolours, Carmelite Vicar Apostolic of Malabar, 94-5

Francis Xavier, St., destined to India, and landed at Goa, 69; in Malabar, 31-3, 176

Franciscans, in India, 69-70, 72; school at Cranganore, 70, 99; in Bassein, 36-8, 176

Franks, Europeans in Asia, 143

Funchal, Padroado bishopric of, 34

Fyzabad, N. India, 131

GABRIEL, Mar, Chaldean Bishop, in Malabar, 92, 143-4

Gabriel, Mar, Jacobite Bishop, in Malabar, 8

Gandhara, 3

Garzia, Francis, Jesuit Archbishop of Cranganore, 78-83

Gazirah, 24; Chaldean Bishopric of, 118; Jesuit College in the Lebanon at, 117

Geevargheese, P.T., see Ivanios, Mar

Gelasius of Cyzica, 7

Gelzer, H., 7

Genoa, 94

George de Christo, Indian Archdeacon of Malabar, 47-8

George de Cruce, Indian Archdeacon of Malabar, 48-9, 53, 55-6, 63

George Warda, hymns of, 62

Germann, on the Indian Syrians, 143

Germany, German, 29, 80, 89, 91, 95, 163

Gesualdo, Cardinal, 72

Ghats, mountains of India, 1, 30, 36, 42, 176

Gheez, liturgical language of Ethiopia, xiii-iv

Giamil S., 10

Goa, Bishops and Archbishops of, 34-5, 37, 42, 44, 46, 47, passim 65-6, 69-71, 89-90, 102, 115, 116; jurisdiction over Malabar from, 34, 37, 55-6, 65, 166; Inquisition at, 33, 36, 39 41, 61, 74, 78, 80, 85; Second

Synod of, 42-3, 69; Third Synod of, 44-5, 165-9, 177; Jesuits at, 70; Carmelites at, 80, 82, 85-7; varia on, 58, 75, 80, 88, 96

Gondaferes, Indo-Parthian King, 2, 6

Gouvea, A. de, Augustinian Friar, on Malabar, 8-9, 49-50, 64-5

Great Britain, 29

Greek, language and literature, xiv, 2, 13; patriarchate of Antioch, 17, 121, 140-1; people, 5, 11-2, 121

Gregorios, Mar, Jacobite Metropolitan, and Malabar, 142

Gregorios, Benedict Mar, Syro-Malankara Archbishop of Trivandrum, 161

Gregory XIII, Pope, 43, 47-8

Gregory of Tours, St., 6, 19

Guduphara see Gondaferes

Gujarat, 8, 21

HABBAN, a Syrian merchant, and India, 4-5

Hanxleden, Ernst, German Jesuit missionary, in Malabar, 91

Henriques, Cardinal, Regent of Portugal, 39

Henry the Navigator, Prince, 29

Hermits of St. Augustine, 49, 56

Himyar, in Ethiopia, 7

Hindus, xiv, 18, 22, 30, 50, 169, 171

Homs, in Syria, 154, 157

Hormisdas, a Chaldean Martyr, 63

Hormizd, Rabban, Chaldean monk, his life, 62; titular patron of the Syro-Malabar church of Angamale, 63; monastery of, 92

Hungary, Calvinists of, 89

Hyacinth of St. Vincent, Carmelite Friar and missionary, 80, 82

IGNATIUS of Loyola, St., 69-70

Ignatius of St. Hyppolitus, Carmelite Friar and missionary, 180

Indian Catholic Bishops, 121-3, 126, 134

Indonesia, 13

Indus, the river, 3, 5

Innocent XII, Pope, 89

Innocent XIII, Pope, 92

Iraq, 120

Iravi Korttan, Syrian merchant, in Malabar, 16

Isaias, Chaldean abbot, his life, 62

Isaias, Nicholas, Catholic Chaldean Patriarch, 110

Ishodenah, Chaldean Bishop of Basrah, his *Book of Chastity*, 62

Ishoyabh II, Chaldean Catholicos, 15

Ishoyabh III, Chaldean Catholicos, 14

Italy, Italian, 29, 30, 66, 68, 80, 89, 95

Ivanios, George Mar, his influence on the Jacobite Church in India, 158-9; founder of the Bethany Congregations, ibid; reunited to the Catholic Church, and first Archbishop of Trivandrum, 159-61, 173

JACOB, Mar, Chaldean Bishop of Malabar, 25, 30, 34; wrote to the Chaldean patriarch, 28; psalter written by, 25; book of Canon law written by, 167; difficulties with the Portuguese, 31-2, 175-6; and the Franciscan school of Cranganore, 69; living at the Franciscan friary of Cochin, 31, 69

Jacob, Mar, Metropolitan of India, 17

Jacobite patriarchate of Antioch, and Malabar, xv-vi, 9-10, 17, 87, 91, 102, 117, 130, 138-9, 141-55, 155-62, 172-4, 184-6

Japanese Bishops, 121

Jathiaikiasangham, joint association of Catholics and Jacobites in Malabar, 155-6

Jerusalem, 9

Jesuits in India and in Malabar, 43-9, 52, 62, 69-70, 72, 76-8, 83, 89-92, 117, 123, 127, *passim*, 131, 176-7

Jewish customs, 169

Jews, in India, 5, 15-6, 20, 22, 169, 171

John Elemosina, Franciscan Friar, and India, 22

John Guriel, Mar Chaldean Bishop of Salmas, 104

John Hormez, Mar, Chaldean Metropolitan of Mosul, 103-4

John, Indian prelate, in Rome, 19

John, Mar, Chaldean Bishop in Malabar, 25, 30-1

John, Mar, Jacobite Bishop, and Malabar, 143

John, Mar, Jacobite Bishop, and Malabar, 144

John, Mar, a Persian Bishop, and the Council of Nicaea, 7

John II, King of Portugal, and the East, 27

John III, King of Portugal, and Malabar, 31-2

John Marignola, Franciscan missionary and traveller, and Malabar, 23

John of Montecorvino, Franciscan missionary and traveller, on India, 20

John XXII, Pope, and the bishopric of Quilon, 22

John Baptist Mary of St. Teresa, Carmelite Vicar Apostolic of Malabar, 92

Jordan Catalani, Dominican Friar and missionary, his visit to Thana, Gujarat, and Malabar, 21; first Latin Bishop of India, 22

Joseph, Mar, Chaldean Metropolitan of Malabar, 35-41, 102, 175-6

Joseph IV, Catholic Chaldean Patriarch, 103-4

Joseph IV, Audo, Catholic Chaldean Patriarch, and Malabar, 105-18; and the Vatican Council, 111-2

Joseph, Metropolitan of Edessa, 10

Joseph, Syro-Malabar priest, 25-6

Joseph of St. Mary Carmelite Friar, Apostolic Commissary, first Vicar Apostolic of Malabar, 80-7, 121

Juda, the Jewish tribe, 4

Judas, name of St. Thomas the Apostle, 2

KADAMATTAM, Jacobite church and Persian cross of, 16

Kadutturutti, Syro-Malabar parish, visited by Archbishop de Menezes, 53-5; Friar Donati at, 76; early reconciliation with the Carmelites, 81; meetings at, 86, 91

Kalacherry, Mar James, Syro-Malabar Bishop of Changanacherry, 159

Kalan, see *Quillah*

Kalapura, Andrew, Syro-Malabar priest, 184

Kalyan, town near Bombay, 13

Kandathil, Mar Augustine, Syro-Malabar Archbishop of Ernakulam, 138-9, 172

Kariatil, Joseph, Syro-Malabar priest, Archbishop of Cranganore, 95-6, 122-3, 145

Kattanars, Syro-Malabar name for priests, 51, 54, 57-8, 77, 106, 109, 110, 117, 123, 141, 142, 146, 166, 176, 177

Kattumangatt, Jacobite priest and monk, *see* Kurillos, Mar

Kawugatt, Mar Matthew, Syro-Malabar Archbishop of Changana-cherry, 127

Khorassan, a region of Persia, 141

Khosroas, Persian Emperor, 11

Kothamangalam, Syro-Malabar diocese of, 136

Kottayam, important Christian centre of Malabar, Persian crosses of, 16; Syro-Malabar apostolic vicariate, 126, *passim*, 134, 172; Syro-Malabar bishopric for the Suddists, 135; reunion of the Jacobites from, 139, 156, 162; dissident Christians of, 129; Jacobite Synod of, 154; Suddist Jacobite bishop near, 154; residence of the Jacobite catholicos at, 155;

Jacobite seminary at, 158; Protestant institutions at, 146; Anglican diocese of, 152

Kunamavu, Syro-Malabar centre, Middle school for girls at, 133; printing-press at, 100, 182, 184

Kurvalangad, an important Syro Malabar parish, visited by the Carmelites, 81; parish priest of, 86

Kurdistan, 112

Kurialacherry, Mar Thomas, Syro-Malabar Bishop of Changanacherry 134, 139

Kurillos Kattumangatt, Mar, Indian Jacobite Metropolitan, founder of the Thozhiur-Anjur community, 144-5

Kurillos, Mar, Jacobite Metropolitan from Syria, and Malabar, 149-50

Kurillos, Mar, Indian Jacobite Metropolitan of Malankara, 153

LA CROZE, Mathurin de, on Malabar and the Synod of Diamper, 57, 145-6

Lateran, IV Council of, 123

Latin, missionaries, priests and faithful, especially in Malabar, 23, 28, 31, 37-8, 47-8, 53-4, 73, 87, 93, 99-100, 102-3, 106, 117; 122, 126, 128, 167, 175-7; language and rite, xvi, 22, 23, 28, 31, 36-7, 40, 45, 54, 56, 64, 66-7, 71, 84, 100, 102, 114, 124-5, 142, 143, 165-73, 175, *passim*, 181, 184; translation of the Bible in, the Vulgate, 59

Lavigne, Bishop Charles, Jesuit Vicar Apostolic of Kottayam, 127-31, 133, 156, 172

Lawrence of St. Mary, Carmelite Friar and missionary, in Malabar, 88

Lebanon, 117, 162, 165

Leo XIII, Pope, xvi, 38, 118, 138

Leonard of St. Louis, Carmelite Vicar Apostolic of Malabar, 100, 115, 117, 124, 171

Leopold I, Emperor of Germany, 89

Leyden, University of, 8

Liber Canonum, 62

Liber Status Animarum, 14, 168

Lima, Rodriguez de, Portuguese Ambassador in Ethiopia, 27

Lisbon, relations with the Syro-Malabar Church, 25, 34-5, 37, 39, 44, 70-1, 82, 85, 87, 94, 95

London, 150

Louis of St. Teresa, Carmelite Vicar Apostolic of Malabar, 105

Louis Mary of Jesus, Carmelite Vicar Apostolic of Malabar, 97

Low Countries, 29

Lyons, Jesuit province of, 117

MACAO, 44, 94

Madras, State of, 1, 135; town of, 148, Jacobites at, 155; University of, 158

Madura, Jesuit mission of, 123

Magistris, Hyacinth de, Jesuit missionary in India, 80, 82

Mahluph, *see* Mylapore

Majid, Arab pilot of Vasco de Gama, 27

Makil, Mar Matthew, Syro-Malabar Vicar General of Kottayam, 128, 130, 134; Vicar Apostolic of Changanacherry, 130, 134, 174; of Kottayam, 134

Malabar, 1, 4-6, 8, 10, 31, 37-9, *passim*; North, 135; Jacobites in, 142, *passim*, 157, 167, 175, 180-1

Malacca Straits, 14

Malankara, 148, *passim*, 162

Malayalam, the Dravidian language, 1, 8, 91, 99, 117; ignorance of, 33, 128; speeches in, 50; profession of faith in, 57; catechism in, 58, 64; Acts of the Diamper Synod in, 63; Te Deum sung in, 64; well spoken by Bishop Roz, 72, 74; printing in, 99-100, 128; papal documents in, 115, 117; schools in, 133; disciplinary

decrees of the Council of Trent in, 164; constitutions of the Jacobites in, 178; liturgy of the Jacobites in, 189-90; Holy Scriptures and Anglican liturgy in, 146; Anglican catechism in, 146

Malayalees, those who speak Malayalam, 1, 158

Maldive Islands, 7

Male, 13

Malpan, Syro-Malabar priest of learning, 99, 105-7, 148

Malta, Maltese 34, 36, 38

Mampully, George, Syro-Malabar priest, Vicar General of Trichur, 132

Mana, 13

Mangalore, Latin diocese of, 100, 106, 135; Seminary of, 129

Mangate, *see* Alangad

Mannamam, Syrian Seminary of, 99; Syrian Carmelite monastery of, 111; meeting at, 116; reception of Bishop Lavigne at, 127; catechumenate at, 130; centre of orthodoxy at, 132; printing-press at, 181-2, 184

Manuel de S. Joachim das Neves, administrator of Cranganore, 105

Maphrian, the Jacobite prelate of Mesopotamia, 14, 140, 143

Maramon, centre of the Mar Thomites 148

Marcel of St. Ivo, Carmelite Friar and missionary, and Malabar, 80

Marcellino da Civezza, 22

Marcellinus of St. Teresa, Carmelite Coadjutor, Bishop of Verapoly, 100, 124

Marco Polo, on Socotra, 12; on India, 19-20

Mardin, Chaldean archbishopric of, 119; Jacobite patriarch near, 148

Mari, 15

Maronites, xvii, 13, 66, 71, 84, 88, 162, 180

Marriage, Sacrament of, in the Syro-Malabar Church, 63, 168-9, 170-1, 183-4

Marseilles, 13

Mar Thomites, Reformed Jacobite community of Malabar, 145, 147, *passim*, 152, 161, 173; liturgy of the, 185

Maruta, Maphrian of Takrit, 14, 140

Mass, Holy Sacrifice of the, *see* Eucharist

Massawah, in Ethiopia, 46

Mattai, Mar, Jacobite monastery of, 143

Mattanchery, suburb of Cochin, 79

Matthew, *see* Mar Athanasios, Mar Thomite Metropolitan

Matthew de Campo, 88

Matthew of St. Joseph, Carmelite Friar and missionary, in Malabar, 80, 82, 87

Medicine of the Persians see Parisman

Medes, 4

Mediterranean sea, 68, 82

Medlycott, Bishop Adolf, Vicar Apostolic of Trichur, 126, 131-3; on St. Thomas in India, 3, 5-6, 133

Melinda, 40, 42

Melkites, Eastern Christians of the Near East, 13, 140-1

Mellano, Joseph Anthony, *see* Leonard of St. Louis

Mello, Francisco de, Portuguese Governor of Cochin, 81

Mello Castro, Antonio de, Viceroy of Goa, 87

Mellus, Mar Elias, Chaldean Bishop, counsellor of Patriarch Joseph Audo, 112; came to Malabar and provoked disturbances, 114, *passim*, 124; returned to Mesopotamia and became Archbishop of Mardin, 119

Mellusians, group of recent dissidents in Malabar, 116, 119-20, 128, 131, 132

Menacherry, Mar John, secretary to Mgr. Medlycott, 134; Vicar Apostolic of Trichur, 134, 138

Menetillo of Spoleto, Dominican Friar and missionary, 20

Menezes, Alexis de, Augustinian Hermit and Archbishop of Goa, his dealings with the Syro-Malabar Christians, 47, 48-68, 70-1, 73, 166, 167-8

Mesopotamia, particularly in relation with India, xiii-v, 2-10, 17-18, 24-5, 30, 34-5, 37, 40, 43, 49, 52, 60, 66, 82, 90, 101-20, 122, 140, 163, 175, 177, 179-81

Meurin, Mgr. Leo, Jesuit Vicar Apostolic of Bombay, and Goa, 115-6; and Malabar, 116-7

Milan, 67

Militia Christi, Portuguese Order, 33

Mingana A., 7

Mohammedans, to Mylapore, 19; in India, 18, 20-1, 23, 27-8, 30, 169, 171; relations with the Portuguese, 29, 33, 175

Molandurte, *see* Molanthurutti

Mongolian armies, xv, 24

Monophysites, in Ethiopia, 30; in Mesopotamia, 141; in India, 141-2

Mooney, Latin Archbishop, Apostolic Delegate in India, 159

Moors, *see* Mohammedans

Moses, Maronite priest, 71

Mosul, 87, 103, 108, 110, 112, 114, 119, 143

Mozambique, 35, 69

Mulanthurutty, Syro-Malabar parish visited by Menezes, 55; Jacobite Synod of, 151

Munro, Colonel, English Resident in Malabar, 145-6

Muslims, *see* Mohammedans

Mutholy, Seminary of, 128; Syrian Carmelite Sisters at, 129; catechumenate at, 130

Muttam, Syro-Malabar parish, and the Carmelites, 81

Muttuchira, Syro-Malabar parish, Persian cross of, 16; and the Carmelites, 81

Muziris, important trade centre, 5-6, see also Cranganore

Mylapore, the place where St. Thomas died and was buried, 4, 6; Persian cross of, 16, 178; visited by monk Theodore, 6,19; by King Alfred's envoys, 19; by Marco Polo, 19-20; by medieval friars and missionaries, 20-3; conversions at, 32; monk Athallah at, 78

Mysore, Latin diocese of, 135

NAIRS, a Hindu caste of Malabar, 63, 164, 171

Namputhiri, see Brahmins

Nau F., 25, 143

Navikarannakar, see Mar Thomites

Nazarene, name of the Syro-Malabar Christians, 22

Nestorian, Nestorianism, xv, 17-8, 37, 45-6, 48, 50-2, 57, *passim*, 62, 71, 92, 102, 103, 110-1, 119-20, 123, 143, 177

Nestorius, 45, 55, 59, 60, 142, 177

Nicaea, Council of, 7

Nicholas de Conti, and India, 23

Nicholas of Pistoia, Dominican Friar and missionary, died at Mylapore, 20

Nidiri, Emmanuel, Syro-Malabar priest, Vicar General of Kottayam, 127-8, 130, 138, 155

Nilamperur, statuette of a Christian personage at, 4

Nineveh, 9

Niranam, Syro-Malabar parish, now Jacobite, 161

Nishabur, 141

Nobili, Robert de, famous Italian Jesuit missionary of Madura, 74

Nomocanon, see Bar Hebraeus

Nordist, the most numerous social group among the Syro-Malabar Christians, 8-10, 127-8, 134

OBLATES of the S. Heart, diocesan congregation of Kottayam, 137

Oderic of Pordenone, Franciscan Friar and missionary, and India, 22

Office, canonical, in the Chaldean and Syro-Malabar rites, 58, 167, 170, 184

Order, Sacrament of, 63, 160, 171, 173, 184

Order of Christ, see *Militia Christi*

Oriental Church, S. Congregation for the, 100, 120, 156, 159-60

Ormuz, 35, 51, 102, 142

Ottoman Empire and Government, 113, 120

PACHECO, Peter, Dominican Bishop of Cochin, 90

Padroado, 29, 71, 73, 83, 89, 105, 111, 112, 116, 122, 125

Palai, Syro-Malabar diocese of, 135-6

Palakal, Thomas, Syro-Malabar priest, one of the founders of the Carmelite Tertiaries, 98

Palayur, ancient Syro-Malabar centre, 4

Pakalomattam, name of the Syro-Malabar archdeacon's family, 150

Pampakuda, Jacobite printing-press of, 185-6

Pandari, Paul, Syro-Malabar priest, and Chaldean Bishop, 103-4

Pantaenus, and India, 6, 10

Paradise of Eden, see Abdisho of Nisibis

Parambil, Chandi, see Alexander de Campo

Paremmakal, Thomas, Syro-Malabar priest, companion of Archbishop Kariatil, and administrator of Cranganore archdiocese, 96, 103, 122-3, 145

Pareparambil, Aloysius, Syro-Malabar priest, Superior General of the Syro-Malabar Sisters, 129; and the reunion of the Jacobites, 130, 138; first Vicar Apostolic of Ernakulam, 134, 172, 182

Pariahs, the Indian outcastes, 63

Parisman, a book condemned by the Diamper Synod, 62

Parsis, in India, 8, 15

Parthia, Parthians, 2-4

Parur, Syro-Malabar centre, church of, 75; new bishopric of, 44, 47; visited by Menezes, 53; by the Carmelites, 81; Mar Gregorios died at, 142

Paul, College of St., Jesuit institution at Goa, 70

Paul III, Pope, 69

Paulinus of St. Bartholomew, Carmelite Friar, missionary and scholar, 94, 97

Payva, Alfonso de, Portuguese discoverer, 27

Penteado, Alvaro, Portuguese priest, and Malabar, 31, 175-6

Perath, d'Maisan, see Basrah

Peregrinatores Christi, society of medieval friars and missionaries, 29

Pereira, Bishop Lawrence, 159

Perez de Covilham, João, Portuguese discoverer, 27

Peroz, Mar, Chaldean Bishop in Malabar, 15-6

Persia, Persian xv, 7-8, 11, 13, 21, 120, 140; Church, 8-11; Gulf, 7, 12, 23, 31, 101; immigrants, in India 15; monks, 14; crosses in India, 16

Persico, Mgr. Ignatius, Capuchin Bishop and visitor, in Malabar, 117-8

Peshitto, the Syriac version of the Holy Scriptures, 2

Peter VII, Ignatius Mar, Jacobite Patriarch, and Malabar, 151-2

Philip III, King of Spain and Portugal, 72

Philostorgos, 7-8

Philoxenos, Mar, Jacobite Metropolitan of Thozhiur, 147

Pimenta, local Queen of Malabar, 54

Pimentel, Antonio, Jesuit Archbishop of Cranganore, 92

Piquet, Francis, French Consul at Aleppo, 84

Pius IV, Pope, 38-41

Pius V, Pope, 41

Pius VI, Pope, 95

Pius IX, Pope, and Chaldean dealing, in Malabar, 110, 114, 116-7

Pius XI, Pope, and Africa and the Far East, 121; and Malabar, 134-5, 138

Pondicherry, 5, 90

Portugal, Portuguese, with special reference to India and Malabar, xiii-xv, 9, 18, 25-9, passim, 121, 125, 163-5, 173, 175, 177, 183

Porukara, Syro-Malabar priest, one of the founders of the Carmelite Tertiaries, 98

Prester John, the kingdom of, 27-8

Propaganda, S. Congregation of, and the Jesuits in Malabar, 76-8; sent Carmelites to Malabar, 80, 83-4, 87-88, 122; confirmed the jurisdiction of the Vicar Apostolic of Malabar, 91-3; approved the Seminary of Verapoly, 93; and the Chaldean dealings in Malabar, 103, passim; and the Syro-Malabar missal, 93, 104 179-80, 182; and the Syro-Malabar ritual, 183-4; concerning the concordat between Rome and Portugal, 111, 125; sent visitors to Malabar, 116-8; and the question of Syro-Malabar prelates, 123, 125-6; West Syrian liturgical books published by, 156-7; concerning the Synod of Diamper, 170 conditions given for the reunion of Mar Thomas VI, 145

Propaganda College, in Rome, 95, 104, 107, 112, 131, 134

Protestants in Malabar, 20, 128, 145, passim, 153, 161, 185

Protoevangelium Jacobi, 61

Ptolomaeus, 11

Puccinelli, Jesuit Missionary in India, on Malabar, 123

Pulincunnu, Syrian Seminary of, 99

Punjab, 2, 5, 6

Puttenchira, Syo-Malabar centre and residence of the Archbishops of Cranganore, 91

Puthenpally, Syrian Seminary of, 99-100, 124, 128; printing-press of, 181-2, 184; parish priest of, 172

QALAH, *see* Qillah

Qamis Bar Qardahe, the hymns of, 62

Qillah, in the Malacca Straits, 14

Quilon, early Christian centre at, 13, 15; first Latin bishopric of, 22-3; conversions at, 32; modern Latin diocese of, 100, 106

RANGEL, Michael Da Cruz, Dominican Bishop of Cochin, 77

Raymond of St. Joseph, Carmelite Vicar Apostolic of Malabar, 97

Rewardashir, in Persia, 14, 18

Ribeiro, John, Jesuit Archbishop of Cranganore, 91

Ricard, Louis, French Jesuit, in Malabar, 128, *passim*, 131

Rickloff, Dutch General and Governor of Cochin, 86

Ring of Solomon, book forbidden by the Synod of Diamper, 62

Rodriguez, Dominican Friar and missionary, at Quilon, 32

Rokos, Mar, Chaldean Bishop, and Malabar, 99, 108-11, 122, 123

Romagyris, catholicosate of, 141

Rome, the Holy See, with special reference to Malabar, xv-vi, 12, 18, 19, 22, 26, 28, 32, 34-5, 39, 41, 42-4, 47, 52, 60, 66-7, 76, 80, 82-4, 86, 87, 88, 90, 94, 95, 102, *passim*, 122, *passim*, 125, *passim*, 141, 144, 145, 157-9, 173, 175, 176, 180, 183

Rosario Gomez, Benedict de, Episcopal Governor of Cranganore, 115

Roz, Francis, Jesuit missionary in Malabar 45-6; Vicar Apostolic of Angamale, 48, 70; adviser to the archdeacon, 48-9, 56; corrected the Syriac Bible and liturgical books, 59, 62, 167-8, 178; first Latin Bishop of the Syro-Malabars, 66, 71-5, 176; prevented Rome from approving the acts of the Synod of Diamper, 66-7; wrote on effects of Latinization, 176

SABRISHO I, Chaldean Catholicos, 14

Sabrisho III, Chaldean Catholicos, 12

Sabrisho, Mar, Chaldean Bishop, and Malabar, 15-6

Salsette, Island of, near Bombay, 21

Santarem, in Portugal, 27

Sapor II, Sassanide Emperor, 5, 8

Sathanam, copper-plates, 15

Schaaf C., and Malabar, 144

Schurhammer, George, Jesuit scholar, and Malabar, 17-8

Sebastiani, *see* Joseph of St. Mary

Seleucia-Ctesiphon, Chaldean Catholicos of, xiii, 9, 18, 24, 30, 51, 101, 121, 141, 165

Serampore, Protestant College of, near Calcutta, 158

Serra, the mountain, Portuguese name given to Malabar, 30

Servants of the Cross, Jacobite brotherhood, 155

Severios, Joseph Mar, Jacobite Metropolitan of Niranam, became Catholic and Bishop of Tiruvalla, 160-1

Sharfe, in the Lebanon, 157

Simon, Mar, Chaldean Metropolitan of Adana, and Malabar, 90

Simon, Mar, Nestorian Bishop, and Malabar, 43-4, 48

Simon V, Chaldean Catholicos, 25

Simon IX Denha, Catholic Chaldean Catholicos, 49, 52

Simon XVII Abraham, Nestorian Catholicos, and Malabar, 110

Simon XIX Benjamin, Nestorian Catholicos, 119

Simon XXI, Nestorian Catholicos, 120

Socotra, Christianity in, 6, 11-3

Sofala, 27

Solomon of Basrah, his *Book of the Bee*, 4

Souza, Antonio de Souza Countinho, Portuguese Governor of Cranganore, 81

Stabellini, Maurilio, Carmelite administrator and Vicar Apostolic of Verapoly, 98, 104

Sublime Porte, *see* Ottoman Government

Suddist, social group among the Syro-Malabar Christians, 8-10, 127-8; Jacobites, 130, 139, 154, 156, 161-2; apostolic vicariate of Kottayam for the, 134; bishopric of Kottayam for, 135-6, 137

Sulaqa, Mar Joseph, Catholic Chaldean Catholicos, 34-5, 39, 41, 176

Sultan, the Turkish, 154, 173

Surat, harbour in India, 78, 85,

Synodicon Orientale, 163

Syria, 71, 72, 80, 140, 147

Syriac, rite and language, xiv, 2, 7, 8, 10, 16, 17, 24, 35, 36, 45, 49, 50, 53, 54, 56, *passim*, 74, *passim*, 84, 99-100, 104, 105, 106, 117, 158, 163, 167-8, 174, 177, 179-80, 183, 185

Syrians in the Near East, 2, 5, 13, 18, 24, 60, 74, 90, 162

Syro-Malabar, main references to the Syro-Malabar Church and Christians, xv-vi, 1, 25, 29-30, 34, 40, 49, 61, 67, 70, 77-80, 87-8, 92-3, 95-100, 105, 109-10, 116-8, 120, 122, *passim*, 134-5, *passim*, 139, 141, 156, 161-2, 164-72, 175-84

Syro-Malankara, Church, rite and Christians, 139, 157-62, 185-6 Canon Law, 172-4

Szoskak, Nicholas, *see* Florentius of Jesus Nazareth

TAKRIT, Maphrian of, 14

Taprobana, *see* Ceylon

Tashkent, in Turkestan, 141

Tauris, in Turkey, 20-1

Tellicherry, Syro-Malabar diocese of, 135-6

Temudo, George, Archbishop of Goa, 42

Tertiaries of St. Francis of Assisi, 129, 137-8

Tevalacara, the copper-plates of, 16

Thana, near Bombay, 21-2

Thayil, Joseph, Syro-Malabar priest, Vicar General of Kottayam, 128

Thekkumbhagar, *see* Suddist

Theodore, Frankish monk, and Mylapore, 6, 19

Theodore of Mopsuestia, xv, 45, 55, 62, 177

Theophilos, James Mar, Bethany monk and Bishop of Tiruvalla, 159-61

Theophilus, an Eastern monk in India, 7-8

Thevara, *see* Ernakulam

Thiruvancode, ancient Syro-Malabar parish, now Jacobite, 32

Thoma, Mar, Nestorian Bishop of Trichur, 120

Thomas, Chaldean Bishop, and Malabar, 15

Thomas, Mar, Chaldean Bishop, and Malabar, 25, 31

Thomas, I, Mar, *see* Thomas de Campo

Thomas II, head of the Syro-Malabar dissidents, 142

Thomas III, head of the Syro-Malabar dissidents, 142-3

Thomas IV, head of the Syro-Malabar dissidents, petition to Rome, 143

Thomas V, head of the Syro-Malabar dissidents, 144

Thomas VI, head of the Syro-Malabar dissidents, 95, 144-5, reunion with Rome, 145

Thomas, Mar, *see* Rokos

Thomas, St., The Apostle, his work in India, xiii, 2-6, 10, 14-5, 72; his tomb at Mylapore, 6, 19, 30; Law of, 49, 52, 55, 60; feast of, 19, 134-5, 175, 182; University College of, at Trichur, 132-3

Thomas de Campo, Archdeacon of Malabar, 78; fake consecration of, 79-80; refused to make peace, 81, 83, 85, 86; became a Jacobite, 87, 89, 102, 122, 141-2

Thomas Cana, in Malabar, 9-10

Thondanatta, Anthony, Syro-Malabar priest, and Mar Rokos, 106-7; consecrated bishop by the Nestorian catholicos, 110; repented, 111; head of the Mellusian dissidents, 118-9, 123

Thozhiur, the Jacobite dissidents of, 144-5, 147, 150

Tibet, 164

Timothy I, Chaldean Catholicos, 14-15, 164

Timothy II, Chaldean Catholicos, 62

Timothy Abimelech, Mar, Nestorian Bishop of Trichur, 119

Timur Leng, xiv

Tiruvalla, episcopal see of, 159-6; printing-press at, 186

Topographia Christiana, *see* Cosmas Indicopleustes

Toulouse, Jesuit province of, 127

Tranquebar, German and Danish missionaries of, on Malabar, 144, 145

Transoxonia, 141

Travancore, King of, 97, 149; State of, 135, 146, 149, 151, 158, 173; Anglican diocese of, 153

Travancore-Cochin, State of, 1

Trent, Council of, 39, 56-7, 61, 67, 166, 168-9

Trichur, Syro-Malabar centre, Seminary of, 100; parish of, 112, 132; residence of Mar Mellus at, 114; Syrian Carmelites at, 115, 138; Nestorian church at, 119-20; Vicar Apostolic of, 126, 131-4, 172; diocese of, 135-6

Tricomia, Titular Bishop of, *see* Medlycott

Trincomalee, 131

Trinitarians, in India, 69

Trivandrum, Syro-Malankara archdiocese, 98, 160-1

Turks, 31

UDAYAMPERUR, *see* Diamper

Uraha, Mar Philipos Jacob, Chaldean Bishop, and Malabar 115, 118

VADAKKUMBHAGAR, *see* Nordist

Vaicom, Syro-Malabar centre, 129

Vaipicotta, Jesuit Seminary of, 45, 49-50, 52, 56, 62-4, 70, 74, 76, 89, 99, 176-7

Valignano, Alexander, Jesuit Visitor of the Asian missions, 44

Vasco da Gama, 27, 30-1

Vasconcellos, Francis de, Jesuit Bishop of Cochin, 92

Vatican Council, 111-2

Vatakkumkur, *see* Pimenta

Vaughan, Cardinal, Archbishop of Westminster, 133

Vazhakulam, Syrian Seminary of, 99

Venice 26, 31

Vengurla, 86

Verapoly, Carmelite monastery of, 91, 95; Seminary of, 89, 93-4, 99; mission and apostolic vicariate of, 97, 98, 100, 105-6, 115-6, 123-4, 126, 136, 179; Archbishop of, 100, 126; Synod of, 172

Vincent de Lagos, Franciscan Friar and missionary, and the school-seminary of Cranganore, 146

Vincent Mary of St. Catherine, Carmelite Friar and missionary, 80-1

Vincent de Paul, St., Syro-Malabar congregation of, 137

Visitation, Tertiary Sisters of the, 129, 138

WICKI, Joseph, Jesuit scholar, 35

Wilson, Daniel, Anglican Bishop of Calcutta, and the Jacobites, 147

YAHBALLAHA III, Chaldean Catholicos, 17, 101

Yahballaha, Chaldean Metropolitan of India, in Malabar, 25, 30-1

Yaqut, Arab geographer, 11

ZACHARIAS, psalter copied at Cranganore by Bar Joseph Bar Zacharias, 17

Zahara, Anthony, Maltese Dominican Friar, in India and Malabar, 35, 38-9

Zeila, 27

Ziegenbalg, Bartholomew, German missionary of Tranquebar, 145

Zoroastrians, see Parsis